C000179131

Little Oxford Dictionary of
Proverbs

EDITED BY
Elizabeth Knowles

UNIVERSITY PRESS

OXFORD
UNIVERSITY PRESS

Great Clarendon Street, Oxford OX2 6DP

Oxford University Press is a department of the University of Oxford.
It furthers the University's objective of excellence in research, scholarship,
and education by publishing worldwide in

Oxford New York

Auckland Bangkok Buenos Aires Cape Town Chennai
Dar es Salaam Delhi Hong Kong Istanbul Karachi Kolkata
Kuala Lumpur Madrid Melbourne Mexico City Mumbai Nairobi
São Paulo Shanghai Taipei Tokyo Toronto

Oxford is a registered trade mark of Oxford University Press
in the UK and in certain other countries

Published in the United States
by Oxford University Press Inc., New York

© Oxford University Press, 2009

The moral rights of the author have been asserted
Database right Oxford University Press (maker)

First edition published 2009

British Library Cataloguing in Publication Data
Data available

Library of Congress Cataloging-in-Publication Data
Data available

Typeset by Macmillan Publishing Solutions
Printed and bound in China
through Asia Pacific Offset Ltd.

ISBN 978-0-19-956802-4
10   9   8   7   6   5

Contents

Introduction

The *Little Oxford Dictionary of Proverbs* brings together a wide range of proverbs and sayings, from the traditional western maxims of biblical and classical tradition, through proverbs from across the wider world, to sayings, catchphrases, and slogans from popular culture. The selection made is based on the diversity of real usage: when reaching today for a saying to use in advice or admonition, we happily draw material from a broad range of sources.

The dictionary is arranged by theme, so that a number of sayings on each topic can be found together. Subjects covered range widely, from **Ambition** ('The smaller the lizard, the greater its hopes of becoming a crocodile') to **Hospitality** ('Treat your guest as a guest for two days; on the third day, give him a hoe'), and from **Opportunity** ('If the camel once gets his nose in the tent, his body will soon follow') to **Trees** ('To plant a tree is to plant hope'). Comments on **Parents** include the child's optimistic view that 'A father is a banker provided by nature.' Within each theme, the proverbs and sayings are arranged alphabetically (initial 'a' and 'the' being ignored). There is a keyword index for essential words from the first part of each saying, allowing the reader to trace a saying to its place in its particular theme.

One of the pleasures of proverbs is in seeing how, in different parts of the world, the same idea may be expressed. Under **Caution**, the traditional warning that you should 'Let sleeping dogs lie' is echoed by the Japanese saying 'Poke a bush, a snake comes out', and reinforced by the catchphrase from *Hill Street Blues*: 'Let's be careful out there.' At **Change**, the familiar saying 'The leopard does not change his spots' can be matched by an African warning that the essential nature of something will not change: 'No matter how long a log floats in the water, it will never become a crocodile.'

Sometimes, of course, different approaches are emphasized. At **Ability**, the idea that someone not naturally suited to a task will perform poorly is traditionally expressed by the proverb 'A sow may whistle, though it has an ill mouth for it.' The African saying 'If you can talk, you can sing, and if you can walk, you can dance' offers a much more positive approach. Views of **Enemies** range from 'The enemy of my enemy is my friend' to the warning 'Do not call a wolf to help you against the dogs.' Traditional proverbs about **Power** often give a simple picture of its merciless exercise: 'Big fish eat little fish' and 'Might is right.' However, an African proverb sees matters from another perspective: 'Power is like an egg: if you hold it too tightly, it breaks, and if you hold it too loosely, it drops and breaks.'

Some new items have come to attention through very high profile use. Addressing the Church of England General Synod in July 2008, Archbishop John Sentamu referred to what he called 'a wonderful African saying', 'He who travels fast, travels alone and he who travels far, travels in the company of others', to be found here at **Cooperation**. When Hillary Clinton as Secretary of State visited Haiti in April 2009, she referred to 'an old Haitian proverb' in her address to President Preval: 'Beyond the mountains, there are mountains'; this saying now appears at **Determination**. In other cases, present-day concerns have highlighted particular sayings: recent events in the worlds of **Business** and finance have brought the view that 'Bull markets climb a wall of worry.' Advice on **Buying and Selling** includes the stock market warning against greed, 'The bulls make money, the bears make money, the hogs get slaughtered.'

One of the fascinating things about language is that we can never really say with certainty that a maxim which has fallen out of use may not reappear. The recommendation of the value of **Patience**, 'With time and patience the mulberry leaf becomes satin', reappeared in July 2003 in a column on football, in which Sir Bobby Robson's signing of Lee Bowyer to Newcastle United was further described as 'adding the proverbial mulberry leaf to his squad'. Similarly, once an item has made an appearance, it may be noticed elsewhere. An obituary from 2009 for the American surrealist Franklin Rosemont cited the surrealist proverb 'Elephants are contagious.' In his autobiographical essay *Still Alive* (1994), the critic Jan Kott, writing of the impact of Ionesco's *Rhinoceros*, had noted that the saying had appealed to him when he encountered it in 1938. 'But in all my prewar innocence I could never have suspected that rhinoceroses too are contagious.'

An Arab proverb advises, 'To understand the people, acquaint yourself with their proverbs', but the enjoyment of compiling a book of this kind is the opportunity it gives to observe not one but a multiplicity of views. I hope that some of this pleasure will have been passed on to the reader.

Acknowledgements

Little Proverbs has drawn particularly from the *Oxford Dictionary of Phrase, Saying, and Quotation* (3/e, 2006), as well as from the *Oxford Dictionary of Proverbs* (5/e, 2008). This material has been augmented by Oxford's Quotations reading programme, the Oxford Corpus, and the Editor's own reading and research. Any book of this kind rests on the research, scholarship, and insight of many others, and I am extremely grateful to have had such a foundation. I have also appreciated a good deal of wise critical advice, and personal encouragement and support, from Ben Harris, a most valued former colleague, who commissioned the book.

Elizabeth Knowles   Oxford, 2009

List of Subjects

Ability

The consensus of proverbial wisdom is that ability (or the lack of it) is innate, although aptitudes may be developed: If you can talk, you can sing; if you can walk, you can dance.

But I know a man who can.
advertising slogan for the Automobile Association.

Genius is an infinite capacity for taking pains.
English proverb, late 19th century.

Horses for courses.
originally (in horse-racing) meaning that different horses are suited to different racecourses, but now used more generally to mean that different people are suited to different roles; English proverb, late 19th century.

If you can talk, you can sing; if you can walk, you can dance.
often used as an encouragement to undertake something new; African (Shona) proverb.

Inside the forest there are many birds.
people are of many different kinds and abilities ('many birds' here = 'birds of many kinds'); Chinese proverb.

Is Saul also among the prophets?

a rhetorical question asked when someone displays unexpected abilities; from the biblical account (1 Samuel 10:11), in which the young Saul's prophesying became one of the signs that he had been chosen as king of Israel.

A sow may whistle, though it has an ill mouth for it.

someone not naturally suited to a task will perform it badly; English proverb, early 19th century.

Absence

See also MEETING AND PARTING

Despite the saying that Absence makes the heart grow fonder, *it is possible that an absent person who is not present to defend themselves may be blamed for something, or simply forgotten.*

Absence is the mother of disillusion.

American proverb, mid 20th century.

Absence makes the heart grow fonder.

affection for a person is strengthened by missing them; English proverb, mid 19th century, derived from a Latin proverb recorded from the 1st century BC.

The absent get farther away every day.

Japanese proverb.

He who is absent is always in the wrong.

someone who is not present cannot defend themselves; English proverb, mid 15th century.

A little absence does much good.
American proverb, mid 20th century.

Out of sight, out of mind.
someone who is not present is easily forgotten; English proverb, mid 13th century.

Where were you in '62?
advertising slogan for the film *American Graffiti* (1973).

Achievement

See also AMBITION, EFFORT, PROBLEMS AND SOLUTIONS, SUCCESS AND FAILURE

Effort and aspiration are both needed for achievement, but even if the goal is reached the outcome may not be satisfactory, since While the grass grows, the steed starves.

Behind an able man there are other able men.
modern saying, said to be a Chinese proverb.

Didn't she [*or* he *or* they] do well?
catchphrase used by Bruce Forsyth in 'The Generation Game' on BBC Television, 1973 onwards.

The difficult is done at once.
slogan of the US Armed Forces; recorded earlier as a comment by the French statesman Charles Alexandre de Calonne (1734–1802), 'Madam, if a thing is possible, consider it done; the impossible?—that will be done.'

The hand will not reach what the heart does not long for.
desire is essential for achievement; Welsh proverb.

He who likes cherries soon learns to climb.
achievement seen as the result of motivation; German proverb.

In a calm sea every man is a pilot.
apparent achievement may not have been tested by circumstances; English proverb, recorded from the early 19th century.

Palmam qui meruit, ferat [**Let him who has won it bear the palm**].
Latin, adopted by Lord Nelson (1758–1805) as his motto, from John Jortin *Lusus Poetici* (3rd ed., 1748), 'Ad Ventos'.

Per ardua ad astra [**Through struggle to the stars**].
Latin, motto of the Mulvany family, quoted and translated by Rider Haggard in his novel *The People of the Mist* (1894), and still in use as a motto of the Royal Air Force, having been approved by King George V in 1913.

Seekers are finders.
success is the result of effort; Persian proverb; compare **Seek and ye shall find** at ACTION AND INACTION.

Seriously, though, he's doing a grand job!
catchphrase used by David Frost in 'That Was The Week That Was', on BBC Television, 1962–3.

Still achieving, still pursuing.

American proverb, mid 20th century, from Henry Wadsworth Longfellow's adjuration, 'Let us, then, be up and doing, With a heart for any fate; Still achieving, still pursuing, Learn to labour and to wait' from the poem 'A Psalm of Life' (1838).

Whatever man has done, man can do.

anything that has been achieved once can be achieved again; English proverb, mid 14th century.

While the grass grows, the steed starves.

by the time hopes or expectations can be satisfied, it may be too late; English proverb, mid 14th century.

You cannot have your cake and eat it.

you cannot have things both ways; English proverb, mid 16th century.

Action and Inaction

See also IDLENESS, WORDS AND DEEDS

While setting out on a planned course is likely to be rewarded, since we are told that Seek and ye shall find, *there are also dangers in not thinking things through:* Action without thought is shooting without aim.

Action is worry's worst enemy.

advocating the control of fruitless worry by taking a decision and acting upon it; American proverb, mid 20th century.

Action this day.
annotation as used by Winston Churchill at the Admiralty
in 1940.

Action without thought is shooting without aim.
American proverb, mid 20th century.

A barking dog never bites.
noisy threats often do not presage real danger; English proverb,
16th century; recorded earlier in French in the 13th century.

Better to light one candle than to curse the darkness.
motto of the American Christopher Society, founded in 1945.

If it ain't broke, don't fix it.
warning against interference with something that is working
satisfactorily; late 20th-century saying.

If you want something done, ask a busy person.
implying that a busy person is most likely to have learned how to
manage their time efficiently; late 20th century saying.

It is as cheap sitting as standing.
often used literally; English proverb, mid 17th century.

Lookers-on see most of the game.
those who are not participating are able to take an overall view;
English proverb, early 16th century.

The road to hell is paved with good intentions.
often used as a comment on well-intentioned actions that have
turned out badly; English proverb, late 16th century (earlier
forms omit the first three words).

Seek and ye shall find.
an active search for something wanted is likely to be rewarded;
English proverb, mid 16th century, from the Bible (Matthew 7:7),
'Ask, and it shall be given you: seek, and ye shall find'; compare
Seekers are finders at ACHIEVEMENT.

When in doubt, do nowt.
advising against taking action when one is unsure of one's
ground; English proverb, mid 19th century.

Adversity
See also MISFORTUNES, SUFFERING

*Adversity is unavoidable, and may in fact be salutary; a modern
saying advises making the best of it:* If life hands you lemons,
make lemonade. *We also, according at least to a Swahili
proverb, have the comfort that adversity is finite:* After hardship comes relief.

Adversity is the foundation of virtue.
Japanese proverb.

Adversity makes strange bedfellows.
shared difficulties may bring together very different people;
English proverb, mid 19th century.

After hardship comes relief.
African proverb (Swahili).

A dose of adversity is often as needful as a dose of medicine.
American proverb, mid 20th century.

If life hands you lemons, make lemonade.
an adjuration to make the best of difficult circumstances; late
20th century saying.

 Advertising

It is tempting to think of advertising as a modern phenomenon, but the awareness that It pays to advertise *goes back a considerable way, as* Good wine needs no bush *shows.*

Any publicity is good publicity.
it is always preferable to have attention focused on a name than
to be unnoticed; English proverb, early 20th century.

Blow your own horn, even if you don't sell a clam.
American saying.

Don't advertise what you can't fulfil.
American proverb, mid 20th century.

Good wine needs no bush.
there is no need to advertise or boast about something of good quality as people will always discover its merits, referring to the bunch of ivy that was formerly the sign of a vintner's shop; English proverb, early 15th century.

It pays to advertise.
American proverb, mid 20th century.

Let's run it up the flagpole and see if anyone salutes it.
recorded as an established expression in the 1960s, suggesting the testing of a new idea or product.

 Advice

Caution should be exercised in the giving and receiving of advice: against the warning Don't teach your grandmother to suck eggs, *we have the reminder that* A fool may give a wise man counsel.

Ask advice, but use your common sense.
American proverb, mid 20th century.

Don't teach your grandmother to suck eggs.
a caution against offering advice to the wise and experienced; English proverb, early 18th century.

A fool may give a wise man counsel.

sometimes used as a warning against overconfidence in one's judgement; English proverb, mid 14th century.

Never give advice unless asked.

German proverb.

Night brings counsel.

sometimes used as a warning against overconfidence in one's judgement; English proverb, mid 14th century.

A nod's as good as a wink to a blind horse.

the slightest hint is enough to convey one's meaning in a particular case; English proverb, late 18th century.

A word to the wise is enough.

only a very brief warning is necessary to an intelligent person; English proverb, early 16th century; earlier in Latin *verbum sat sapienti* [a word is sufficient to a wise man]'.

Age

See also YOUTH

The consensus on the latter part of life is that experience is likely to have brought wisdom: the 'fool at forty' is an exception to the view that The older the ginger the more pungent its flavour.

A fool at forty is a fool indeed.

someone who has not learned wisdom by the age of forty will never learn it; in this form from Edward Young's *Universal Passions* (1725), 'Be wise with speed; A fool at forty is a fool indeed'; English proverb, early 16th century.

For the unlearned, old age is winter; for the learned, it is the season of harvest.

Jewish saying.

The fox may grow grey, but never good.

ageing will not change a person's essential nature; English proverb; compare **The wolf may lose his teeth, but never his nature** below.

The gods send nuts to those who have no teeth.

opportunities or pleasures often come too late to be enjoyed; English proverb, early 20th century.

Life begins at forty.

English proverb, mid 20th century, from the title of a book (1932) by Walter B. Pitkin.

The older the ginger the more pungent its flavour.
older people have more knowledge and experience than the
young; Chinese proverb.

An old horse does not spoil the furrow.
Russian proverb; compare **There's many a good tune played on
an old fiddle** below.

There's many a good tune played on an old fiddle.
someone's abilities do not depend on their being young; English
proverb, early 20th century; compare **An old horse does not
spoil the furrow** above.

There's no fool like an old fool.
often used to suggest that folly in an older person, who should be
wiser, is particularly acute; English proverb, mid 16th century.

**When an elder dies, it is as if a whole library has
burned down.**
African proverb.

The wolf may lose his teeth, but never his nature.
age may affect physical strength, but not a dangerous nature; English
proverb; compare **The fox may grow grey, but never good** above.

Ambition

See also ACHIEVEMENT, SUCCESS AND FAILURE

Although There is always room at the top *is encouraging,
proverbial wisdom warns that the results of pursuing one's
goals may be less than happy:* Many go out for wool and
come home shorn.

Aut Caesar, aut nihil [Caesar or nothing].
motto coined by Cesare Borgia (1476–1507), and inscribed on
his sword.

Hasty climbers have sudden falls.
the over-ambitious often fail to take necessary precautions;
English proverb, mid 15th century.

**The higher the monkey climbs the more he shows
his tail.**
the further an unsuitable person is advanced, the more their
inadequacies are apparent; English proverb, late 14th century.

It's ill waiting for dead men's shoes.
often used of a situation in which one is hoping for a position currently
occupied by another; English proverb, mid 16th century; compare **A
bloody war and a sickly season** at ARMED FORCES.

Many go out for wool and come home shorn.
many who seek to better themselves or make themselves rich
end by losing what they already have; English proverb, late 16th
century.

The smaller the lizard, the greater its hopes of becoming a crocodile.

lack of power may be a spur to ambition; African proverb.

There is always room at the top.

as a response to being advised against joining the overcrowded legal profession, it is also attributed to the American politician and lawyer Daniel Webster (1782–1852); English proverb, early 20th century.

 # Anger

Losing your temper is unproductive, since Anger improves nothing but the arch of a cat's back; *traditional advice suggests using soft answers to deflect the anger of others, and counting to a hundred to avoid becoming angry yourself.*

Anger improves nothing but the arch of a cat's back.

American proverb, mid 20th century.

He that will be angry for anything will be angry for nothing.

frequent anger is likely to be prompted by petty reasons; Scottish proverb.

A little pot is soon hot.

a small person soon becomes angry or passionate; English proverb, mid 16th century.

HE THAT WILL BE

ANGRY FOR

ANYTHING WILL BE

ANGRY FOR NOTHING

A soft answer turneth away wrath.
with allusion to the Bible (Proverbs 15:1); English proverb, late Middle English.

When angry count a hundred.
advising against precipitate response (the number proposed varies, and sometimes the advice is '... recite the alphabet'); English proverb, late 16th century.

 Apology and Excuses

Making excuses to avoid blame is regarded poorly, since He who excuses himself, accuses himself, *and we are told that* A bad workman blames his tools. *However, it may be right to try to make some kind of explanation:* A bad excuse is better than none.

Apology is only egoism wrong side out.
American proverb, mid 20th century.

A bad excuse is better than none.
It is better to attempt to give some kind of explanation, even a weak one; English proverb, mid 16th century.

A bad workman blames his tools.
often used as a comment on someone's excuses for their lack of success; English proverb, early 17th century, late 13th century in French; (compare **One who cannot dance blames the uneven floor** at DANCE).

Don't make excuses, make good.
American proverb, mid 20th century.

Excuse (or pardon) my French.
an informal apology for swearing.

He who excuses himself, accuses himself.
often used to mean that attempts to excuse oneself show a guilty conscience; English proverb, early 17th century.

It is easy to find a stick to beat a dog.
it is easy to find reasons to criticize someone who is vulnerable; English proverb, mid 16th century.

When you are in a hole, stop digging.
complicated explanations and attempts to exculpate oneself often make a bad situation worse; late 20th century saying; often associated with the British Labour politician Denis Healey.

 # Appearance
See also BEAUTY, THE BODY

The idea that Appearances are deceptive *is reflected in a number of sayings. While it may be true that* A carpenter is known by his chips, *we are cautioned in a number of ways against judging by the outward look.*

Appearances are deceptive.
the outward form of something may not be a true guide to its real nature; English proverb, mid 17th century.

A blind man's wife needs no paint.

there is no point in making efforts that cannot be appreciated;
English proverb, mid 17th century.

A carpenter is known by his chips.

the nature of a person's occupation or interest is demonstrated
by the traces left behind; English proverb, mid 16th century.

The cowl does not make the monk.

warning against judging nature and moral character by appearance; English proverb, late 14th century.

Distance lends enchantment to the view.

English proverb, late 18th century, from the lines ''Tis distance
lends enchantment to the view, and robes the mountain in its
azure hue', by Thomas Campbell (1777–1844) in *Pleasures of
Hope* (1799).

Do not judge a tree by its bark.

a warning against making assumptions based on the outward
appearance; Italian proverb.

A fair skin hides seven defects.

Japanese proverb; compare **Beauty is only skin deep** at BEAUTY.

A good horse cannot be of a bad colour.

colour is not an indicator of a horse's quality; English proverb,
early 17th century.

Keep that schoolgirl complexion.

advertising slogan for Palmolive soap, from 1917.

A man without culture is like a zebra without stripes.
African proverb (Masai).

Merit in appearance is more rewarded than merit itself.
American proverb, mid 20th century.

Never choose your women or linen by candlelight.
warning against being deceived by apparent attractions seen in a
poor light; English proverb, late 16th century.

What you see is what you get.
used generally to mean that the function and value of something
can be deduced from its outward appearance, and that there are
no hidden drawbacks or advantages; late 20th century computing
expression, from which the acronym *wysiwyg* derives.

You can't tell a book by its cover.
outward appearance is not a guide to a person's real nature;
English proverb, early 20th century.

 # Architecture

*Building is likely to involve expense, although the 17th-century
view that* Building and marrying of children are great
wasters *may be thought too severe.*

The arch never sleeps.
saying, meaning that an arch constantly thrusts against keystone
and walls.

Building and marrying of children are great wasters.
comparing two major sources of expense for the head of a
household; English proverb.

**In settling an island, the first building erected by a
Spaniard will be a church; by a Frenchman, a fort; by a
Dutchman, a warehouse; and by an Englishman, an
alehouse.**
English proverb, late 18th century.

It is easier to build two chimneys than to maintain one.
the cost of using and maintaining a building may be much
greater than the cost of building it; English proverb, mid 16th
century.

No good building without a good foundation.
English proverb, late 15th century.

***Si monumentum requiris, circumspice* [If you seek a
monument, gaze around].**
Latin inscription in St Paul's Cathedral, London, applied to
Sir Christopher Wren, its architect, and attributed to Wren's son.

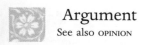

Argument

See also OPINION

Positive injunctions to avoid quarrelling, such as Birds in their little nests agree, *are reinforced by pragmatic reflections as to the dangers of indulging in disagreement:* While two dogs are fighting for a bone, a third runs away with it.

Birds in their little nests agree.

used as a direction that young children should not argue among themselves; a nursery proverb from Isaac Watts *Divine Songs* (1715).

Do not argue against the sun.

there is no point in disputing what is obvious; saying, of Latin origin.

It takes two to make a quarrel.

some responsibility for a disagreement rests with each party to it; English proverb, early 18th century.

The more arguments you win, the less friends you will have.

American proverb, mid 20th century.

The only thing a heated argument ever produced is coolness.

American proverb, mid 20th century.

While two dogs are fighting for a bone, a third runs away with it.

while the attention of two disputants is on their quarrel, they may lose possession of what they are fighting over to a third party; English proverb, late 14th century, which gave rise to the phrase 'bone of contention'.

 # The Armed Forces

See also WARFARE

A number of sayings reflect life within the armed forces over several centuries, from the naval toast A bloody war and a sickly season *from the time of the Napoleonic wars, to the advice to soldiers in the Second World War:* If it moves, salute it; if it doesn't move, pick it up; and if you can't pick it up, paint it.

The army knows how to gain a victory but not how to make proper use of it.

American proverb, mid 20th century.

An army of stags led by a lion would be more formidable than one of lions led by a stag.

courage and tenacity can be negated by poor leadership, while a strong leader can provide crucial encouragement for weak forces; English military saying, of classical origin.

A bloody war and a sickly season.

naval toast in the time of Nelson, when an increased death rate meant more rapid promotion; compare **It's ill waiting for**

---

dead men's shoes at AMBITION and **a willing foe and sea room** below.

Daddy, what did you do in the Great War?
small daughter to father, in First World War recruiting poster; compare **Your King and Country need you** below.

The first duty of a soldier is obedience.
English proverb, mid 19th century.

If it moves, salute it; if it doesn't move, pick it up; and if you can't pick it up, paint it.
1940s military saying.

Old soldiers never die.
English proverb, early 20th century.

One of our aircraft is missing.
title of film (1941), an alteration of the customary formula used by BBC news in the Second World War, 'one of our aircraft failed to return.'

Providence is always on the side of the big battalions.
English proverb, early 19th century; a similar thought can be found earlier in other languages, as the words of the Roman senator and historian Tacitus, '*Deos fortioribus adesse* [The gods are on the side of the stronger]', and the comment in a letter of the French soldier and poet the Comte de Bussy Rabutin (1618–93), 'As you know, God is usually on the side of the big squadrons against the small.'

A singing army and a singing people can't be defeated.
American proverb, mid 20th century.

A soldier of the Great War known unto God.
adopted by the War Graves Commission as the standard epitaph
for the unidentified dead of World War One.

A willing foe and sea room.
naval toast in the time of Nelson (compare **a bloody war and a
sickly season** above).

Your King and Country need you.
1914 recruiting advertisement, showing Lord Kitchener with
pointing finger; compare **Daddy, what did you do in the Great
War?** above.

**Your soul may belong to God, but your ass belongs to
the army.**
American saying to new recruits, mid 20th century.

 Art

Even a talented painter needs to practise their art: the advice
Not a day without a line *goes back to the classical world.*

Every painter paints himself.
Italian proverb, said to be of Renaissance origin.

A good painter can draw a devil as well as an angel.
English proverb, late 16th century.

Not a day without a line.
traditional saying, attributed to the Greek artist Apelles (fl. 325 BC) by Pliny the Elder.

 # Autumn
See also SPRING, SUMMER, WINTER

There are notably fewer proverbs about Autumn than the other seasons, and those in use today sound a cautionary note.

All autumns do not fill granaries.
Estonian proverb.

Chickens are counted in the autumn.
Russian proverb; compare **Don't count your chickens before they are hatched** at OPTIMISM, and **May chickens come cheeping** at SPRING.

If you do not sow in the spring, you will not reap in the autumn.
Irish proverb.

September blow soft till the fruit's in the loft.
expressing the hope that fine weather often customary in September will hold until a crop of apples or other fruit has been picked and stored; English proverb, late 16th century.

Beauty

See also APPEARANCE, THE BODY

The early 20th-century advertising slogan Beauty is power
*reflects a traditional awareness of the force of physical attrac-
tion, but as far back as the 17th century we have also been
warned that* Beauty is only skin deep.

Beauty draws with a single hair.
asserting the powerful attraction of a woman's beauty (often
shown as outdoing great physical strength); English proverb, late
16th century.

Beauty is a good letter of introduction.
American proverb, mid 20th century.

Beauty is in the eye of the beholder.
beauty is not judged objectively, but according to the beholder's
estimation; English proverb, early 17th century.

Beauty is only skin deep.
physical beauty is no guarantee of a good character or temper-
ament; English proverb, early 17th century; compare **A fair skin
hides seven defects** at APPEARANCE.

Beauty is power.
advertising slogan for Helena Rubinstein's Valaze Skin Food, 1904.

Black is beautiful.
slogan of American civil rights campaigners, mid 1960s.

It is the beautiful bird that gets caged.

beauty has its own dangers; Chinese proverb.

**Mirror, mirror on the wall, Who is the fairest of
them all?**

the customary invocation of Snow White's wicked stepmother,
which in due time received the response that Snow White rather
than the Queen was now the most beautiful of all; in the early
19th-century translation of the Grimm Brothers' *Fairytales*.

Monday's child is fair of face.

first line of a traditional rhyme, mid 19th century (compare
qualities associated with birth on other days at entries under
GIFTS, SORROW, TRAVEL, and WORK).

Please your eye and plague your heart.

contrasting the pleasure given by the appearance of a beautiful
person with the heartache they may cause; English proverb,
early 17th century.

Beginning

See also CHANGE, ENDING

Starting well is important, as we are told that A good
beginning makes a good ending, *but it is also wise to consider whether the course on which you are embarking is a wise
one:* It is easier to raise the Devil than to lay him.

Are you sitting comfortably? Then we'll begin.

introduction to stories on *Listen with Mother*, BBC Radio programme for small children, 1950–82, coined by the presenter
Julia Lang (1921–).

Beginning is easy; continuing is hard.
a good start is not enough, since success requires pertinacity;
modern saying, said to be a Japanese proverb.

First impressions are the most lasting.
English proverb, early 18th century.

The golden rule of life is, make a beginning.
American proverb, mid 20th century.

A good beginning makes a good ending.
getting things right at the outset is likely to ensure success;
English proverb, early 14th century.

It is easier to raise the Devil than to lay him.
sometimes used to mean that it is easier to start a process than to
stop it; English proverb, mid 17th century.

It is the first step that is difficult.
English proverb, late 16th century.

It was a dark and stormy night.
one variant of an opening line intended to convey a threatening
and doom-laden atmosphere; in this form used by the novelist
Edward Bulwer-Lytton (1803–73) in his novel *Paul Clifford* (1830).

I've started so I'll finish.
said by Magnus Magnusson when a contestant's time ran out
while a question was being put, on *Mastermind*, BBC television
(1972–97).

The longest journey begins with a single step.
often used to emphasize how important a single decision may be;
late 20th-century saying, ultimately derived from words of the

Chinese philosopher Lao Tzu (*c*.604–*c*.531 BC) in the *Tao-te Ching*, 'A tower of nine storeys begins with a heap of earth. The journey of a thousand *li* starts from where one stands.'

The sooner begun, the sooner done.
used as a warning against putting off a necessary but unwanted task; English proverb, late 16th century.

There is always a first time.
English proverb, late 16th century.

Well begun is half done.
emphasizing the importance of a successful beginning to the completion of a project; English proverb, early 15th century.

Behaviour
See also MANNERS, WORDS AND DEEDS

While there is a traditional emphasis on the importance of right action, as in Do as I say, not as I do, *there is also a certain scepticism about what may be only the appearance of good behaviour:* Handsome is as handsome does.

Be what you would seem to be.
English proverb, late 14th century; earlier in classical sources, as in *Seven against Thebes* by the Greek tragedian Aeschylus (*c*.525–456 BC), 'He wishes not to appear but to be the best.'

By a sweet tongue and kindness, you can drag an elephant by a hair.
Middle Eastern proverb, commonly found in this form in Arabic; the equivalent proverb in Persian has 'drag a snake'.

Cleanliness is next to godliness.

next here means 'immediately following', as in serial order, and is now often used humorously to mean 'the second most desirable quality possible'; English proverb, late 18th century.

Do as I say, not as I do.

often used with an imputation of hypocrisy; English proverb, mid 16th century.

Evil communications corrupt good manners.

proper conduct is harmfully influenced by false information or knowledge; the saying is also sued to assert the deleterious effect of bad example; English proverb, early 15th century, from the Bible (1 Corinthians 15:33).

Good behaviour is the last refuge of mediocrity.

American proverb, mid 20th century.

Handsome is as handsome does.

handsome here referred to chivalrous or genteel behaviour, although it is often popularly taken to refer to good looks; English proverb, late 16th century; compare **Pretty is as pretty does** below.

He is a good dog who goes to church.

good character is shown by moral custom and practice; English proverb, early 19th century.

It is one thing to keep your morals on high plane; it's another to keep up with them.

American proverb, mid 20th century.

Never do evil that good may come of it.
the prospect of a good outcome cannot justify wrongdoing;
English proverb, late 16th century.

Pretty is as pretty does.
American proverb, mid 19th century, equivalent of **Handsome is
as handsome does** above.

When in Rome, do as the Romans do.
English proverb, late 15th century; ultimately deriving from a
passage in a letter of St Ambrose, AD *c*.400, 'When I go to Rome,
I fast on Saturday, but here [Milan] I do not. Do you also follow
the custom of whatever church you attend, if you do not want to
give or receive scandal.'

 Belief
See also CERTAINTY AND DOUBT

Belief may relate to religious faith as in Faith will move mountains, *but some traditional sayings deal with more general questions of how you should approach the world around you:* Believe
nothing of what you hear, and only half of what you see.

**Believe nothing of what you hear, and only half of
what you see.**
English proverb, mid 19th century; a related Middle English
saying warns that you should not believe everything that is said
or that you hear.

A believer is a songless bird in a cage.
American proverb, late 19th century.

Believing has a core of unbelieving.
American proverb, mid 19th century.

Don't strain at a gnat, and swallow a camel.
do not make difficulties over a small matter, when you have
already accepted something of much greater importance; saying
with biblical allusion, to Matthew 23:24, 'Ye blind guides, which
strain at a gnat, and swallow a camel.'

Faith will move mountains.
with the help of faith something naturally impossible can be
achieved; English proverb, late 19th century, in allusion to the
Bible (Matthew 17:20, 'If ye have faith as a grain of mustard seed,
ye shall say unto this mountain, Remove hence to yonder place;
and it shall remove').

Ohhh, I don't believe it.
catchphrase used by Victor Meldrew (played by Richard Wilson)
in *One Foot in the Grave* (BBC television series, 1989–2000), written by David Renwick.

Pigs may fly, but they are very unlikely birds.
English proverb, mid 19th century.

Seeing is believing.
acceptance of the existence of something depends on actual
demonstration; English proverb, early 17th century.

Tell that to the marines.
a scornful expression of disbelief, from the saying *that will do for
the marines but the sailors won't believe it* (the marines were

originally soldiers enlisted and trained to serve aboard ship); the expression is recorded from the early 19th century, although a late 19th-century hoax attributing the origin to a remark made by Charles II to Samuel Pepys has been widely reprinted.

 ## Birds

Sayings relating to birds are likely to reflect the associations of particular species, from the English magpies whose gathering may foretell sorrow or mirth, to the rare white heron of New Zealand.

Birds of prey do not sing.
German proverb.

A mockingbird has no voice of his own.
the mockingbird is known for its mimicry of the calls and songs of other birds; American proverb, mid 19th century.

One for sorrow; two for mirth; three for a wedding, four for a birth.
a traditional rhyme found in a variety of forms, referring to the number of magpies seen on a particular occasion; English proverb, mid 19th century.

The robin and the wren are God's cock and hen; the martin and the swallow are God's mate and marrow.
there was a traditional belief that the robin and the wren were sacred birds, and that to harm them in any way would be

unlucky (*marrow* = 'companion'); English proverb, late 18th century.

The white heron is a bird of a single flight.
the white heron is very rare; Maori proverb.

 # The Body
See also APPEARANCE, BEAUTY, THE SENSES

Physical characteristics may give a clue to inner qualities, from Cold hands, warm heart *to* The larger the body, the bigger the heart.

Cold hands, warm heart.
an outward sign may contradict an inward reality; English proverb, early 20th century.

The eyes are the window of the soul.
it is in the eyes that a person's true nature may be discerned; English proverb, mid 16th century.

The larger the body, the bigger the heart.
American proverb, mid 20th century.

Books

See also READING, WRITING

While not every book is admirable (A great book is a great evil), the consensus of proverbial wisdom is in favour of the written word: A book is like a garden carried in the pocket.

Beware of the man of one book.
warning against the person who places too much confidence in a single authority; Latin proverb.

A book is like a garden carried in the pocket.
Middle Eastern saying.

A great book is a great evil.
a long book is likely to be verbose and badly written; English proverb, early 17th century; a contraction of Callimachus (*c.*305–*c.*240 BC), 'The great book is equal to a great evil.'

A library is a repository of medicine for the mind.
American proverb, mid 20th century.

Borrowing

See DEBT AND BORROWING

British Towns and Regions

Local pride is an enduring quality, whether expressed in a traditional saying such as Kirton was a borough town when Exon was a vuzzy down, *or a 20th-century slogan such as* Glasgow's miles better.

Essex stiles, Kentish miles, Norfolk wiles, many a man beguiles.
traditional saying, early 17th century.

From Hell, Hull, and Halifax, good Lord deliver us.
traditional saying, late 16th century.

Glasgow's miles better.
slogan introduced by Provost Michael Kelly, 1980s.

Kirton was a borough town when Exon was a vuzzy down.
on the relative ages of Crediton (*Kirton*) and Exeter (*Exon*); traditional saying.

Lincoln was, London is, and York shall be.
referring to which is the greatest city; traditional saying, late 16th century.

**London Bridge is broken down
My fair lady.**
traditional nursery rhyme, early 18th century.

May God in His mercy look down on Belfast.
traditional refrain.

Northamptonshire for squires and spires.
traditional saying, late 19th century.

Peebles for pleasure.
the town of Peebles in the Scottish Borders has traditionally been a favoured holiday resort; traditional saying, late 19th century.

Some places of Kent have health and no wealth, some wealth and no health, some health and wealth.
referring to the north and east part of the county, Romney Marsh, and the Weald respectively; traditional saying, late 16th century.

Sussex won't be druv.
asserting that Sussex people have minds of their own, and cannot be forced against their will (*druv* is a dialect version of *drove*, meaning *driven*); English proverb, early 20th century.

Take away Aberdeen and twelve miles round, and where are you?
Scottish saying, reflecting local pride in the city.

There are more saints in Cornwall than in heaven.
traditional saying, relating to the number of West Country saints known through their local cult.

What Manchester says today, the rest of England says tomorrow.
English proverb, late 19th century, occurring in a variety of forms.

Yorkshire born and Yorkshire bred, strong in the arm and weak in the head.

the names of other (chiefly northern) English counties and towns are also used instead of Yorkshire; English proverb, mid 19th century.

 # Broadcasting

The early days of broadcasting are associated with the high-minded aspirations of Nation shall speak peace unto nation; *later years brought a somewhat more flippant approach, as in the American advice* Always turn the radio on before you listen to it.

Always turn the radio on before you listen to it.

American saying, mid 20th century.

Assistant heads must roll!

traditional solution to management problems in broadcasting.

Nation shall speak peace unto nation.

motto of the BBC, adapted from the Bible (Isaiah 2:4, 'Nation shall not lift up sword against nation, neither shall they learn war any more') by Montague John Rendall (1862–1950).

So much chewing gum for the eyes.

small boy's definition of certain television programmes, 1950.

Business

See also BUYING AND SELLING

While not all sayings go as far as the modern Business is war, *there is a consensus in favour of determined application:* Business before pleasure, *and* Business neglected is business lost.

Bull markets climb a wall of worry.
signs of recovery from a recession are treated with scepticism; modern saying.

Business before pleasure.
often used to encourage a course of action; English proverb, mid 19th century.

Business goes where it is invited and stays where it is well treated.
American proverb, mid 20th century.

Business is like a car: it will not run by itself except downhill.
American proverb, mid 20th century.

Business is war.
modern saying, sometimes said to be of Japanese origin.

Business neglected is business lost.
North American proverb, mid 20th century.

The customer is always right.

English proverb, early 20th century; compare a saying of the Swiss hotel proprietor César Ritz (1850–1918), '*Le client n'a jamais tort* [The customer is never wrong].'

He that cannot abide a bad market does not deserve a good one.

to be successful in business you must be able to deal with bad times as well as good; English proverb, late 17th century.

If you don't speculate, you can't accumulate.

outlay (and some degree of risk) is necessary if real gain is to be achieved; English proverb, mid 20th century.

I liked it so much, I bought the company!

advertising slogan for Remington Shavers, coined by the owner Victor Kiam (1926–2001).

Keep your own shop and your shop will keep you.

recommending attention to what is essential to one's livelihood; English proverb, early 17th century.

Never knowingly undersold.

motto, from *c*.1920, of the John Lewis partnership.

No cure, no pay.

known principally from its use on Lloyd's of London's Standard Form of Salvage Agreement; English proverb, late 19th century.

No penny, no paternoster.

if you want a thing you must pay for it (the allusion is to priests insisting on being paid for performing services); English proverb, late 16th century.

Pay beforehand was never well served.

payment in advance removes the incentive to finish the work; English proverb, late 16th century.

Pile it high, sell it cheap.

slogan coined by Jack Cohen (1898–1979), founder of the Tesco supermarket chain.

There are tricks in every trade.

the practice of every skill is likely to involve some trickery or dishonesty; English proverb, mid 17th century.

Trade follows the flag.

commercial development is likely to follow military intervention; English proverb, late 19th century.

Buying and Selling

See also BUSINESS

The warning Let the buyer beware, *drawn ultimately from the classical world, enshrines a core belief about the world of commerce. More explicit advice along the same lines is found in the saying,* The buyer has need of a hundred eyes, the seller of but one.

The bulls make money, the bears make money, but the hogs get slaughtered.

money can be made through buying or selling stock, but greed is fatal; modern saying.

The buyer has need of a hundred eyes, the seller of but one.

stressing the responsibility of a purchaser to examine the goods on offer; English proverb, mid 17th century.

Buy in the cheapest market and sell in the dearest.

sometimes with an implication of sharp practice; English proverb, late 16th century.

Let the buyer beware.

warning that it is up to a buyer to establish the nature and value of a purchase before completing the transaction; English proverb, early 16th century; the saying is also found in the form of the Latin tag *caveat emptor*.

Sell in May and go away (come back on St Leger's Day).

saying related to the cycle of activity on the London Stock Exchange. May, shortly after the start of the financial year, was traditionally a busy time, but during the summer months trading was slack as Londoners (including stockbrokers) took their holiday breaks away from the capital. The full form of the saying refers to the classic St Leger horse race, taken as marking the end of the English summer social calendar.

You buy land, you buy stones; you buy meat, you buy bones.

every purchase has its drawbacks; English proverb, late 17th century.

Cats

See also DOGS

Sayings about cats emphasize not only their independence of humankind, but also their capacity to survive: A cat always lands on its feet.

A cat always lands on its feet.
a cat's natural agility typifies its ability to escape from trouble; traditional saying.

A cat has nine lives.
traditional saying.

A cat may look at a king.
even someone in a lowly position has a right to observe a person of power and influence; English proverb, mid 16th century.

Feed a dog for three days and he will remember your kindness for three years. Feed a cat for three years and she will forget your kindness in three days.
Japanese proverb.

Touch not the cat but a glove.
but = without, and the cat referred to here is a wild cat; Scottish proverb, early 19th century.

Causes and Consequences

Deliberate choice will have a result which may be unwelcome, as in After the feast comes the reckoning. *However, traditional wisdom also emphasizes that something of apparent unimportance may have significant consequences:* The mother of mischief is no bigger than a midge's wing.

After the feast comes the reckoning.
a period of pleasure or indulgence has to be paid for; English proverb, early 17th century, but now chiefly in modern North American use.

As you bake, so shall you brew.
as you begin, so shall you proceed; English proverb, late 16th century.

As you brew, so shall you bake.
your circumstances will be shaped by your own initial actions; English proverb, late 16th century.

As you make your bed, so you must lie upon it.
as you begin, so shall you proceed; English proverb, late 16th century.

As you sow, so you reap.
you will have to endure the consequences of your actions; English proverb, late 15th century; compare **They that sow the wind, shall reap the whirlwind** below.

A fence between makes love more keen.
impediments between lovers are likely to increase fondness;
German proverb.

Good seed makes a bad crop.
something which has a sound basis will do well; English proverb,
mid 16th century.

Great oaks from little acorns grow.
great results may ensue from apparently small beginnings;
English proverb, late 14th century.

He who plants thorns must not expect to gather roses.
Arabic proverb.

If you want to see heaven, you have to die yourself.
Indian proverb.

Kill the chicken to scare the monkey.
make an example of those in a weak position to frighten possible
stronger opponents; Chinese saying.

The mother of mischief is no bigger than a midge's wing.
the origin of difficulties can be very small; English proverb, early
17th century.

Sow much, reap much; sow little, reap little.
Chinese proverb.

There is reason in the roasting of eggs.

however odd an action may seem, there is a reason for it; English proverb, mid 17th century.

They that sow the wind, shall reap the whirlwind.

those who have initiated a dangerous course must suffer the consequences; English proverb, late 16th century; compare **As you sow, so you reap** above.

Who won't be ruled by the rudder must be ruled by the rock.

a ship which is not being steered on its course will run on to a rock; English proverb, mid 17th century.

 Caution

See also DANGER

We may put ourselves at risk through lack of caution, but someone who adheres too closely to the advice Better be safe than sorry *may miss out on possible benefits, since* A cat in gloves catches no mice.

Better be safe than sorry.

urging the wisdom of taking precautions; English proverb, mid 19th century.

A bird in the hand is worth two in the bush.

it is better to accept what one has than to try to get more and risk losing everything; English proverb, mid 15th century.

HE WHO FIGHTS

AND RUNS AWAY

LIVES TO FIGHT

ANOTHER DAY

Call on God, but row away from the rocks.

make an effort to avoid a dangerous situation; Indian proverb.

A cat in gloves catches no mice.

deliberate restraint and caution (or 'pussyfooting') often result in failure to achieve anything; English proverb, late 16th century.

Caution is the parent of safety.

American proverb, early 18th century.

Delhi is far away.

warning that unexpected events may intervene in apparently dangerous circumstances; Indian proverb, deriving from the response of the 14th-century Sufi mystic Nizamuddin Aulia to a threat from the Sultan of Delhi (the Sultan in fact died before returning home); compare **God is high above, and the tsar is far away** and **The mountains are high, and the emperor is far away** at GOVERNMENT.

Discretion is the better part of valour.

often used to explain cautious action, and sometimes with allusion to Shakespeare's 1 *Henry IV* (1597), 'The better part of valour is discretion'; English proverb, late 16th century.

Don't put all your eggs in one basket.

you should not chance everything on a single venture, but spread the risk; English proverb, mid 17th century.

Don't put up your umbrella before it rains.
do not take defensive action before it becomes necessary; modern saying.

Duck and cover.
US advice in the event of a missile attack, c.1950; associated particularly with the children's cartoon character 'Bert the Turtle'.

Full cup, steady hand.
used especially to caution against spoiling a comfortable or otherwise enviable situation by a careless action; English proverb, early 11th century.

Go in, stay in, tune in.
British government advice on preparing for emergencies, 2004.

He who fights and runs away, lives to fight another day.
English proverb, mid 16th century.

He who has been scalded by hot milk, blows even on cold lassi before drinking it.
lassi = an Indian drink, traditionally based on diluted buttermilk or yoghurt, and usually served chilled; Indian proverb; compare **Once bitten by a snake, a man will be afraid of a piece of rope for three years** below.

He who sups with the devil should have a long spoon.
one should be cautious when dealing with dangerous persons;
English proverb, late 14th century.

If you can't be good, be careful.
often used as a humorous warning; English proverb, early 20th
century; the same idea is found in 11th-century Latin, *si non caste
tamen caute*.

Let's be careful out there.
catchphrase from *Hill Street Blues* (police procedural
television series, 1981–7), written by Steven Bochco and
Michael Kozoll.

Let sleeping dogs lie.
something which may be dangerous or difficult to handle is
better left undisturbed; English proverb, late 14th century;
compare **Poke a bush, a snake comes out** below.

Let well alone.
often used as a warning against raising problems which will then
be difficult to resolve; English proverb, late 16th century;
compare **Never trouble trouble till trouble troubles you** below.

Look before you leap.
used to advise caution before committing oneself to a course of
action; English proverb, mid 14th century.

The more you stir it [a turd] the worse it stinks.
disturbance of something naturally unpleasant will only make it
more disagreeable; English proverb, mid 16th century.

Never trouble trouble till trouble troubles you.

another version of the advice that one should let well alone; English proverb, late 19th century.

Once bitten by a snake, a man will be afraid of a piece of rope for three years.

Chinese proverb; compare **He who has been scalded by hot milk, blows even on cold lassi before drinking it** above, and **Once bitten, twice shy** at EXPERIENCE.

Poke a bush, a snake comes out.

warning against unnecessary disturbance; Japanese proverb; compare **Let sleeping dogs lie** above.

Safe bind, safe find.

something kept securely will be readily found again; English proverb, mid 16th century.

Second thoughts are best.

it is dangerous to act on one's first impulse without due thought; English proverb, late 16th century.

Steady as she goes!

injunction to hold carefully to the course set; nautical saying.

A stitch in time saves nine.

a small but timely intervention will ensure against the need for much more substantial repair later; English proverb, early 18th century.

Stop-look-and-listen.
road safety slogan, current in the US from 1912.

Those who play at bowls must look out for rubbers.
one must beware of difficulties associated with a particular
activity; *rubber* here is an alteration of *rub*, an obstacle or impe-
diment to the course of a bowl; English proverb, mid 18th
century.

Trust in Allah, but tie up your camel.
Arab proverb; compare **Put your trust in God, and keep your
powder dry** at PRACTICALITY.

We won't make a drama out of a crisis.
advertising slogan for Commercial Union insurance.

Certainty and Doubt
See also BELIEF, FAITH, INDECISION

We may be urged to be definite in our views, but proverbially
Nothing is certain but death and taxes.

Does she ... or doesn't she?
advertising slogan for Clairol hair colouring, 1950s.

Don't be vague, ask for Haig.
advertising slogan for Haig whisky, *c.*1936.

The eyes believe themselves; the ears believe other people.
others may persuade us not to believe the evidence of our own eyes; Greek proverb.

Nothing is certain but death and taxes.
summarizing what in life is inevitable and inescapable; English proverb, early 18th century.

 # Chance and Luck

Against the view that Blind chance sweeps the world along, *there are suggestions that there are ways to make your own fortune:* Diligence is the mother of good luck. *Occasionally, too, the right patronage may be helpful:* The Devil looks after his own.

Accidents will happen (in the best regulated families).
the most orderly arrangements cannot prevent accidents from occurring; English proverb, mid 18th century.

Blind chance sweeps the world along.
American proverb, mid 20th century.

The devil looks after his own.

often used to comment on the good fortune of someone undeserving; English proverb, early 18th century.

The devil's children have the devil's luck.

commenting on the good fortune of someone undeserving; English proverb, late 17th century.

Diligence is the mother of good luck.

success results more from application and practice than from good fortune; English proverb, late 16th century.

Fools for luck.

a foolish person is traditionally fortunate; English proverb, mid 19th century.

A great fortune depends on luck; a smaller one on diligence.

for outstanding success we need good luck as well as the capacity for hard work; Chinese proverb.

The harder I work, the luckier I get.

modern saying, often as a response to having success attributed to good fortune.

If you want to live and thrive, let the spider run alive.

It was traditionally unlucky to harm a spider or a spider's web; English proverb, mid 19th century.

It could be you.

advertising slogan for the British national lottery, 1994.

It is better to be born lucky than rich.

often with the implication that riches can be lost or spent, but that good luck gives one the capacity of improve one's fortunes; English proverb, mid 17th century.

Lightning never strikes the same place twice.

often used as an encouragement that a particular misfortune will not be repeated; English proverb, mid 19th century.

Lucky at cards, unlucky in love.

suggesting that good fortune in gambling is balanced by lack of success in love; English proverb, mid 19th century.

Moses took a chance.

used to urge someone to take a risk; American proverb, mid 20th century.

See a pin and pick it up, all the day you'll have good luck; see a pin and let it lie, bad luck you'll have all day.

extolling the virtues of thrift in small matters; English proverb, mid 19th century.

There is luck in odd numbers.

English proverb, late 16th century.

The third time is the charm.

modern saying; compare **Third time lucky** below.

Third time lucky.

reflecting the idea that three is a lucky number; often used to suggest making another effort after initial failure; English proverb, mid 19th century; compare **The third time is the charm** above.

Throw a lucky man into the sea, and he will come up with a fish in his mouth.

a fortunate person will have further luck; Arabic proverb.

You have two chances, Buckley's and none.

Australian proverb; in Australia, *Buckley's chance* means a slim chance or no chance at all, and is sometimes said to derive from the name of William Buckley (died 1856), who, despite dire predictions as to his chances of survival, lived with the Aboriginals for many years.

 # Change

See also BEGINNING, ENDING

Change may be refreshing (A change is as good as a rest)*, or tiring* (Three removals are as bad as a fire)*. However, perhaps more importantly, there is an awareness that some things cannot be changed:* No matter how long a log floats in the river, it will never become a crocodile.

Always something new out of Africa.

English proverb, mid 16th century; from Pliny the Elder (AD 23–79)'s words '*Semper aliquid novi Africam adferre* [Africa always brings [us] something new]', originally referring to the hybridization of African animals.

And now for something completely different.

catchphrase popularized in *Monty Python's Flying Circus* (BBC TV programme, 1969–74).

Be sure you can better your condition before you make a change.

American proverb, mid 20th century.

A change is as good as a rest.

suggesting that a change of activity can be refreshing; English proverb, late 19th century.

It is never too late to mend.

one can always try to improve; English proverb, late 16th century.

The leopard does not change his spots.

a person cannot change their essential nature, from the Bible (Jeremiah 13:23), 'Can the Ethiopian change his skin, or the leopard his spots?'; English proverb, mid 16th century; compare **By seeing one spot, you know the entire leopard** at CHARACTER.

Never say never.

used as a warning against over-confidence that circumstances cannot change; late 20th century saying; compare **Never is a long time** and TIME.

New brooms sweep clean.

often used in the context of someone newly appointed to a post who is making changes in personnel and procedures; English proverb, mid 16th century.

New lords, new laws.

new authorities are likely to change existing rules; English proverb, mid 16th century.

No matter how long a log floats in the river, it will never become a crocodile.

essential characteristics will not change; African proverb; compare **Feeding a snake with milk will not change its poisonous nature** at CHARACTER.

No more Mr Nice Guy.

said to assert that one will no longer be amiable or cooperative; mid 20th-century saying.

Nothing is for ever.

late 20th-century saying.

Other times, other manners.

used in resignation or consolation; English proverb, late 16th century.

Semper eadem.

Latin, meaning 'Ever the same', the motto of Elizabeth I (1533–1603).

There are no birds in last year's nest.

circumstances have changed, and former opportunities are no longer there; English proverb, early 17th century.

Three removals are as bad as a fire.

moving house is so disruptive and unsettling, that the effects of doing it three times are as devastating as a house fire; English proverb, mid 18th century.

Times change and we with time.

we adapt in response to changes in the world around us; English proverb, late 16th century.

To change, and change for the better, are two different things.

German proverb.

Turkeys, heresy, hops, and beer came into England all in one year.

perhaps referring to 1521. The *turkey*, found domesticated in Mexico in 1518, was soon afterwards introduced into Europe; in 1521, the Pope conferred on Henry VIII the title Defender of the Faith, in recognition of his opposition to the Lutheran *heresy*; the *hop*-plant is believed to have been introduced into the south of England from Flanders between 1520 and 1524; and *beer* as the name of hopped malt liquor became common only in the 16th century; English proverb, late 16th century.

Variety is the spice of life.

English proverb, late 18th century, originally with allusion to William Cowper's *The Task* (1785), 'Variety's the very spice of life,/ That gives it all its flavour.'

You can't put new wine in old bottles.

often used in relation to the introduction of new ideas or practices; English proverb, early 20th century, from the Bible (Matthew 9:17), 'Neither do men put new wine into old bottles: else the bottles break, and the wine runneth out, and the bottles perish.'

When the music changes, so does the dance.
a reminder that we need to change with the times; African proverb.

Character

See also THE HUMAN RACE, REPUTATION

A number of sayings reflect on essential characteristics displayed through outward appearance: By seeing one spot, you know the entire leopard. *However, there is some warning against making too ready assumptions from outer circumstances:* The man who is born in a stable is not a horse.

An ape's an ape, a varlet's a varlet, though they be clad in silk or scarlet.
inward nature cannot be overcome by outward show; English proverb, mid 16th century.

A bad penny always turns up.
referring to the inevitable return of an unwanted or disreputable person; English proverb, mid 18th century.

The bee sucks honey where the spider sucks poison.
we make the best or worst of things depending on our own nature; English proverb.

IT TAKES ALL
SORTS TO MAKE
A WORLD

Better a good cow than a cow of a good kind.

good character is more important than distinguished lineage;
English proverb, early 20th century.

By seeing one spot, you know the entire leopard.

Japanese proverb; compare **The leopard does not change his
spots** at CHANGE.

*Cet animal est très méchant: Quand on l'attaque, il se
défend* ['**This animal is very vicious: when attacked, it
defends itself**'].

ironic recognition that a natural urge to defend yourself may be
interpreted as aggression; French proverb.

**Character is what we are; reputation is what others
think we are.**

American proverb, mid 20th century.

The child is the father of the man.

asserting the unity of character from childhood to adult life;
English proverb, early 19th century; from Wordsworth's lines
'The Child is father of the Man; And I could wish my days to be
Bound each to each by natural piety.'

Diamond cuts diamond.

used of persons who are evenly matched in wit or cunning (only
a diamond is hard enough to cut another diamond); English
proverb, early 17th century.

Eagles don't catch flies.
great or important persons do not concern themselves with trifling matters; English proverb, mid 16th century.

Feeding a snake with milk will not change its poisonous nature.
kindness will not alter a bad character; Indian proverb; compare
No matter how long a log floats in the river, it will never become a crocodile at CHANGE.

Iron sharpens iron.
friends of the same calibre can strengthen one another; modern saying, with biblical allusion to Proverbs 27:17, 'Iron sharpeneth iron; so a man sharpeneth the countenance of his friend.'

It takes all sorts to make a world.
often used in recognition that a particular group may encompass a wide range of character and background; English proverb, early 17th century.

Like a fence, character cannot be strengthened by whitewash.
American proverb, mid 20th century.

The man who is born in a stable is not a horse.
sometimes attributed to the Duke of Wellington, who asserted that being born in Ireland did not make him Irish; English proverb, mid 19th century.

Once a —, always a —.

a particular way of life produces traits that cannot be eradicated; English proverb, early 17th century; compare **Once a priest, always a priest** at CLERGY.

The same fire that hardens the egg melts the butter.

different people will react in different ways to the same experiences; modern saying, but the idea is found in the early 17th century in the words of Francis Bacon (1561–1623), 'In one and the same fire, clay grows hard and wax melts.'

A sleeping fox counts hens in his dreams.

particular characteristics affect all we do; Russian proverb.

Still waters run deep.

now commonly used to assert that a placid exterior hides a passionate nature; English proverb, early 15th century; compare **Where the river is deepest, it makes the least noise** below.

A stream cannot rise above its source.

used to suggest that a person's natural level is set by their ultimate origin; English proverb, mid 17th century.

The style is the man.

one's chosen style reflects one's essential characteristics; English proverb, early 20th century, although a similar thought is found earlier in French, in the Comte de Buffon's words to the Académie Française on 25 August 1753, 'These things [subject matter] are external to the man; style is the man.'

There's many a good cock come out of a tattered bag.

something good may emerge from unpromising surroundings (the reference is to cockfighting); English proverb, late 19th century.

The tree is known by its fruit.

a person is judged by what they do and produce; English proverb, early 16th century.

What can you expect from a pig but a grunt?

used rhetorically of coarse or boorish behaviour; English proverb, mid 18th century.

What's bred in the bone will come out in the flesh.

inherent characteristics will in the end become apparent; English proverb, late 15th century.

When the going gets tough, the tough get going.

pressure acts as a stimulus to the strong; English proverb, mid 20th century, often used by Joseph Kennedy (1888–1969) as an injunction to his children.

Where the river is deepest, it makes the least noise.

Italian proverb; compare **Still waters run deep** above.

You cannot dream yourself into a character, you must forge one out for yourself.

American proverb, mid 20th century.

You dirty rat.
frequently attributed to James Cagney in a gangster part, but not
found in this precise form in any of his films.

 Charity
See also GENEROSITY

Together with praise for the natural springs of charity, The
roots of charity are always green, *there may be a note of self-
interest:* Keep your own fish-guts for your own sea-maws.

Charity begins at home.
you should look first to needs in your immediate vicinity; English
proverb, late 14th century.

**Charity is not a bone you throw to a dog but a bone
you share with a dog.**
the recipient of one's charity should not be treated as an inferior;
American proverb, mid 20th century.

Charity sees the need, not the cause.
true charity succours need regardless of whether the needy
person is responsible for their own situation; German proverb.

Give a man a fish, and you feed him for a day; show him how to catch fish, and you feed him for a lifetime.

mid 20th century saying, perhaps deriving from a Chinese saying; compare **Who teaches me for a day, is my father for a lifetime** at TEACHING.

If everyone gives a thread, the poor man will have a shirt.

a little from each person makes an effective whole; Russian proverb.

Keep your own fish-guts for your own sea-maws.

any surplus product should be offered first to those in need who are closest to you; Scottish proverb, early 18th century.

The roots of charity are always green.

true generosity constantly renews itself; American proverb, mid 20th century.

Service is the rent we pay for our room on earth.

modern saying, deriving from the admission ceremony of Toc H, a society, originally of ex-servicemen and women, founded by Tubby Clayton (1885–1972) after the First World War to promote Christian fellowship and social service.

Children
See also THE FAMILY, PARENTS, YOUTH

Changes in attitude have moved the focus on child-rearing from the repressive Children should be seen and not heard *and* Spare the rod, and spoil the child *to the duty of society to nurture as expressed by the African saying,* It takes a village to raise a child.

And the child that is born on the Sabbath day,
Is bonny, and blithe, and good and gay.
line from a traditional rhyme (compare qualities associated with birth on other days at entries under BEAUTY, GIFTS, SORROW, TRAVEL, and WORK).

The art of being a parent consists of sleeping when the baby isn't looking.
American proverb, mid 20th century.

Children: one is one, two is fun, three is a houseful.
American proverb, mid 20th century.

Children should be seen and not heard.
originally applied specifically to (young) women; English proverb, early 15th century.

It takes a village to raise a child.
many in the community have a role in a child's development; African proverb (Yoruba).

Jeannie Jeannie, full of hopes
Read a book by Marie Stopes
But to judge from her condition
She must have read the wrong edition.

1920s skipping rhyme; Marie Stopes (1880–1958) was a Scottish birth-control campaigner.

Little children, little sorrows; big children, great sorrows.

even when grown up, children are likely to be a source of concern to their parents; Danish proverb.

No moon, no man.

recording the traditional belief that a child born at the time of the new moon or just before its appearance will not live to grow up; English proverb, late 19th century.

Spare the rod and spoil the child.

the result of not disciplining a child is to spoil it; English proverb, early 11th century, sometimes with allusion to the Bible (Proverbs 13:24), 'He that spareth his rod hateth his son.'

Choice

See also INDECISION

Choice may be inevitable, as in A door must be either shut or open, *but it is noticeable how often the view is that we find ourselves choosing between unpalatable options:* Small choice in rotten apples.

Better red than dead.

slogan of nuclear disarmament campaigners, late 1950s.

Different strokes for different folks.

different ways of doing something are appropriate for
different people (the saying is of US origin, and *strokes* here
means 'comforting gestures of approval'); late 20th-century
saying.

A door must be either shut or open.

said of two mutually exclusive alternatives; English proverb, mid
18th century.

He that has a choice has trouble.

choosing between two things or persons may cause difficulties;
American proverb, mid 20th century.

No man can serve two masters.

English proverb, early 14th century.

The obvious choice is usually a quick regret.

selection on outward appearance alone soon disappoints;
American proverb, mid 20th century.

Of two evils choose the less.

English proverb, late 14th century.

Small choice in rotten apples.

if all options are unpalatable there is little choice to be had;
English proverb, late 16th century.

They offered death so you would be happy with a fever.
a worse possibility makes something inherently unwelcome acceptable; Persian proverb.

Whose finger do you want on the trigger?
headline in the *Daily Mirror* 21 September 1951, alluding to the atom bomb, apropos the failure of both the Labour and Conservative parties to purge their leaders of proven failures.

You pays your money and you takes your choice.
said when there is little or nothing to choose between two options; English proverb, mid 19th century.

The Christian Church

See also CLERGY, GOD, RELIGION

The essential strength of the Church is seen in its capacity to withstand persecution: The church is an anvil which has worn out many hammers.

The blood of the martyrs is the seed of the Church.
persecution causes the Church to grow; English proverb, mid 16th century, perhaps ultimately deriving from the *Apologeticus* of the Roman theologian Tertullian (*c.* AD 160–*c.*225), 'As often as we are mown down by you, the more we grow in numbers; the blood of Christians is the seed.

Christ has no body now on earth but yours, no hands but yours, no feet but yours, yours are the eyes through which he looks compassion on this world, yours are the feet with which he is to go about doing good.

modern saying, often attributed to St Teresa of Ávila (1512–82), but not found in her writings.

The Christians to the lions!

saying reported by the Roman theologian Tertullian (*c.* AD 160–*c.*225) in his *Apologeticus*, 'If the Tiber rises, if the Nile does not rise, if the heavens give no rain, if there is an earthquake, famine, or pestilence, straightway the cry is . . .'

The church is an anvil which has worn out many hammers.

the passive strength of Christianity will outlast aggression; English proverb, mid 19th century.

A church is God between four walls.

American proverb, mid 20th century.

Meat and mass never hindered man.

indicating human need for physical and spiritual sustenance; English proverb, early 17th century.

The nearer the church, the farther from God.

sometimes used to indicate a lack of true spirituality where it is most likely to be found; English proverb, early 14th century.

You can't build a church with stumbling-blocks.
members of a church need to work together in fellowship;
American proverb, mid 20th century.

 Christmas

*Sayings about Christmas give particular emphasis to prepara-
tions for celebration, from the gifts appropriate to the Twelve
Days to the anticipated feasting:* Christmas is coming, and
the goose is getting fat.

**Christmas comes but once a year, and when it comes it
brings good cheer.**
traditional saying, going back to the 16th century.

Christmas is coming, and the goose is getting fat.
from a traditional rhyme, recorded from the 19th century (goose
was traditional Christmas fare).

A green Yule makes a fat churchyard.
a mild winter is traditionally unhealthy (*Yule* is an archaic term
for Christmas); English proverb, mid 17th century.

Only — shopping days to Christmas.
the imminence of Christmas expressed in commercial terms.

On the first day of Christmas my true love sent to me A partridge in a pear tree.

opening lines of 'The Twelve Days of Christmas', a traditional song listing gifts sent on each day of the Christmas season.

 ## Circumstance and Situation

See also CHANGE

It is as well to come to terms with circumstances, a consensus expressed in the advice offered by the Indian proverb, If you live in the river, you should make friends with the crocodile.

Although the branch is broken off, the trunk remains.

damage, while unpleasant, is not necessarily disastrous; Maori saying.

Circumstances alter cases.

a general principle may be modified in the light of particular circumstances; English proverb, late 17th century.

If you do not know where you have been, you cannot know where you are going.

understanding of your own situation is essential for effective action; African proverb.

If you live in the river, you should make friends with the crocodile.

Indian proverb.

May you live in interesting times.
used ironically, as eventful times are often dangerous or
unpleasant; modern saying, said to derive from a Chinese curse,
but likely to be apocryphal.

New circumstances, new controls.
American proverb, mid 20th century.

No rose without a thorn.
even the pleasantest circumstances have their drawbacks; English
proverb, mid 15th century.

One day honey, one day onions.
Arab proverb.

One man's loss is another man's gain.
often said by the gainer in self-congratulation; English proverb,
early 16th century.

A rolling stone gathers no moss.
used to imply that someone who does not settle down will not
prosper, or form lasting ties; English proverb, mid 14th century.

There's a time and place for everything.
often used as a warning against doing or saying something at a
particular time or in a particular situation; English proverb, early
16th century.

There's no great loss without some gain.
said in consolation or resignation; English proverb, mid 17th
century.

The wheel has come full circle.
the situation has returned to what it was in the past, as if completing a cycle, with reference to Shakespeare's *King Lear* 'The wheel is come full circle.'

Cities
See TOWNS AND CITIES

Clergy
See also THE CHRISTIAN CHURCH

Sayings relating to the clerical profession include the rather bleak assessment of the likely pressure on a cleric's family: Clergyman's sons always turn out badly. *However, there is no going back:* Once a priest, always a priest.

Clergymen's sons always turn out badly.
the implication is that the weight of expectation on clergymen's children is often itself damaging; English proverb, late 19th century.

Like people, like priest.
English proverb, late 16th century; from the Bible (Hosea 4:9), 'And there shall be like people, like priest.'

Nobody is born learned; bishops are made of men.
American proverb, mid 20th century.

Once a priest, always a priest.
English proverb, mid 19th century; compare **Once a —, always a — at** CHARACTER.

 # Computing
See also TECHNOLOGY

Sayings about the world of computing date from early days of the technology, when the instruction Do not fold, spindle or mutilate *was an important warning. However, some sayings are timeless:* Garbage in, garbage out *remains true through all developments.*

Do not fold, spindle or mutilate.
instruction on punched cards (1950s, and in differing forms from the 1930s).

Don't be evil.
informal slogan for the search engine Google.

Garbage in, garbage out.
in computing, incorrect or faulty input will always cause poor output; mid 20th century saying.

If you can't do it in Fortran, do it in assembly language. If you can't do it in assembly language, it's not worth doing.
saying on computer programming (*Fortran* = a high-level programming language used especially for scientific calculations).

It's not a bug, it's a feature.
bug = an error in a computer program or system; late 20th-century saying.

No manager ever got fired for buying IBM.
IBM advertising slogan.

To err is human but to really foul things up requires a computer.
late 20th-century saying; compare **to err is human (to forgive divine)** at MISTAKES.

 ## Conscience
See also FORGIVENESS

Proverbial wisdom tends to dwell on the uncomfortable effects of a bad conscience. While A clean conscience is a good pillow, permitting easy sleep, awareness of guilt makes the waking life unpleasant: Evil doers are evil dreaders.

A clean conscience is a good pillow.
a clear conscience enables its possessor to sleep soundly; English proverb, early 18th century.

Conscience gets a lot of credit that belongs to cold feet.
American proverb, mid 20th century.

Do right and fear no man.
English proverb, mid 15th century.

Evil doers are evil dreaders.
someone engaged in wrongdoing is likely to be nervous and
suspicious of others; English proverb, mid 16th century.

A guilty conscience needs no accuser.
awareness of one's own guilt has the same effect as an accusa-
tion; English proverb, late 14th century.

Let your conscience be your guide.
American proverb, mid 20th century.

A quiet conscience sleeps in thunder.
someone with an untroubled conscience will sleep
undisturbed whatever the noise; English proverb, late 16th
century.

Consequences
See CAUSES AND CONSEQUENCES

Cooking
See also EATING, FOOD

Good equipment is important (A cook is no better than her
stove), *but you cannot always judge by outward appearances:*
All are not cooks who sport white caps and carry long
knives.

**All are not cooks who sport white caps and carry long
knives.**
American proverb, mid 20th century.

A cook is no better than her stove.
American proverb, mid 20th century.

Fish, to taste good, must swim three times—in water, in butter, and in wine.
the best way to cook fish; Polish proverb.

God sends meat, but the Devil sends cooks.
anything which is in itself good or useful may be spoiled or perverted by the use to which it is put; English proverb, mid 16th century.

It is a poor cook that cannot lick his own fingers.
a good cook assesses their food with their own sense of taste; English proverb.

Keep one eye on the frying-pan, and one on the cat.
Italian proverb.

 # Cooperation

Sayings about cooperation emphasize the positive side of working with others, as in When spider webs unite, they can tie up a lion. *However, the dangers of not cooperating are also considered:* If you don't believe in cooperation, watch what happens to a wagon when one wheel comes off.

All arts are brothers; each is a light to the other.
American proverb, mid 19th century.

DOG DOES NOT EAT DOG

A chain is no stronger than its weakest link.
often used when identifying a particular point of vulnerability;
English proverb, mid 19th century; compare **You are the
weakest link … goodbye** at STRENGTH AND WEAKNESS.

Dog does not eat dog.
people of the same profession should not attack each other;
English proverb, mid 16th century.

Each of us at a handle of the basket.
Maori proverb.

Every little helps.
English proverb, early 17th century.

Four eyes see more than two.
two people are more observant than one alone; English proverb,
late 16th century.

Hawks will not pick out hawks' eyes.
powerful people from the same group will not attack one
another; English proverb, late 16th century.

**He who travels fast, travels alone, and he who travels
far, travels in the company of others.**
African proverb.

**If you don't believe in cooperation, watch what
happens to a wagon when one wheel comes off.**
American proverb, mid 20th century.

If you think cooperation is unnecessary, just try running your car a while on three wheels.

American proverb, mid 20th century.

It takes two to make a bargain.

often used to imply that both parties must be prepared to give some ground; English proverb, late 16th century.

It takes two to tango.

meaning that a cooperative venture requires a contribution from both participants; mid 20th-century saying, from the 1952 song by Al Hoffman and Dick Manning.

Little birds that can sing and won't sing must be made to sing.

those who refuse to obey or cooperate will be forced to do so; English proverb, late 17th century.

Many hands make light work.

often used as an encouragement to join in with assistance; English proverb, mid 14th century.

One good turn deserves another.

English proverb, early 15th century.

One hand washes the other.

referring to cooperation between two closely linked persons or organizations; English proverb, late 16th century.

Phone a friend.

advice to contestants uncertain of the correct answer, said by Chris Tarrant, host of the ITV quiz show *Who Wants to be a Millionaire* (1998–).

A single arrow is easily broken, but not ten in a bundle.

when people combine, they can resist attack; Japanese proverb.

A single bracelet does not jingle.

to make an effect we need the help of others; African proverb.

There is honour among thieves.

sometimes used ironically; English proverb, early 19th century.

A trouble shared is a trouble halved.

discussing a problem will lessen its impact; English proverb, mid 20th century.

Union is strength.

English proverb, mid 17th century; *unity* is a popular alternative for *union*, especially when used as a trade-union slogan.

United we stand, divided we fall.

a watchword of the American Revolution, English proverb, late 18th century.

When spider webs unite, they can tie up a lion.

African proverb.

With your food basket, and with my food basket, the guest will have enough.

Maori proverb.

Corruption

Sayings such as A golden key can open any door *remind us that there is always likely to be someone who is open to bribery—and that the practice may spread, given that* The rotten apple injures its neighbour.

Corruption will find a dozen alibis for its evil deeds.
American proverb, mid 20th century.

Every man has his price.
everyone is susceptible to the right bribe; English proverb, mid 18th century.

A golden key can open any door.
any access is guaranteed if enough money is offered; English proverb, late 16th century.

If gold rusts, what will iron do?
if someone of admirable character succumbs to temptation, what is likely to happen to a person of less upright character; English proverb.

It's not what you know, it's who you know.
stressing the importance of personal influence; late 20th century saying.

The rotten apple injures its neighbour.
often used to mean that one corrupt person in an organization is likely to affect others; English proverb, mid 14th century.

When money speaks, the truth keeps silent.
Russian proverb.

 # Countries and Peoples

Sayings about countries and peoples may reflect either a cherished self-image (An Englishman's word is his bond), or a less flattering opinion from someone who does not belong to the people concerned: Scratch a Russian and you find a Tartar.

Advance Australia.
catchphrase used as a patriotic slogan or motto, mid 19th century onwards; the national anthem of Australia (officially adopted in 1984) includes the lines, 'In joyful strains then let us sing Advance Australia fair.'

A mare usque ad mare.
Latin, meaning 'From sea unto sea'; motto of Canada, taken from the Bible (Psalm 72), 'He shall have dominion also from sea to sea, and from the river unto the ends of the earth.'

America is a tune. It must be sung together.
American proverb, mid 20th century.

Australians wouldn't give a XXXX for anything else.
advertising slogan for Castlemaine lager, 1986 onwards.

England is the paradise of women, the hell of horses, and the purgatory of servants.
English proverb, late 16th century.

England's difficulty is Ireland's opportunity.
associated with the aspirations of Irish nationalism; English proverb, mid 19th century.

An Englishman's word is his bond.
a promise given is regarded as having the force of a legal agreement; English proverb, early 16th century.

Every land has its own law.
Scottish proverb, early 17th century, used to emphasize the individuality of a nation or group.

Every Turk is born a soldier.
Turkish saying.

Good Americans when they die go to Paris.
coinage attributed to Thomas Gold Appleton (1812–84); American proverb, mid 19th century.

It is a striking coincidence that the word American ends in *can*.
American proverb, mid 20th century.

The Mounties always get their man.
unofficial motto of the Royal Canadian Mounted Police.

A nation without a language is a nation without a heart.
Welsh proverb.

Scratch a Russian and you find a Tartar.

if a person is harmed their real national character will be
revealed; English proverb, early 19th century.

 # The Country and the Town

*The contrast between urban and rural life embodies what is
often seen as a key cultural division.*

An everyday story of country folk.

traditional summary of the BBC's long-running radio soap opera
The Archers.

God made the country and man made the town.

contrasting rural and urban life; English proverb, mid 17th
century, in this form from William Cowper's poem *The
Task* (1785).

**If you have not lived in the country, you do not know
what hardship means.**

contrasting rural and urban poverty; Chinese proverb.

**You can take the boy out of the country but you can't
take the country out of the boy.**

even when a person moves away from the place they were
brought up in, they retain its essential manners and customs;
English proverb, mid 20th century.

Courage

See also DANGER, FEAR

Courage may be admirable itself, but proverbial wisdom also stresses the practical advantages that it may bring: Fortune favours the brave.

Attack is the best form of defence.
English proverb, late 18th century; compare **The best defence is a good offence** below.

The best defence is a good offence.
late 20th-century American version of **Attack is the best form of defence** above.

A bully is always a coward.
English proverb, early 19th century.

Courage is fear that has said its prayers.
American proverb, mid 20th century.

Courage without conduct is like a ship without ballast.
American proverb, mid 20th century.

Don't cry before you're hurt.
sometimes used as a warning against appealing for sympathy on the assumption of an unpleasant outcome; English proverb, mid 16th century.

Faint heart never won fair lady.
often used as an encouragement to action; English proverb, mid 16th century.

For every Pharaoh there is a Moses.

a liberator will arise against every oppressor; Middle Eastern proverb.

Fortune favours the brave.

a person who acts bravely is likely to be successful; English proverb, late 14th century, originally often with allusion to *Phormio* by the Roman comic dramatist Terence, 'Fortune assists the brave', and Virgil *The Aeneid*, 'Fortune assists the bold.'

None but the brave deserve the fair.

English proverb, late 17th century, from Dryden's poem *Alexander's Feast* (1697), 'None but the brave deserves the fair.'

You never know what you can do till you try.

often used as encouragement to the reluctant; English proverb, early 19th century.

 # Crime and Punishment

See also GUILT, JUSTICE, THE LAW, MURDER

From Ill gotten goods never thrive *in the 16th century,* *to* Crime doesn't pay *in the 20th century, there is a consensus that wrongdoing is unlikely benefit the perpetrator—even if society does not follow the kind of draconian practice enshrined in the recommendation,* Hang a thief when he's young, and he'll no steal when he's old.

A conservative is a liberal who's been mugged.

American saying, 1980s.

THREE STRIKES
AND YOU'RE OUT

Crime doesn't pay.
American proverb, early 20th century; a slogan of the FBI and the cartoon detective Dick Tracy.

Crime leaves a trail like a water-beetle.
Malay proverb.

Crime must be concealed by crime.
American proverb, mid 20th century.

Hang a thief when he's young, and he'll no steal when he's old.
Scottish proverbial saying, early 19th century.

If there were no receivers, there would be no thieves.
English proverb, late 14th century.

Ill gotten goods never thrive.
something which is acquired dishonestly is unlikely to be the basis of lasting prosperity; English proverb, early 16th century.

Little thieves are hanged, but great ones escape.
sufficient power and influence can ensure that a wrongdoer is not punished; English proverb, mid 17th century.

Opportunity makes a thief.
often used to imply that the carelessness of the person who is robbed has contributed to the crime; English proverb, early 13th century.

Three strikes and you're out.

referring to legislation which provides that an offender's third felony is punishable by life imprisonment or other severe sentence; deriving from the terminology of baseball, in which a batter who has had three strikes, or three fair opportunities of hitting the ball, is out; late 20th-century saying.

When thieves fall out, honest men come by their own.

meaning that it is through thieves quarrelling over their stolen goods that they are likely to be caught, and the goods recovered; English proverb, mid 16th century.

You'll die facing the monument.

warning of the end of a life of crime; in Glasgow, prisoners were hanged facing Nelson's Monument on Glasgow Green; Scottish proverb.

 # Criticism

See also LIKES AND DISLIKES

While self-examination can be a wholesome discipline, we should not be too ready to criticize others: Don't judge a man till you've walked two moons in his moccasins.

The best place for criticism is in front of your mirror.

judge yourself before others; American proverb, mid 20th century.

Criticism is something you can avoid by saying nothing, doing nothing, and being nothing.

abstaining from criticism will result in complete inaction; American proverb, mid 20th century.

Don't judge a man till you've walked two moons in his moccasins.

warning against judging without understanding circumstances; modern saying, said to be of Native American origin.

 ## Custom and Habit

Sayings about custom tend towards the negative: there is a perception that enshrined practice is likely to lead to someone being less able to deal with changes: You can't teach an old dog new tricks.

A bad custom is like a good cake, better broken than kept.

we should use our judgement to decide whether a custom is worthy of respect; English proverb.

Custom is mummified by habit and glorified by law.

American proverb, mid 20th century.

Old habits die hard.
it is difficult to break long-established habits; English proverb,
mid 18th century.

Sow an act, and reap a habit.
recommending the development of good practice; English proverb.

What is new cannot be true.
used to imply that innovation is less soundly based than custom
which has been proved by experience; English proverb, mid 17th
century.

You cannot shift an old tree without it dying.
often used to suggest the risk involved in moving an elderly
person who has lived in the same place for many years; English
proverb, early 16th century.

You can't teach an old dog new tricks.
someone who is already set in their ways is not able to learn new
ways of doing things; English proverb, mid 16th century.

 Dance

Dancing may require some innate ability—You need more than dancing shoes to be a dancer—*but dancing is still seen as a natural form of expression:* We're fools whether we dance or not, so we might as well dance.

One who cannot dance blames the uneven floor.
Indian proverb; compare **A bad workman blames his tools** at APOLOGY AND EXCUSES.

We're fools whether we dance or not, so we might as well dance.
modern saying, claimed to be a Japanese proverb.

When you go to dance, take heed whom you take by the hand.
English proverb, early 17th century.

You need more than dancing shoes to be a dancer.
American proverb, mid 20th century.

ONE WHO CANNOT

DANCE BLAMES THE

UNEVEN FLOOR

Danger

See also CAUTION, COURAGE, FEAR

A risk may be taken rightly, since The post of honour is the post of danger, *but peril can result from overconfidence:* When the lion shows its teeth, don't assume that it is smiling.

Adventures are to the adventurous.

the person who wants exciting things to happen must take the initiative; English proverb, mid 19th century.

A common danger causes common action.

American proverb, mid 20th century.

Heaven protects children, sailors, and drunken men.

often used (in a number of variant forms) to imply that someone unable to look after themselves has been undeservedly lucky; English proverb, mid 19th century.

He who rides a tiger is afraid to dismount.

once a dangerous or troublesome venture is begun, the safest course is to carry it through to the end; English proverb, late 19th century.

If you play with fire you get burnt.

if you involve yourself with something potentially dangerous you are likely to be hurt; English proverb, late 19th century.

It is the calm and silent water that drowns the man.

the greatest danger may be concealed beneath an innocent appearance; African proverb.

Just when you thought it was safe to go back in the water.

advertising copy for the film *Jaws 2* (1978), featuring the return of the great white shark to bathing beaches.

Light the blue touch paper and retire immediately.

traditional instruction for lighting fireworks.

More than one yew bow in Chester.

you may escape danger once, but not a second time (*Chester* representing the English, the traditional enemy for Wales); Welsh proverb.

The post of honour is the post of danger.

English proverb, mid 16th century.

Three things are not to be trusted; a cow's horn, a dog's tooth, and a horse's hoof.

one may be gored, bitten, or kicked, without warning; English proverb, late 14th century.

We have no friends but the mountains.

inhospitable terrain is more reliable than an ally as a source of safety; Kurdish proverb.

When the lion shows its teeth, don't assume that it is smiling.

a warning sign from a source of power should not be taken lightly; Arab proverb.

Who dares wins.
motto of the British Special Air Service regiment; from 1942.

The wolves are well fed and the sheep are safe.
when a predator's immediate needs have been satisfied, there is
temporary safety for the prey; Russian proverb.

Women and children first.
order given on a ship in difficulty, indicating that women and
children should be allowed onto the lifeboats before men; in
allusive (and often humorous) use, warning of a risky or
unpleasant situation; from the mid 19th century.

 # Death
See also MOURNING

The end of life may offer an escape from some pressures, since
Death pays all debts, *but the main note is one of resignation
in the face of the inevitable:* There is a remedy for everything except death.

**After the game, the king and the pawn go into the
same box.**
rank is no protection against death; Italian proverb.

As a tree falls, so shall it lie.
one should not alter one's long-established practices and customs
because of approaching death; English proverb, mid 16th
century, from the Bible (Ecclesiastes 11:3), 'In the place where
the tree falleth, there it shall be.'

Blessed are the dead that the rain rains on.
English proverb, early 17th century.

[Death is] Nature's way of telling you to slow down.
American life insurance saying, in *Newsweek* 25 April 1960.

Death is the great leveller.
all people will be equal in death, whatever their material prosperity; English proverb, early 18th century.

Death pays all debts.
the death of a person cancels out their obligations; English proverb, early 17th century.

Et in Arcadia ego.
Latin tomb inscription, 'And I too in Arcadia', of disputed meaning, often depicted in classical paintings, notably by Poussin in 1655.

One funeral makes many.
sometimes with the implication that attendance at a deathbed or funeral may have fatal consequences; English proverb, late 19th century.

Stone-dead hath no fellow.
traditionally used by advocates of the death penalty, to suggest that only when a dangerous person is dead can one be sure that they will pose no further threat; English proverb, mid 17th century.

There is a remedy for everything except death.

English proverb, mid 15th century.

This ae nighte, This ae nighte,
—*Every nighte and alle,*
Fire and fleet and candle-lighte,
And Christe receive thy saule.

refrain from a traditional ballad, the 'Lyke-Wake Dirge'; *fleet* is a
corruption of *flet* meaning 'a dwelling, a house'.

You can only die once.

used to encourage someone in a dangerous or difficult
enterprise; English proverb, mid 15th century.

Young men may die, but old men must die.

death is inevitable for all, and can at best be postponed until old
age; English proverb, mid 16th century.

 # Debt and Borrowing
See also THRIFT

Credit card slogans such as Access—your flexible friend
*may strike an upbeat note, but earlier sayings stress the dangers
of getting into debt, summed up generally in the 15th-century
assertion* He that goes a-borrowing, goes a-sorrowing.

Access—your flexible friend.

advertising slogan for Access credit card, 1981 onwards.

American Express? ... That'll do nicely, sir.
advertising slogan for American Express credit card, 1970s.

Have a horse of your own, and you may borrow another's.
evidence that you have resources of your own makes it more likely that you will be lent something; English proverb.

He that goes a-borrowing, goes a-sorrowing.
involving oneself in debt is likely to lead to unhappiness; English proverb, late 15th century.

Lend your money and lose your friend.
debt puts a strain on friendship; English proverb, late 15th century.

A man in debt is caught in a net.
American proverb, mid 20th century.

A national debt, if it is not excessive, will be to us a national blessing.
American proverb; often attributed to the American politician Alexander Hamilton (c.1755–1804).

Neither a borrower, nor a lender be.
advising caution in financial dealings with others; English proverb, early 17th century, from the words of Polonius to his son Laertes in Shakespeare *Hamlet* (1601), 'Neither a borrower, nor a lender be, For loan oft loses both itself and friend.'

Out of debt, out of danger.

someone in debt is vulnerable and at risk from others; English proverb, mid 17th century.

Short reckonings make long friends.

the prompt settlement of any debt between friends ensures that their friendship will not be damaged; English proverb, mid 16th century.

 # Deception
See also LIES

Deception may not benefit the perpetrator, since we are told that Cheats never prosper, *but there is also a warning that we have some responsibility for ensuring that we are not deceived:* Fool me once, shame on you; fool me twice, shame on me.

Cheats never prosper.

English proverb, early 19th century.

Deceit is a lie, that wears a smile.

American proverb, mid 20th century.

Fool me once, shame on you; fool me twice, shame on me.

if someone is deceived twice by the same person, their own stupidity is to blame; late 20th-century saying.

Deeds

See WORDS AND DEEDS

Defiance

See also DETERMINATION

Apart from the traditional reflection that You can take a horse to water, but you can't make him drink, *defiance is often expressed through a slogan, from the 17th-century* No surrender! *to the anti-Poll Tax cry* Can't pay, won't pay *of the early 1990s.*

Burn, baby, burn.
black extremist slogan in use during the Los Angeles riots, August 1965.

Can't pay, won't pay.
anti-Poll Tax slogan, *c.*1990.

Ils ne passeront pas.
French, 'They shall not pass', slogan used by the French army at the defence of Verdun in 1916; variously attributed to Marshal Pétain and to General Robert Nivelle, and subsequently taken up by Republicans in the Spanish Civil War in the form *No pasarán!*

Nemo me impune lacessit.
Latin, 'No one provokes me with impunity', motto of the Crown of Scotland and of all Scottish regiments.

No surrender!

Protestant Northern Irish slogan originating with the defenders of Derry against the Catholic forces of James II in 1689.

They haif said: Quhat say they? Lat thame say.

motto of the Earl Marischal of Scotland, inscribed at Marischal College, Aberdeen, 1593; a similarly defiant motto in Greek has been found engraved in remains from classical antiquity.

You can take a horse to the water, but you can't make him drink.

even if you create the right circumstances you cannot persuade someone to do something against their will; English proverb, late 12th century.

 # Delay

See HASTE AND DELAY

 # Determination

See also DEFIANCE

Refusal to be deterred by apparent failure can overcome both disappointment, as in the encouraging Fall seven times, stand up eight, *and difficult circumstances, since* A determined fellow can do more with a rusty monkey wrench than a lot of people can with a machine shop.

The best fish swim near the bottom.

patience and persistence are necessary for the best results; English proverb.

LITTLE STROKES FELL

GREAT OAKS

Beyond mountains there are more mountains.
overcoming the first obstacle is likely to bring you face to face
with another; Haitian proverb.

Constant dropping wears away a stone.
primarily used to mean that persistence will achieve a difficult or
unlikely object; English proverb, mid 13th century.

**A determined fellow can do more with a rusty
monkey wrench than a lot of people can with a
machine shop.**
American proverb, mid 20th century.

Fall seven times, stand up eight.
Japanese proverb; compare If at first you don't succeed, try,
try, try again below.

He that will to Cupar maun to Cupar.
if someone is determined on an end they will not be dissuaded
(*Cupar* is a town in Fife, Scotland); Scottish traditional saying,
early 18th century.

He who wills the end, wills the means.
someone sufficiently determined upon an outcome will also be
ready to accept whatever is necessary to achieve it; English
proverb, late 17th century.

If at first you don't succeed, try, try, try again.
English proverb, mid 19th century; compare **Fall seven times,
stand up eight** above.

It is idle to swallow the cow and choke on the tail.

when a serious matter has been accepted, there is no point in quibbling over a trifle; when a great task is almost completed, it is senseless to give up; English proverb, mid 17th century.

It's dogged as does it.

steady perseverance will bring success; English proverb, mid 19th century.

Just say no.

motto of the Nancy Reagan Drug Abuse Fund, founded 1985.

Little strokes fell great oaks.

a person of size and stature can be brought down by a series of small blows; English proverb, early 15th century.

Nil *carborundum illegitimi*.

cod Latin for 'Don't let the bastards grind you down', in circulation during the Second World War, though possibly of earlier origin.

Put a stout heart to a stey brae.

determination is needed to climb a steep ('stey') hillside; Scottish proverb, late 16th century.

Revenons à ces moutons.

an exhortation to stop digressing and get back to the subject in hand; French, literally 'Let us return to these sheep', with allusion to the confused court scene in the Old French *Farce de Maistre Pierre Pathelin* (c.1470).

The show must go on.
American proverb, mid 19th century.

Slow and steady wins the race.
from the story of the race between the hare and the tortoise, in Aesop's *Fables*, in which the winner was the slow but persistent tortoise and not the swift but easily distracted hare; mid 18th-century saying.

A stern chase is a long chase.
a *stern chase* is a chase in which the pursuing ship follows directly in the wake of the pursued; English proverb, early 19th century.

The third time pays for all.
success after initial failure makes up for earlier disappointment; English proverb, late 16th century.

We shall not be moved.
title of labour and civil rights song (1931), adapted from an earlier gospel hymn.

We shall overcome.
title of song, originating from before the American Civil War, adapted as a Baptist hymn ('I'll Overcome Some Day', 1901) by C. Albert Tindley; revived in 1946 as a protest song by black tobacco workers, and in 1963 during the black civil rights campaign.

Where there's a will there's a way.
anything can be done if one has sufficient determination; English proverb, mid 17th century.

A wilful man must have his way.
a person set on their own ends will disregard advice in pursuing
their chosen course; English proverb, early 19th century.

Difference
See SIMILARITY AND DIFFERENCE

Discontent
See SATISFACTION AND DISCONTENT

Dislikes
See LIKES AND DISLIKES

Dogs
See also CATS, HORSES

The idea of the dog as protector goes back to the Cave canem
of the classical world, and is reinforced by the Persian proverb,
The dog is a lion in his own house.

Cave canem.
Latin, 'beware of the dog', deriving originally from the Roman
satirist Petronius (d. 65), '*Canis ingens, catena vinctus, in pariete
erat pictus superque quadrata littera scriptum "Cave Canem."*
[A huge dog, tied by a chain, was painted on the wall and over it
was written in capital letters "Beware of the dog." ']

The dog is a lion in his own house.
Persian proverb.

A dog is for life, not just for Christmas.
slogan of the National Canine Defence League (now Dogs Trust), from 1978.

Love me, love my dog.
English proverb, early 16th century.

There is no good flock without a good shepherd, and no good shepherd without a good dog.
motto of the International Sheep Dog society, said to derive from a Scottish proverb.

 # Doubt
See CERTAINTY AND DOUBT

 # Dreams
See also SLEEP

Apart from the warning from 19th-century America that Dreams retain the infirmities of our character, *dreams are traditionally seen as predictive, if they can be correctly interpreted.*

Dream of a funeral and you hear of a marriage.
English proverb, mid 17th century.

Dreams go by contraries.
English proverb, early 15th century.

Dreams retain the infirmities of our character.
American proverb, late 19th century.

Morning dreams come true.
English proverb, mid 16th century, recording a traditional
superstition.

To dream of the dead is a sign of rain.
traditional saying.

 # Dress
See also APPEARANCE

*Dress may be important as protection from the elements
(Ne'er cast a clout till May be out), or as allowing us to
make a good impression: If you want to get ahead, get
a hat.*

Blue and green should never be seen.
traditional warning against wearing the two colours
together.

Clothes make the man.
what one wears is taken by others as an essential signal of status;
English proverb, early 20th century.

Fine feathers make fine birds.

beautiful clothes confer beauty or style on the wearer; English proverb, late 16th century.

If you want to get ahead, get a hat.

advertising slogan for the British Hat Council, 1965.

It takes 40 dumb animals to make a fur coat, but only one to wear it.

slogan of an anti-fur campaign poster, 1980s; sometimes attributed to the English photographer David Bailey (1938–).

Ne'er cast a clout till May be out.

warning against leaving off old or warm clothes until the end of the month of May (the saying is sometimes mistakenly understood to refer to hawthorn blossom or *may*); English proverb, early 18th century.

Nine tailors make a man.

literally, a gentleman must select his attire from a number of sources (later also associated with bell-ringing, with the *nine tailors* or *tellers* indicating the nine knells traditionally rung at the death of a man); English proverb, early 17th century.

Drink

See also DRUNKENNESS, FOOD

Sayings about drink often emphasize the attractions or characteristics of a particular form of alcohol, whether it be beer, vodka, or a dry Martini.

Alcohol will preserve anything but a secret.
American proverb, mid 20th century.

Don't ask a man to drink and drive.
British road safety slogan, from 1964.

Guinness is good for you.
reply universally given to researchers asking people why they drank Guinness; advertising slogan for Guinness, from *c.*1929.

Heineken refreshes the parts other beers cannot reach.
slogan for Heineken lager, from 1975 onwards.

I'm only here for the beer.
slogan for Double Diamond beer, 1971 onwards.

Let's get out of these wet clothes and into a dry Martini.
line coined in the 1920s by the press agent for the American humorist Robert Benchley, and adopted by Mae West in *Every Day's a Holiday* (1937 film).

Vodka is an aunt of wine.
Russian proverb.

 # Drunkenness
See also DRINK

Apart from the risks of becoming addicted (The drunkard's cure is to drink again)*, there are other dangers in falling under the influence of alcohol:* When the wine is in, the wit is out.

The drunkard's cure is drink again.
American proverb, mid 20th century.

He that drinks beer, thinks beer.
warning against the effect of intoxication; English proverb, early 19th century.

There is truth in wine.
a person who is drunk is more likely to speak the truth; English proverb, mid 16th century (the saying is found earlier in Latin as *in vino veritas*).

When the wine is in, the wit is out.
when one is drunk one is likely to be indiscreet or to speak or act foolishly; English proverb, late 14th century.

WHEN THE WINE

IS IN, THE WIT

IS OUT

Eating

See also COOKING, FOOD, HEALTH

*In the 21st century, the saying You are what you eat has
gained a new prominence, but earlier proverbs may be
more likely to reflect a world in which eating was not
something to be taken for granted: Hunger is the
best sauce.*

After dinner rest a while, after supper walk a mile.
the implication is that dinner is a heavy meal, while supper is a
light one; English proverb, late 16th century.

After meat, mustard.
traditional comment on some essential ingredient which is
brought too late to be of use; English proverb, late 16th
century.

**Breakfast like a king, lunch like a prince, and dine like
a pauper.**
modern saying, recommending lighter meals as you move
through the day.

Eat to live, not live to eat.
distinguishing between necessity and indulgence; English proverb, late 14th century.

Fingers were made before forks.

commonly used as a polite excuse for eating with one's hands at table; English proverb, mid 18th century; the earlier variant 'God made hands before knives' is found in the mid 16th century.

Go to work on an egg.

advertising slogan for the British Egg Marketing Board, from 1957; perhaps written by Fay Weldon or Mary Gowing.

Hunger is the best sauce.

food which is needed will be received most readily; English proverb, early 16th century.

The way one eats is the way one works.

Czech proverb; compare **You are what you eat** below.

We must eat a peck of dirt before we die.

often used as a consolatory remark in literal contexts; English proverb, mid 18th century.

You are what you eat.

English proverb, mid 20th century; in the early 19th century, the French jurist and gourmet Anthelme Brillat-Savarin (1755–1826) wrote, 'Tell me what you eat and I will tell you what you are'; compare **The way one eats is the way one works** above.

Education

See also KNOWLEDGE, TEACHING

The saying As the twig is bent, so is the tree inclined
*reflects an awareness of the importance of early
influences, but for late developers there is the
encouragement,* It is never too late to learn.

As the twig is bent, so is the tree inclined.
early influences have a permanent effect; English proverb, early
18th century.

**Education doesn't come by bumping your head against
the school house.**
American proverb, mid 20th century.

Genius without education is like silver in the mine.
American proverb, mid 18th century.

**Give me a child for the first seven years, and you may
do what you like with him afterwards.**
traditionally regarded as a Jesuit maxim; recorded in Lean's *Collectanea* vol. 3 (1903).

**The ink of a scholar is holier than the blood of a
martyr.**
modern saying, said to derive from an Arab proverb, but of
uncertain origin.

It is never too late to learn.
English proverb, late 17th century.

Lady Margaret Hall for ladies,
St Hugh's for girls,
St Hilda's for wenches,
Somerville for women.
Oxford saying, c.1930s.

Never let your education interfere with your
intelligence.
American proverb, mid 20th century.

Never too old to learn.
English proverb, late 16th century.

No more Latin, no more French,
No more sitting on a hard board bench.
traditional children's rhyme for the end of a school term.

Teachers open the door, but you must enter by
yourself.
learning requires effort on the part of the student; Chinese
proverb.

There is no royal road to learning.
English proverb, early 19th century, deriving from the words
of the Greek mathematician Euclid (fl. c.300 BC) addressed
to Ptolemy I of Egypt, 'There is no "royal road" to
geometry.'

When the pupil is ready, the master arrives.
Indian proverb, deriving from Sanskrit.

 ## Effort
See also ACHIEVEMENT

Proverbs such as He that would eat the fruit must climb
the tree *and* No pain, no gain *emphasize how essential
effort is to achievement. There is comparatively little
concern that the effort might be expended ineffectually,
although by implication we are warned to set our
sights on an achievable goal:* If the sky falls, we shall
catch larks.

And all because the lady loves Milk Tray.
advertising slogan for Cadbury's Milk Tray chocolates, 1968
onwards, showing the obstacles and dangers overcome to deliver
the box of chocolates.

Easy come, easy go.
something which is acquired without effort will be lost without
regret; English proverb, mid 17th century.

He that would eat the fruit must climb the tree.

someone who wishes to attain success must first make the necessary effort; English proverb, mid 17th century.

I didn't get where I am today without —.

managerial catchphrase of 'C.J.' in the BBC television series *The Fall and Rise of Reginald Perrin* (1976–80), written by David Nobbs.

If a thing's worth doing, it's worth doing well.

if something is worth any effort at all, it should be taken seriously; English proverb, mid 18th century.

If the sky falls we shall catch larks.

used dismissively to indicate that something will be attainable only in the most unlikely circumstances; English proverb, mid 15th century.

Much cry and little wool.

referring to a disturbance without tangible result; in early usage, the image was that of shearing a pig, which would cry loudly but yield no wool; English proverb, late 15th century.

No pain, no gain.

nothing worth having can be achieved without effort; English proverb, late 16th century.

One cannot become a good sailor sailing in a tranquil sea.

a person must be disciplined and educated to become a useful citizen; Chinese proverb.

We're number two. We try harder.

advertising slogan for Avis car rentals.

 # Employment

See also MANAGEMENT

One saying from the 18th century and one saying from the 20th offer very different views of employment: the belief that The eye of a master does more work than both his hands *contrasts with the cynical comment from Soviet Russia:* We pretend to work, and they pretend to pay us.

The eye of a master does more work than both his hands.

employees work harder when the person who is in charge is present; English proverb, mid 18th century.

Jack is as good as his master.

'Jack' is used variously as a familiar name for a sailor, a member of the common people, a serving man, and one who does odd jobs; English proverb, early 18th century.

Jack of all trades and master of none.
a person who tries to master too many skills will learn none of them properly; English proverb, early 17th century.

We pretend to work, and they pretend to pay us.
Russian saying of the Soviet era.

 Ending
See also BEGINNING, CHANGE

Whether or not an ending is as successful as that implied by
The end crowns the work, *it will inevitably arrive.*
However, we should not assume too quickly that something
has been completed: The opera isn't over till the
fat lady sings.

All good things must come to an end.
nothing lasts; although the addition of 'good' is a later development; English proverb, mid 15th century.

All's well that ends well.
often used with the implication that difficulties have been successfully negotiated; English proverb, late 14th century.

And they all lived happily ever after.
traditional ending for a fairy story.

The end crowns the work.
the fulfilment of a process is its finest and most notable part;
English proverb, early 16th century.

End good, all good.
a good outcome means that the work has been worthwhile;
German proverb.

Everything has an end.
no condition lasts for ever; English proverb, late 14th century.

In my end is my beginning.
motto of Mary, Queen of Scots (1542–87).

The opera isn't over till the fat lady sings.
using an informal description of the culmination of a traditional
opera to indicate that a process is not yet complete; late 20th
century saying.

Enemies

See also DANGER

While we should be cautious in our dealings with an enemy
(Do not call a wolf to help you against the dogs), *shared
enmity can be useful:* The enemy of my enemy is my friend.

Dead men don't bite.
killing an enemy puts an end to any threat they may pose;
English proverb, mid 16th century.

Do not call a wolf to help you against the dogs.
advising against making alliance with someone likely to destroy
you in your turn; Russian proverb.

The enemy of my enemy is my friend.
shared enmity provides common ground; American proverb,
mid 20th century, often said to be 'an old Arab proverb'; compare **My brother and I against my cousin and my cousin and I
against the stranger** at FAMILY.

Love your enemy—but don't put a gun in his hand.
indicating the practical limitations of charity; American proverb,
mid 20th century.

Strike the serpent's head with your enemy's hand.
use one opponent to defeat another; English proverb.

There is no little enemy.
any enemy can be dangerous; English proverb, mid
17th century.

 The Environment

In recent years political slogans such as Think globally, act
locally *and sayings believed to derive from cultures in touch
with a pre-industrial way of living such as* Touch the earth
lightly *have combined to urge sensitivity and care in dealing
with the natural world.*

The earth is man's only friend.
Bulgarian proverb.

The earth laughs at him who calls a place his own.
Indian proverb.

**However high a bird may soar, it seeks its food
on earth.**
Danish proverb.

WE DO NOT

INHERIT THE EARTH

FROM OUR PARENTS,

WE BORROW IT FROM

OUR CHILDREN

Kills all known germs.

advertising slogan for Domestos bleach, 1959.

Save the whale.

environmental slogan associated with the alarm over the rapidly declining whale population which led in 1985 to a moratorium on commercial whaling.

Think globally, act locally.

Friends of the Earth slogan, c.1985.

Touch the earth lightly.

modern saying, said to derive from an Australian Aboriginal proverb.

We do not inherit the earth from our parents, we borrow it from our children.

modern saying, said to be of Native American origin.

When the last tree is cut, the last river poisoned, and the last fish dead, we will discover that we can't eat money.

Canadian saying, sometimes said to be of Native American origin.

Envy

While being envied may sustain our pride, to feel envy is likely to make us discontented: The grass is always greener on the other side of the fence.

Better be envied than pitied.
even if one is unhappy it is preferable to be rich and powerful rather than poor and vulnerable; English proverb, mid 16th century.

Envy feeds on the living; it ceases when they are dead.
American proverb, mid 20th century.

The grass is always greener on the other side of the fence.
something just out of reach always appears more desirable than what one already has; English proverb, mid 20th century.

If envy were a fever, all the world would be ill.
Envy is a common vice; Danish proverb.

Excellence

True excellence may be seldom encountered, since If something sounds too good to be true, it probably is.

Corruption of the best becomes the worst.
translation of the Latin saying *Corruptio optimi pessima*; English proverb, early 19th century.

If something sounds too good to be true, it probably is.
late 20th-century saying.

Excess
See also MODERATION

The idea that You can have too much of a good thing *occurs in many cultures, from the medieval English warning that* The pitcher will go to the well once too often, *to the Chinese* Do not add legs to the snake after you have finished drawing it.

Do not add legs to the snake after you have finished drawing it.
advising against making superfluous and undesirable additions; Chinese proverb.

Even nectar is a poison, if taken to excess.
too much of anything is inadvisable; Hindu proverb.

It is the last straw that breaks the camel's back.
the addition of one quite minor problem may prove crushing to someone who is already overburdened; English proverb, mid 17th century.

The last drop makes the cup run over.
the addition of something in itself quite minor causes an excess; English proverb, mid 17th century.

Overpaid, overfed, oversexed, and over here.
of American troops in Britain during the Second World War; associated with the comedian Tommy Trinder (1909–89), but probably not his invention.

The pitcher will go to the well once too often.
one should not repeat a risky action too often, or push one's luck too far; English proverb, mid 14th century.

You can have too much of a good thing.
excess even of something which is good in itself can be damaging; English proverb, late 15th century.

Excuses

See APOLOGY AND EXCUSES

Experience

While there is no doubt that experience is worth having
(Experience is the father of wisdom), *it may be gained at the
cost of some unpleasantness:* A burnt child dreads the fire.

Appetite comes with eating.

desire or facility increases as an activity proceeds; English
proverb, mid 17th century.

A burnt child dreads the fire.

the memory of past hurt may act as a safeguard in the future;
English proverb, mid 13th century.

Experience is the best teacher.

sometimes used with the implication that learning by experience
may be painful; English proverb, mid 16th century.

Experience is the comb which fate gives a man when his hair is all gone.

American proverb, mid 20th century.

Experience is the father of wisdom.
real understanding of something comes only from direct
experience of it; English proverb, mid 16th century.

Experience keeps a dear school.
lessons learned from experience can be painful; English proverb,
mid 18th century.

Good soup is made in an old pot.
successful results are due to age and experience; French proverb.

Live and learn.
often as a resigned or rueful comment on a disagreeable experience; English proverb, early 17th century.

Once bitten, twice shy.
someone who has suffered an injury will in the future be very
cautious of the cause; English proverb, mid 19th century;
compare **Once bitten by a snake, a man will be afraid of a
piece of rope for three years** at CAUTION.

**Some folks speak from experience; others, from
experience, don't speak.**
American proverb, mid 20th century.

They that live longest, see most.
often used to comment on the experience of old age; English
proverb, early 17th century.

Walking ten thousand miles is better than reading ten thousand books.

theoretical knowledge must be consolidated by practical experience; Chinese proverb; compare **Walking ten thousand miles; reading ten thousand books** at KNOWLEDGE.

You cannot catch old birds with chaff.

the wise and experienced are not easily fooled; English proverb, late 15th century.

You cannot put an old head on young shoulders.

you cannot expect someone who is young and inexperienced to show the wisdom and maturity of an older person; English proverb, late 16th century.

You should make a point of trying every experience once, excepting incest and folk-dancing.

20th-century saying, repeated by Arnold Bax in *Farewell my Youth* (1943), quoting 'a sympathetic Scot'.

Extravagance
See THRIFT AND EXTRAVAGANCE

Fact

See HYPOTHESIS AND FACT

Failure

See SUCCESS AND FAILURE

Fame

See also REPUTATION

Lasting fame is not easily achieved, since even if it is
well founded, without a written record it may be forgotten:
Brave men lived before Agamemnon.

Brave men lived before Agamemnon.
to be remembered the exploits of a hero must be recorded;
English proverb, early 19th century, from Horace (65–8 BC) *Odes*,
'Many brave men lived before Agamemnon's time, but they are
all, unmourned and unknown, covered by the long night,
because they lack their sacred poet.'

Common fame is seldom to blame.
reputation is generally founded on fact rather than rumour;
English proverb, mid 17th century.

If any man seek for greatness, let him forget greatness
and seek truth.
American proverb, mid 20th century.

More people know Tom Fool than Tom Fool knows.

English proverb, mid 17th century; *Tom Fool* was a name given to the part of the fool in a play or morris dance.

A tall tree attracts the wind.

fame may make you the subject of hostile attention; Chinese proverb.

Who he?

an editorial interjection after the name of a (supposedly) little-known person, associated particularly with Harold Ross (1892–1951), editor of the *New Yorker*; repopularized in Britain by the satirical magazine *Private Eye*.

 # Familiarity
See also NEIGHBOURS

While it may be safer to stick with what you know (Better the devil you know, than the devil you don't), *it may be difficult to recognize the virtues of the familiar. Without the enchantment lent by distance,* Local ginger is not hot.

Better the devil you know than the devil you don't.

understanding of the nature of a danger may give one an advantage, and is preferable to something which is completely unknown, and which may well be worse; English proverb, mid 19th century.

Better wed over the mixen than over the moor.

it is better to marry a neighbour than a stranger (a *mixen* is a midden); English proverb, early 17th century.

Blue are the hills that are far away.

a distant view lends enchantment; English proverb, early 20th century.

Come live with me and you'll know me.

the implication is that only by living with a person will you learn their real nature; English proverb, early 20th century.

Familiarity breeds contempt.

we value least the things which are most familiar; English proverb, late 14th century.

If you lie down with dogs, you will get up with fleas.

asserting that human failings, such as dishonesty and foolishness, are contagious; English proverb, late 16th century (earlier in Latin).

Local ginger is not hot.

modern saying, said to derive from a Chinese proverb; compare **a prophet is not without honour save in his own country** below.

A man is known by the company he keeps.

originally used as a moral maxim or exhortation in the context of preparation for marriage; English proverb, mid 16th century.

No man is a hero to his valet.

English proverb, mid 18th century, found earlier in French, in a letter from the society hostess Mme Cornuel (1605–94).

A prophet is not without honour save in his own country.

English proverb, late 15th century, from the Bible (Matthew 13:57), 'A prophet is not without honour, save in his own country, and in his own house'; compare **Local ginger is not hot** above.

There is nothing new under the sun.

English proverb, late 16th century, from the Bible (Ecclesiastes 1:9), 'The thing that hath been, it is that which shall be; and that which is done is that which shall be done: and there is no new thing under the sun.'

 # The Family
See also CHILDREN, PARENTS

Proverbial wisdom on the subject of the family finds a consensus in the view that Blood will tell. *The idea is expressed in detail in the Chinese saying,* Dragons beget dragons, phoenixes beget phoenixes, and burglars' children learn how to break into houses.

The apple never falls far from the tree.

family characteristics will assert themselves; English proverb, mid 19th century.

Blood is thicker than water.
in the end family ties will always count; English proverb, mid 19th century.

Blood will tell.
family characteristics or heredity will in the end be dominant; English proverb, mid 19th century.

The child of a frog is a frog.
Japanese proverb.

Children are certain cares, but uncertain comforts.
emphasizing the continuing responsibility and anxiety of parenthood; English proverb, mid 17th century.

Dragons beget dragons, phoenixes beget phoenixes, and burglars' children learn how to break into houses.
Chinese proverb; see **Like father, like son** below.

I belong by blood relationship; therefore I am.
on the importance of family ties in one's sense of identity; African proverb.

A large family, quick help.
those related to you will provide ready help in time of need; Serbian proverb.

Like father, like son.
often used to call attention to similarities in behaviour; English proverb, mid 14th century.

Like mother, like daughter.

English proverb, early 14th century; the ultimate allusion is to the Bible (Ezekiel 16:44), 'As is the mother, so is her daughter.'

My brother and I against my cousin and my cousin and I against the stranger.

Arab proverb; compare **The enemy of my enemy is my friend** at ENEMIES.

The shoemaker's son always goes barefoot.

the family of a skilled or knowledgeable person are often the last to benefit from their expertise; English proverb, mid 16th century.

Fate

See also THE FUTURE

Views on fate see it as unlikely to be altered by human intervention: Man proposes, God disposes. *The only strongly contrary assessment is found in the modern American saying,* Fate can be taken by the horns, like a goat, and pushed in the right direction.

Every hog has its Martinmas.

everyone has their destiny; *Martinmas*, the feast of St Martin, 11 November, was the season at which pigs and other domestic animals were slaughtered before winter; traditional saying.

WHAT GOES UP
MUST COME
DOWN

Fate can be taken by the horns, like a goat, and pushed in the right direction.

with sufficient determination one need not be a helpless victim of fate; American proverb, mid 20th century.

Hanging and wiving go by destiny.

an expression of fatalism about the course of one's life; English proverb, mid 16th century.

If you're born to be hanged then you'll never be drowned.

used to qualify apparent good luck which may have an unhappy outcome; English proverb, late 16th century.

Man proposes, God disposes.

often now said in consolation or resignation when plans have been disrupted; English proverb, mid 15th century.

The mills of God grind slowly, yet they grind exceeding small.

English proverb, mid 17th century; in its current form, it derives from Henry Wadsworth Longfellow's translation of *Sinnegedichte* by Friedrich von Logau, 'Though the mills of God grind slowly, yet they grind exceeding small; Though with patience He stands waiting, with exactness grinds he all' (Von Logau's first line is itself a translation of an anonymous verse in Sextus Empiricus *Adversus Mathematicos*).

Sour, sweet, bitter, pungent, all must be tasted.

We have to experience both happiness and sadness in life; Chinese proverb.

**We're here
Because
We're here
Because
We're here
Because we're here.**
soldiers' song of the First World War, sung to the tune of 'Auld
Lang Syne'.

What goes up must come down.
commonly associated with wartime bombing and anti-aircraft
shrapnel, and often used with the implication that an
exhilarating rise must be followed by a fall; early 20th-century
saying.

What must be, must be.
used to acknowledge the force of circumstances; English proverb, late 14th century.

Fear
See also COURAGE, DANGER

*A fearful person is likely to suffer from more than just the effects
of the danger they fear:* Cowards die many times before
their death.

Be afraid. Be very afraid.
advertising slogan for the film *The Fly* (1986).

Cowards may die many times before their death.
English proverb, late 16th century; in this form, a misquotation from Shakespeare *Julius Caesar* (1599) 'Cowards die many times before their deaths; / The valiant never taste of death but once.'

Fear makes the wolf bigger than he is.
Fear exaggerates what we are afraid of; German proverb.

From ghoulies and ghosties and long-leggety beasties
And things that go bump in the night,
Good Lord, deliver us!
'The Cornish or West Country Litany'

In space no one can hear you scream.
advertising copy for the film *Alien* (1979).

 Feelings
See also LOVE

Good feeling is seen as something without which there can be little real enjoyment: Better a dinner of herbs than a stalled ox where hate is. *Beyond this, ill will directed against another may rebound on the perpetrator:* Curses, like chickens, come home to roost.

Better a dinner of herbs than a stalled ox where hate is.
simple food accompanied by goodwill and affection is preferable to luxury in an atmosphere of ill will; English proverb, mid 16th century, with allusion to the Bible (Proverbs 15:17), 'Better a dinner of herbs where love is, than a stalled ox with hatred therewith.'

Curses, like chickens, come home to roost.
ill will directed at another is likely to rebound on the originator;
English proverb, late 14th century.

Out of the fullness of the heart the mouth speaks.
overwhelming feeling will express itself in speech; English
proverb, late 14th century, originally with allusion to the
Bible (Matthew 12:34), 'Out of the abundance of the heart the
mouth speaketh.'

Sing before breakfast, cry before night.
warning against overconfidence in early happiness presaging a
reversal of good fortune; English proverb, early 17th century.

Flattery
See PRAISE AND FLATTERY

Flowers
See also GARDENS

*Flowers are a natural source of enjoyment, but they require
nurturing and protection:* It is not enough for a gardener to
love flowers; he must also hate weeds.

All the flowers of tomorrow are in the seeds of today.
Indian proverb; compare **A seed hidden in the heart of an apple
is an orchard invisible** at TREES.

It is not enough for a gardener to love flowers; he must also hate weeds.

American proverb, mid 20th century.

Say it with flowers.

slogan for the Society of American Florists, from 1917.

 Food

See also COOKING, DRINK, EATING

Some sayings focus on particular foodstuffs, as in the traditional warning Don't eat oysters unless there is an R in the month. *However, and more importantly, food is recognized as the most basic necessity:* No dinner without bread.

An apple-pie without some cheese is like a kiss without a squeeze.

traditional saying, early 20th century.

Don't eat oysters unless there is an R in the month.

from the tradition that oysters were likely to be unsafe to eat in the warmer months between May and August.

Every pomegranate has one seed that has come from heaven.

Arabic proverb.

God never sends mouths but He sends meat.
used in resignation or consolation; English proverb, late 14th century.

A hungry man is an angry man.
someone deprived of a basic necessity will not be easily placated; English proverb, mid 17th century.

It's ill speaking between a full man and a fasting.
someone in need is never on good terms with someone who has all they want; English proverb, mid 17th century.

The more butter, the worse cheese.
the more cream used for butter, the less available for cheese; traditional saying.

No dinner without bread.
Russian proverb.

Of soup and love, the first is best.
Spanish proverb.

Oxo gives a meal man-appeal.
advertising slogan for Oxo beef extract, *c.*1960.

Stop me and buy one.
Wall's ice cream, from spring 1922.

Twice-cooked cabbage is death.
Latin proverb.

Fools

Despite the hopeful note struck by the saying Fortune favours fools, *the consensus is that a foolish person is more likely to be unfortunate:* A fool and his money are soon parted.

Ask a silly question and you get a silly answer.
often used to indicate that the answer is so obvious that the question should not have been asked; English proverb, early 14th century.

Empty vessels make the most sound.
foolish and empty-headed people make the most noise; English proverb, mid 15th century.

A fool and his money are soon parted.
English proverb, late 16th century.

Fools build houses and wise men live in them.
a shrewd person chooses to save themselves trouble, and benefit from the effort expended by another; English proverb, late 17th century.

Fortune favours fools.
a foolish person is traditionally fortunate; English proverb, mid 16th century.

A wise man changes his mind, a fool never.
obstinacy is a mark of folly; Spanish proverb.

Foresight

See also THE FUTURE

Foresight is seen as desirable (Prevention is better than cure), *but hard to achieve—while conversely,* It's easy to be wise after the event.

He who can see three days ahead will be rich for three thousand years.
even limited foresight is of great value; Japanese proverb.

If a man's foresight were as good as his hindsight, we would all get somewhere.
American proverb, mid 20th century.

It is easy to be wise after the event.
the difficult thing is to make a correct judgement without the benefit of hindsight; English proverb, early 17th century.

It's too late to shut the stable-door after the horse has bolted.
preventive measures taken after things have gone wrong are of little effect; English proverb, mid 14th century.

Nothing is certain but the unforeseen.
warning against an overconfident belief in a future occurrence; English proverb, late 19th century.

Prevention is better than cure.
English proverb, early 17th century.

Forgiveness

See also CONSCIENCE, GUILT

Not only should we be ready to seek forgiveness (A fault confessed is half redressed)*, refusal to forgive is associated with the likelihood that we have wronged another:* Offenders never pardon.

Charity covers a multitude of sins.

charity as a virtue outweighs many faults; English proverb, early 17th century.

A fault confessed is half redressed.

by confessing what you have done wrong you have begun to make amends; English proverb, mid 16th century.

Forgiving the unrepentant is like drawing pictures on water.

forgiveness is meaningless unless there is true repentance on the part of the offender; Japanese proverb.

Good to forgive, best to forget.

it is even better to forget that you have been injured than to forgive the injury; North American proverb, mid 20th century.

Never let the sun go down on your anger.

recommending a swift reconciliation after a quarrel; from the Bible (Ephesians 4:26), 'Be ye angry and sin not: let not the sun go down upon your wrath.'

Offenders never pardon.
the experience of having wronged someone often fosters a
continuing resentment of the victim; English proverb,
mid 17th century.

To know all is to forgive all.
English proverb, mid 20th century; the idea is found earlier in
French, in Mme de Staël *Corinne* (1807), '*Tout comprendre rend très
indulgent* [To be totally understanding makes one very indulgent].'

 Friendship

*Although the good intentions of our friends can sometimes be a
burden* (Save us from our friends), *we depend on having
them*: A friend in need is a friend indeed.

**Be kind to your friends: if it weren't for them, you
would be a total stranger.**
American proverb, mid 20th century.

A friend in need is a friend indeed.
a *friend in need* is one who helps when someone is in need or
difficulty; English proverb, mid 11th century.

Hold a true friend with both your hands.
real friendship is something to be cherished; African proverb.

Life without a friend, is death without a witness.
friendship gives meaning to life; Spanish proverb.

Oh, the comfort—the inexpressible comfort of feeling safe with a person, having neither to weigh thoughts, nor measure words, but pouring them all out, just as they are, chaff and grain together; knowing that a faithful hand will take and sift them—keep what is worth keeping—and with the breath of kindness blow the rest away.

19th-century saying, often attributed to George Eliot or Dinah Mulock Craik (1826–87).

Save us from our friends.

the earnest help of friends can sometimes be unintentionally damaging; English proverb, late 15th century.

Two is company, but three is none.

often used with the alternative ending 'three's a crowd'; English proverb, early 18th century.

 # Futility

See also ACHIEVEMENT

There are a number of ways of invoking the picture of a futile course of action, from Dogs bark, but the caravan goes on *to* You can't make a silk purse out of a sow's ear.

Dogs bark, but the caravan goes on.

trivial criticism will not deflect the progress of something important; English proverb, late 19th century.

Do not push the river, it will flow by itself.

typifying pointless activity; Polish proverb.

Hot water does not burn down the house.

typifying ineffective action; African proverb.

In vain the net is spread in the sight of the bird.

a person who has seen the process by which someone intends to harm them is unlikely to be in danger; English proverb, late 14th century.

Sue a beggar and catch a louse.

it is pointless to try to obtain restitution from someone without resources; English proverb, mid 17th century.

You cannot carry two watermelons in one hand.

typifying an attempted action that is bound to fail; modern saying, said to be an Arabic proverb.

You cannot get a quart into a pint pot.

used of any situation in which the prospective contents are too large for the container; English proverb, late 19th century.

You cannot get blood from a stone.

often used, as a resigned admission, to mean that it is hopeless to try to extort money or sympathy from those who have none; English proverb, mid 17th century.

You cannot make bricks without straw.

nothing can be made or achieved if one does not have the correct materials; English proverb, mid 17th century, with allusion to the

Bible (Exodus) in Pharaoh's decree to the taskmasters set over the Israelites in Egypt, 'Ye shall no more give the people straw to make brick, as heretofore: let them go and gather straw for themselves.'

You can put lipstick on a pig, but it will still be a pig.
superficial improvements will not alter the fundamental structure; modern saying.

You can't make a silk purse out of a sow's ear.
inherent nature cannot be overcome by nurture; English proverb, early 16th century.

You can't unscramble scrambled eggs.
the results of some actions cannot be undone; modern saying.

The Future
See also FORESIGHT, THE PAST, THE PRESENT

The future may be bright (or indeed, Orange), but too much focus on it may mean that we lose sight of what is actually happening: There is no future like the present.

Coming events cast their shadow before.
some initial effects indicating the nature of an event may be felt before it takes place; English proverb, early 19th century.

The future's bright, the future's Orange.
advertising slogan for Orange telecom company, mid 1990s.

He that follows freits, freits will follow him.

someone who looks for portents of the future will find himself dogged by them (*freits* are omens); Scottish proverb, early 18th century.

An inch ahead is darkness.

we have no knowledge of the future; Japanese proverb.

There is no future like the present.

American proverb, mid 20th century.

Today you; tomorrow me.

often used in the context of the inevitability of death to each person; English proverb, mid 13th century.

Tomorrow is another day.

English proverb, early 16th century.

Tomorrow is often the busiest day of the year.

commenting on the tendency to put off necessary work; Spanish proverb.

Tomorrow never comes.

used in the context of something which is constantly predicted to be imminent, but which never comes; English proverb, early 16th century.

Gardens

See also FLOWERS

Gardening is seen as a source of joy, but also one that requires a good deal of attention, especially where keeping control of weeds is concerned: One's years seeding makes seven years' weeding.

The answer lies in the soil.
traditional gardening advice.

Dig for victory.
Second World War slogan, encouraging production of food in gardens and allotments.

If you would be happy for a week take a wife; if you would be happy for a month kill a pig; but if you would be happy all your life plant a garden.
the saying exists in a variety of forms, but marriage is nearly always given as one of the ephemeral forms of happiness; English proverb, mid 17th century.

Life begins on the day you start a garden.
modern saying, claimed to be a Chinese proverb.

More things grow in the garden than the gardener sows.
some plants will appear as part of the natural process; Spanish proverb.

One year's seeding makes seven years' weeding.
the allusion is to the danger of allowing weeds to grow and seed
themselves; English proverb, late 19th century.

Parsley seed goes nine times to the Devil.
parsley is often slow to germinate, and there was a superstition
that it belonged to the Devil, and had to be sown nine times
before it would come up; English proverb, mid 17th century.

**Select a proper site for your garden and half your work
is done.**
Chinese proverb.

Sow corn in clay, and plant vines in sand.
Spanish traditional saying.

Sow dry and set wet.
seeds should be sown in dry ground and then given water;
English proverb, mid 17th century.

Walnuts and pears you plant for your heirs.
both trees are tradionally slow growing, so that the benefit will
be felt by future generations; English proverb, mid 17th century.

Generosity

See also GRATITUDE

Generosity is seen as an obligation (It is better to give than to receive), *and one which should be readily fulfilled:* He gives twice who gives quickly.

A bird never flew on one wing.

frequently used to justify a further gift, especially another drink; early 18th-century proverb, mainly Scottish and Irish.

Friday's child is loving and giving.

English proverb, mid 19th century, from a traditional rhyme (compare qualities associated with birth on other days at entries under BEAUTY, SORROW, TRAVEL, and WORK).

Give a thing, and take a thing, to wear the devil's gold ring.

a school children's rhyme, chanted when a person gives something and then asks for it back; English proverb, late 16th century.

He gives twice who gives quickly.

associating readiness to give with generosity; English proverb, mid 16th century.

It is better to give than to receive.

English proverb, late 14th century, ultimately with allusion to the Bible (Acts 20:35), 'It is more blessed to give than to receive.'

It is easy to be generous with other people's property.

traditional saying, of classical origin.

 # God

While God may be omnipotent (All things are possible with God), *we are expected to make some efforts on our own behalf:* God helps them that helps themselves.

All things are possible with God.

English proverb, late 17th century, from the Bible (Matthew 19:26), 'With men this is impossible; but with God all things are possible.'

God helps them that help themselves.

often used in urging someone to action; English proverb.

God writes straight with crooked lines.

God can use any instrument to achieve His ends; Portuguese proverb.

The nature of God is a circle of which the centre is everywhere and the circumference is nowhere.

medieval saying, said to have been traced to a lost treatise of Empedocles; quoted in the *Roman de la Rose*, and by St Bonaventura in *Itinerarius Mentis in Deum*.

**There's probably no God. Now stop worrying and
enjoy your life.**
slogan for a secular poster campaign on London buses,
January 2009.

 # Good and Evil
See also VIRTUE

Although some goodness is unassailable (The sun loses
nothing by shining into a puddle), *there is an insistence on
the corrupting effects of evil:* He that touches pitch shall
be defiled.

The greater the sinner, the greater the saint.
a sinner who has reformed is likely to be more virtuous that
someone who is morally neutral; English proverb, late 18th
century.

He that touches pitch shall be defiled.
a person who chooses to put themselves in contact with
wrongdoing will be marked by it; English proverb, early 14th
century, with allusion to the Bible (Ecclesiasticus 13:1), 'He that
toucheth pitch shall be defiled therewith.'

Honi soit qui mal y pense.
French, 'Evil be to him who evil thinks', the motto of the Order
of the Garter, originated by Edward III, probably on 23 April of
1348 or 1349.

Ill weeds grow apace.

used to comment on the apparent success enjoyed by an ill-doer; English proverb, late 15th century.

Satan rebuking sin.

originally meaning that the worst possible stage has been reached; in later use, an ironic comment on the nature of the person delivering the rebuke; English proverb, early 17th century.

The sun loses nothing by shining into a puddle.

something which is naturally clear and radiant cannot be tainted or diminished by association; English proverb, early 14th century, of classical origin.

Two blacks don't make a white.

one injury or instance of wrongdoing does not justify another; English proverb, early 18th century.

Two wrongs don't make a right.

a first injury does not justify a second in retaliation; English proverb, late 18th century.

What is got under the Devil's back is spent under his belly.

what is gained improperly will be spent on folly and debauchery; English proverb, late 16th century.

Where God builds a church, the Devil will build a chapel.

the establishment of something which is itself good may also create the opening for something evil; English proverb, mid 16th century.

Gossip

See also REPUTATION, SECRECY

While gossip may be seen as a natural part of human relations (Gossip is the lifeblood of society), it is more generally seen as likely to be damaging: according to the wartime security slogan, Careless talk costs lives.

Careless talk costs lives.
Second World War security slogan.

A dog that will fetch a bone will carry a bone.
someone given to gossip carries talk both ways; English proverb, early 19th century.

Give a dog a bad name and hang him.
once a person's reputation has been blackened his plight is hopeless; English proverb, early 18th century.

Gossip is the lifeblood of society.
American proverb, mid 20th century.

Gossip is vice enjoyed vicariously.
American proverb, early 20th century.

The greater the truth, the greater the libel.
English proverb, late 18th century.

Loose lips sink ships.
American Second World War security slogan.

A tale never loses in the telling.

implying that a story is often exaggerated when it is repeated; English proverb, mid 16th century.

Those who live in glass houses shouldn't throw stones.

it is unwise to criticize or slander another if you are vulnerable to retaliation; English proverb, mid 17th century.

What the soldier said isn't evidence.

hearsay evidence alone cannot be relied on; English proverb, mid 19th century, originally from Charles Dickens *Pickwick Papers* (1837), 'You must not tell us what the soldier, or any other man, said . . . it's not evidence.'

Whoever gossips to you will gossip about you.

a warning against enjoyment of gossip; Spanish proverb.

Government

See also POLITICS, SOCIETY

From the point of view of the subject, government is seen not only as powerful but also often as out of reach: God is high above, and the tsar is far away.

The cat, the rat, and Lovell the dog, rule all England under the hog.

contemporary rhyme referring to William *Catesby*, Richard *Ratcliffe*, and Francis *Lovell*, favourites of Richard III, whose personal emblem was a white boar.

Divide and rule.

government control is more easily exercised if possible
opponents are separated into factions; English proverb, early
17th century.

God is high above, and the tsar is far away.

the source of central power is out of the reach of local interests;
Russian proverb; compare **The mountains are high, and the
emperor is far away** below, and **Delhi is far away** at CAUTION.

The mountains are high, and the emperor is far away.

the source of central power is out of the reach of local interests;
Chinese proverb; compare **God is high above, and the tsar is
far away** above, and **Delhi is far away** at CAUTION.

No fist is big enough to hide the sky.

there are limits to the powers of even the most repressive
regime; African saying.

Gratitude

See also GENEROSITY

*The ungrateful person may discover too late the value of what
they have received:* You never miss the water till the well
runs dry.

The Devil was sick, the Devil a saint would be.

promises made in adversity may not be kept in prosperity;
English proverb, early 17th century.

YOU NEVER MISS THE

WATER TILL THE

WELL RUNS DRY

Don't overload gratitude, if you do, she'll kick.
American proverb, mid 18th century.

Never look a gift horse in the mouth.
warning against questioning the quality or use of a lucky chance or gift; referring to the fact that it is by a horse's teeth that its age is judged; English proverb, early 16th century.

The river that forgets its source will dry up.
ingratitude brings its own punishment; African proverb.

When you drink water, remember who dug the well.
a warning against taking the efforts of others for granted; modern saying, said to be a Chinese proverb.

You never miss the water till the well runs dry.
applied to situations in which it is only when a source of support or sustenance has been withdrawn that its importance is understood; English proverb, early 17th century.

 # Greed
See also MONEY

When we give in to greed we are likely to find the appetite insatiable: Much would have more.

The more you get the more you want.
English proverb, mid 14th century.

Much would have more.

the ownership of substantial possessions creates in the owner the desire for still more; English proverb, mid 14th century.

Need makes greed.

Scottish proverb.

Pigs get fat, but hogs get slaughtered.

used as a warning against greed; modern saying.

The sea refuses no river.

the sea's capacity is so great that anyone who chooses may find a place there; English proverb, early 17th century.

Where the carcase is, there shall the eagles be gathered together.

English proverb, mid 16th century, from the Bible (Matthew 24:28), 'Wheresoever the carcase is, there will the eagles be gathered together.'

 Guilt

See also CRIME AND PUNISHMENT

The experience of guilt is likely to be intolerable (The guilty man always runs)*; we may as well,* Confess and be hanged.

Confess and be hanged.
guilt must be confessed and the due punishment accepted for
true repentance; English proverb, late 16th century.

The guilty flee when no man pursueth.
saying, with biblical allusion to Proverbs 28:1, 'The wicked
flee when no man pursueth; but the righteous are bold
as a lion.'

The guilty one always runs.
American proverb, mid 20th century.

Not guilty, but don't do it again.
comment on what is taken as a lucky escape from conviction;
informal legal saying.

We are all guilty.
supposedly typical of the liberal view that all members of
society bear responsibility for its wrongs; used particularly as a
catchphrase by the psychiatrist 'Dr Heinz Kiosk', created by the
satirist Peter Simple (pseudonym of Michael Wharton,
1913–2006).

We name the guilty men.
supposedly now a cliché of investigative journalism; *Guilty
Men* was the title of a tract by Michael Foot, Frank Owen,
and Peter Howard, published under the pseudonym of
'Cato', which attacked the supporters of the Munich
agreement and the appeasement policy of Neville
Chamberlain.

Habit

See CUSTOM AND HABIT

Happiness

See also HOPE

The unwise person will recognize happiness only when it is lost (Blessings brighten as they take their flight). *An alternative way is to find reasons for happiness in unpromising circumstances:* It is a poor heart that never rejoices.

Blessings brighten as they take their flight.
it is only when something is lost that one realizes its value; English proverb, mid 18th century.

Call no man happy till he dies.
traditionally attributed to the Athenian statesman and poet Solon (*c.*640–after 556 BC) in the form 'Call no man happy before he dies, he is at best but fortunate'; English proverb, mid 16th century.

A good time was had by all.
title of a collection of poems published in 1937 by Stevie Smith (1902–71), taken from the characteristic conclusion of accounts of social events in parish magazines.

Happiness is the only thing we can give without having.
modern saying.

Happiness is what you make of it.
American proverb, mid 19th century.

Hell is where heaven is not.
English proverb, late 16th century.

If I keep a green bough in my heart a singing bird will come.
we have some role in creating our own happiness; Chinese proverb.

It is a poor heart that never rejoices.
often used to explain a celebratory action, and implying that circumstances are not in general unrelievedly bad; English proverb, mid 19th century.

 Haste and Delay

While the hurried action associated with lack of thought is likely to be ineffectual (More haste, less speed), *procrastination in itself is not an answer:* Delays are dangerous.

Always in a hurry, always behind.
North American proverb, mid 20th century.

Delays are dangerous.

used as a warning against procrastination; English proverb, late 16th century.

Don't hurry—start early.

American proverb, mid 20th century.

Haste is from the Devil.

often used to mean that undue haste results in work being done badly or carelessly; English proverb, mid 17th century.

Haste makes waste.

hurried work is likely to be wasteful; English proverb, late 14th century.

Make haste slowly.

advising a course of careful preparation; English proverb, late 16th century; the idea is found in the classical world in the words of the Roman Emperor Augustus (63 BC–AD 14), 'Festina lente [Make haste slowly].'

More haste, less speed.

speed here meant originally 'success' rather than 'swiftness', and the meaning is that hurried work is likely to be less successful; English proverb, mid 14th century.

Never put off till tomorrow what you can do today.

English proverb, late 14th century.

Procrastination is the thief of time.

someone who continually puts things off ultimately achieves
little; English proverb, mid 18th century, from Edward Young
Night Thoughts (1742–5).

Health

See also EATING, MEDICINE, SICKNESS

*The preservation of health is seen as lying in our own hands,
though the medium of adopting a sensible lifestyle:* Early to
bed and early to rise, makes a man healthy, wealthy,
and wise.

An apple a day keeps the doctor away.

eating an apple each day keeps one healthy; English proverb, mid
19th century; compare **Eat leeks in March and ramsons in May,
and all the year after physicians may play** below.

Don't die of ignorance.

Aids publicity campaign, 1987.

Drinka Pinta Milka Day.

advertising slogan for the National Dairy Council, 1958; coined
by Bertrand Whitehead.

**Early to bed and early to rise, makes a man healthy,
wealthy, and wise.**

linking a healthy and sober lifestyle with material success;
English proverb, late 15th century.

Eat leeks in March and ramsons in May, and all the year after physicians may play.

ramsons = wild garlic; Welsh proverb; compare **An apple a day keeps the doctor away** above.

Even your closest friends won't tell you.

advertising slogan for Listerine mouthwash, US, 1923.

Every good quality is contained in ginger.

Indian proverb.

I was a seven-stone weakling.

advertising slogan for Charles Atlas body-building, originally in US.

More die of food than famine.

American proverb, mid 20th century.

Slip, slop, slap.

sun protection slogan, meaning slip on a T-shirt, slop on some suncream, slap on a hat; Australian health education programme, 1980s.

Those who do not find time for exercise will have to find time for illness.

traditional saying.

Your food is your medicine.

Indian proverb.

History

*To make a mark on history is not necessarily something
to be sought:* Happy is the country which has no
history. *Beyond this, the objectivity of history is
seen rather sceptically:* Until the lions produce their
own historian, the story of the hunt will gratify the hunter.

Happy is the country which has no history.
memorable events are likely to be unhappy and disruptive;
English proverb, early 19th century; compare a comment
attributed to the French political philosopher Montesquieu
(1689–1755) by Thomas Carlyle, 'Happy the people whose annals
are blank in history-books!'

History is a fable agreed upon.
American proverb, mid 20th century.

History is fiction with the truth left out.
American proverb, mid 20th century.

History is written by the victors.
modern saying.

History repeats itself.
English proverb, mid 19th century.

**Until the lions produce their own historian, the story
of the hunt will glorify the hunter.**
African proverb.

The Home

See also HOUSEWORK

There are various ways of expressing the importance of having a home, from East, west, home's best, *to the Chinese assertion that* Falling leaves have to return to their roots.

East, west, home's best.
English proverb, mid 19th century.

An Englishman's home is his castle.
a person has the right to refuse entry to his home; reflecting a legal principle, as formulated by the English jurist Edward Coke (1552–1634), 'For a man's house is his castle, *et domus sua cuique est tutissimum refugium* [and each man's home is his safest refuge]'; English proverb, late 16th century.

Every cock will crow upon his own dunghill.
everyone is confident and at ease on their home; English proverb, mid 13th century.

Falling leaves have to return to their roots.
everything must ultimately return to its origins; Chinese proverb.

Home is home though it's never so homely.
no place can compare with one's own home; English proverb, mid 16th century.

Home is where the heart is.

one's true home is wherever the person one loves most is; English proverb, late 19th century.

Home is where the mortgage is.

American proverb, mid 20th century.

Lang may yer lum reek!

long may your chimney smoke, often used as a toast; Scottish saying.

There's no place like home.

English proverb, late 16th century; the saying is found earlier in Greek, in the work of the Greek poet Hesiod (*c*.700 BC).

Honesty

See also CORRUPTION, DECEPTION, LIES, TRUTH

Honesty is essential in even the smallest actions (It's a sin to steal a pin), *although it is not always realistically to be expected* (Honesty is more praised than practised). *However, apart from moral duty there may be pragmatic reasons for adopting it:* Honesty is the best policy.

Children and fools tell the truth.

implying that they lack the cunning to see possible danger; tradition sometimes adds drunkards; English proverb, mid 16th century.

Confession is good for the soul.

confession is essential to repentance and forgiveness; English proverb, mid 17th century.

He who steals an egg will steal a camel.

someone who is guilty of petty dishonesty is likely to be guilty of more serious theft; modern saying, said to be an Arabic proverb.

Honesty is more praised than practised.

it is easier to advise another person to be honest than to be honest oneself; American proverb, mid 20th century.

Honesty is the best policy.

as well as being right, to be honest may also achieve a more successful outcome; English proverb, early 17th century.

A howlin' coyote ain't stealin' no chickens.

American proverb, mid 20th century.

It's a sin to steal a pin.

even if what is stolen is of little value, the action is still wrong; English proverb, late 19th century.

Nothing is stolen without hands.

if money or goods are missing, someone has stolen them; English proverb, early 17th century.

Sell honestly, but not honesty.

a play on words meaning that honesty is the essential virtue in commerce; American proverb, mid 20th century.

Hope

See also HAPPINESS, OPTIMISM AND PESSIMISM

Hope may make difficult circumstances bearable (If it were not for hope, the heart would break), *but over-indulgence in its promises will not lead to happiness:* He that lives in hope dances to an ill tune.

Blessed is he who expects nothing, for he shall never be disappointed.

English proverb, early 18th century, originally with allusion to Alexander Pope (1688–1744), ' "Blessed is the man who expects nothing, for he shall never be disappointed" was the ninth beatitude.'

A drowning man will clutch at a straw.

when hope is slipping away one grasps at the slightest chance; English proverb, mid 16th century.

He that lives in hope dances to an ill tune.

hoping for something better may constrain one's freedom of action; English proverb, late 16th century.

Hope deferred makes the heart sick.

implying that it is worse to have had one's hopes raised and then dashed, than to have been resigned to not having something; English proverb, late 14th century, from the Bible (Proverbs 13:12), 'Hope deferred maketh the heart sick: but when the desire cometh, it is a tree of life.'

Hope is a good breakfast but a bad supper.
while it is pleasant to begin something in a hopeful mood, the hopes need to have been fulfilled by the time it ends; English proverb, mid 17th century.

Hope is the pillar of the world.
African proverb.

Hope springs eternal.
English proverb, mid 18th century, from Alexander Pope (1688–1744) *An Essay on Man* (1733), 'Hope springs eternal in the human breast: /Man never Is, but always To be blest.'

If it were not for hope, the heart would break.
referring to the role of hope in warding off complete despair; English proverb, mid 13th century.

In the kingdom of hope, there is no winter.
Russian proverb.

It is better to travel hopefully than to arrive.
often with the implication that something long sought may be disappointing when achieved; English proverb, late 19th century; from Robert Louis Stevenson *Virginibus Puerisque* (1881), 'To travel hopefully is a better thing than to arrive, and the true success is to labour.'

While there's life there's hope.
often used as encouragement not to despair in an unpromising situation; English proverb, mid 16th century.

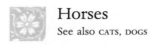

Horses

See also CATS, DOGS

*Sayings about horses reflect interests in choosing, and keeping,
a horse, with an emphasis on personal judgement and management*: Care, and not fine stables, makes a good horse.

Care, and not fine stables, makes a good horse.
Danish proverb.

No foot, no horse.
relating to horse care, and recorded in North America as 'no
hoof, no horse'; English proverb, mid 18th century.

**One white foot, buy him; two white feet, try him; three
white feet, look well about him; four white feet, go
without him.**
on horse-dealing, categorizing features in a horse which are
believed to be unlucky; English proverb, recorded in various
forms from the 15th century.

Pace makes the race.
from horse racing, relating to the setting of odds; modern
saying.

**There is nothing so good for the inside of a man as the
outside of a horse.**
recommending the healthful effects of horse-riding; English
proverb, early 20th century.

Hospitality

Hospitality is a natural source of enjoyment (It is merry in hall when beards wag all), *but guests can overstay their welcome. An African proverb recommends a way of dealing with this:* Treat your guest as a guest for two days; on the third day give him a hoe.

An ace caff with quite a nice museum attached.
advertising slogan for the Victoria and Albert Museum, February 1989.

Always leave the party when you are still having a good time.
implying that pleasure of this kind is transient; American proverb, mid 20th century.

The company makes the feast.
the success of a social occasion depends on those present rather than on the food and drink provided; English proverb, mid 17th century.

The first day a guest, the second day a guest, the third day a calamity.
Indian proverb.

Fish and guests stink after three days.
one should not outstay one's welcome; English proverb, late
16th century.

Food without hospitality is medicine.
American proverb, mid 20th century.

A guest is like the morning dew.
a good guest does not stay very long; African proverb.

**Hospitality and medicine must be confined to
three days.**
Indian proverb.

It is merry in hall when beards wag all.
when conversation is in full flow; English proverb, early 14th
century.

The pot boils; friendship lives.
some friendships will not outlast the provision of hospitality;
proverb of classical origin.

**There isn't much to talk about at some parties until
after one or two couples leave.**
American proverb, mid 20th century.

**Treat your guest as a guest for two days; on the third
day give him a hoe.**
African proverb.

Housework

See also THE HOME

Apart from slogans promoting cleaning devices such as Hoover's It beats as it sweeps as it cleans, *sayings about housework tend to focus on it as the traditional sphere of activity for women:* A woman's work is never done.

He that will thrive must first ask his wife.
the husband's material welfare depends on the way in which his wife manages the household; English proverb, late 15th century.

It beats as it sweeps as it cleans.
advertising slogan for Hoover vacuum cleaners, 1919.

Persil washes whiter—and it shows.
advertising slogan for Persil washing powder, 1970s.

They that wash on Monday
Have all the week to dry;
They that wash on Tuesday
Are not so much awry;
They that wash on Wednesday
Are not so much to blame;
They that wash on Thursday
Wash for very shame;
They that wash on Friday
Wash in sorry need;
And they that wash on Saturday,
Are lazy folk indeed.

traditional rhyme.

A woman's work is never done.

reflecting the traditional responsibilities of the housewife; English proverb, late 16th century.

 # The Human Race

The view that Man is the measure of all things *can be traced back to the classical world, but later sayings suggest more of a limitation:* The best of men are but men at best, *or even the dialect summary,* There's nowt so queer as folk.

All mankind is divided into three classes: those that are immovable, those that are movable, and those that move.

modern saying, said to be an Arabic proverb.

Am I not a man and a brother?

motto on the seal of the British and Foreign Anti-Slavery Society,
1787, depicting a kneeling slave in chains uttering these words
(subsequently a popular Wedgwood cameo).

The best of men are but men at best.

even someone of great moral worth is still human and fallible;
English proverb, late 17th century.

**God sleeps in the stone, dreams in the plant, stirs in the
animal, and awakens in man.**

traditional saying, frequently said to be of Indian origin; the
wording varies in different languages.

Man is a wolf to man.

English proverb, mid 16th century, from the Roman comic dramatist Plautus (c.250–184 BC), 'A man is a wolf rather than a man
to another man, when he hasn't yet found out what he's like.'

Man is the measure of all things.

everything could be understood in terms of humankind; English
proverb, mid 16th century; found earlier in the classical world in
the words of the Greek sophist Protagoras (b. c.485 BC), 'That
man is the measure of all things.'

There's nowt so queer as folk.

English proverb, early 20th century.

We are not alone.

advertising copy for the science-fiction film *Close Encounters of the
Third Kind* (1977).

What is the most important thing in life? It is people, people, people.

Maori proverb.

Young saint, old devil.

unnaturally good and moral behaviour at an early age is likely to change in later life; English proverb, early 15th century.

 ## Hypothesis and Fact

See also SCIENCE, THINKING

While Facts are stubborn things, *they will not always be reached through speculation: the question* How many angels can dance on the head of a pin? *has become a type of fruitless hypothesis.*

The exception proves the rule.

originally this meant that the recognition of something as an exception proved the existence of a rule, but it is now more often used or understood as justifying divergence from a rule (compare **There is an exception to every rule** below); English proverb, mid 17th century.

Facts are stubborn things.

used to indicate a core of reality that cannot be adjusted to people's wishes; English proverb, early 18th century.

How many angels can dance on the head of a pin?
regarded satirically as a characteristic speculation of
scholastic philosophy, particularly as exemplified by
'Doctor Scholasticus' (Anselm of Laon, d. 1117) and as used in
medieval comedies.

Nullius in verba.
Latin, 'in the word of none', motto of the Royal Society,
emphasizing reliance on experiment rather than authority;
adapted from the Roman poet Horace *Epistles*, 'Not bound to
swear allegiance to any master, wherever the wind takes me I
travel as a visitor.'

One story is good till another is told.
doubt may be cast on an apparently convincing account by a
second told from a different angle; English proverb, late 16th
century.

The proof of the pudding is in the eating.
the truth of an assertion will be demonstrated by how things
actually turn out; proof here means 'test'; English proverb, early
14th century.

There is an exception to every rule.
English proverb, late 16th century; compare **The exception
proves the rule** above.

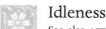

Idleness

See also ACTION AND INACTION, WORDS AND DEEDS

Idleness is not only seen as damaging and dangerous in itself (An idle brain is the devil's workshop), it is not even necessarily enjoyable for the person who gives way to it: Idle people have the least leisure.

As good be an addled egg as an idle bird.
an idle person will produce nothing; English proverb, late 16th century.

Better be idle than ill doing.
Scottish proverb.

Better to wear out than to rust out.
it is better to remain active than to succumb to idleness; in this form frequently attributed to Richard Cumberland, Bishop of Peterborough (1631–1718); English proverb, mid 16th century.

The devil finds work for idle hands to do.
someone who has no work to do will get into mischief; English proverb, early 18th century.

Doing nothing is doing ill.
failing to do anything is effectively wrong-doing; traditional saying.

An idle brain is the devil's workshop.
those who do not apply themselves to their work are most likely to get into trouble; English proverb, early 17th century.

Idleness is never enjoyable unless there is plenty to do.

American proverb, mid 20th century; the idea is found in the Jerome K. Jerome *Idle Thoughts of an Idle Fellow* (1886), 'It is impossible to enjoy idling thoroughly unless one has plenty of work to do.'

Idleness is the root of all evil.

English proverb, early 15th century; the idea has been attributed to the French theologian, monastic reformer, and abbot St Bernard of Clairvaux (1090–1153); compare **Money is the root of all evil** at MONEY.

Idle people have the least leisure.

lazy people are the least able to manage their time efficiently; English proverb, late 17th century.

If you won't work you shan't eat.

essential sustenance is seen as a reward for industry; English proverb, mid 16th century; from the Bible (II Thessalonians 3:10), 'If any would not work, neither should he eat.'

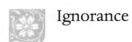

Ignorance

Ignorance is not necessarily seen as an unhappy state:
Ignorance is bliss *from the 18th century finds an echo from a
Russian saying of the Soviet era,* The less you know, the
better you sleep.

The husband is always the last to know.
relating to marital infidelity; English proverb, early
17th century.

Ignorance is bliss.
English proverb, mid 18th century, from Thomas Gray *Ode on a
Prospect of Eton College* (1747), 'Where ignorance is bliss,'Tis folly
to be wise.'

Ignorance is voluntary misfortune.
one has chosen not to remedy the condition; American proverb,
mid 20th century.

It is dark at the foot of the lighthouse.
we often miss what is closest to us; Japanese proverb.

The last one to know about the sea is the fish.
the person with most reason to know about something
often knows least; modern saying, claimed to be a Chinese
proverb.

The less you know, the better you sleep.
Russian saying of the Soviet era.

Man is the enemy of that of which he is ignorant.
fear is a common response to the unknown; Arab proverb.

Nothing so bold as a blind mare.
those who know least about a situation are least likely to be
deterred by it; English proverb, early 17th century.

A slice off a cut loaf isn't missed.
if someone has already been diminished or damaged, further
damage may go unnoticed; English proverb, late 16th century
(first recorded in Shakespeare's *Titus Andronicus*, 1592).

What the eye doesn't see, the heart doesn't grieve over.
now sometimes used with the implication that information is
being withheld to prevent difficulties; English proverb, mid 16th
century.

What you don't know can't hurt you.
English proverb, late 16th century.

**When the blind lead the blind, both shall fall into
the ditch.**
when a person is guided by someone equally inexperienced, both
are likely to come to grief; English proverb, late 9th century,
from the Bible (Matthew 15:14), 'They be blind leaders of the
blind. And if the blind lead the blind, both shall fall into
the ditch.'

Inaction

See ACTION AND INACTION

Indecision

See also CERTAINTY AND DOUBT

The consensus on indecision is that the person who cannot make a choice is likely to lose by it: Between two stools one falls to the ground.

Between two stools one falls to the ground.
inability to choose between, or accommodate oneself to, alternative viewpoints or courses of action may end in disaster; English proverb, late 14th century.

The cat would eat fish, but would not wet her feet.
commenting on a situation in which desire for something is checked by unwillingness to risk discomfort in acquiring it; English proverb, early 13th century.

Councils of war never fight.
people discussing matters in a group never reach the decision to fight, which an individual would make; English proverb, mid 19th century.

First thoughts are best.
advice to trust an instinctive reaction, often used as a warning against indecision; English proverb, early 20th century.

He who hesitates is lost.

often used to urge decisive action on someone; English proverb, early 18th century; early usages refer specifically to women, as in Joseph Addison *Cato* (1713), 'The woman that deliberates is lost.'

If you run after two hares you will catch neither.

one must decide on one's goal; English proverb, early 16th century.

Indecision is fatal, so make up your mind.

American proverb, mid 20th century.

Journalism

See NEWS AND JOURNALISM

Justice

See also CRIME AND PUNISHMENT, THE LAW

*Fairness and honest dealing are desirable in themselves
(Fair play's a jewel), but beyond this there are serious con-
sequences in making it difficult for anyone to obtain justice:
Justice delayed is justice denied.*

All's fair in love and war.

in certain conditions rules do not apply, and any measures are
acceptable; English proverb, early 17th century.

Be just before you're generous.

often used in the context of advising that one should settle any
obligations before indulging in generosity; English proverb, mid
18th century.

A fair exchange is no robbery.

sometimes used of an action regarded as cancelling out an
obligation which has been incurred; English proverb, mid
16th century.

Fair play's a jewel.

applauding the value of honest dealing; English proverb, early
19th century.

The fox should not be on the jury at the goose's trial.
a member of a jury must be unbiased; English proverb.

Give and take is fair play.
English proverb, late 18th century.

Give the Devil his due.
one should acknowledge the strengths and capabilities of even the most unpleasant person; English proverb, late 16th century.

Justice delayed is justice denied.
English proverb, late 20th century; compare a clause from Magna Carta (1215), 'To no man will we sell, or deny, or delay, right or justice.'

One law for the rich and another for the poor.
English proverb, mid 19th century.

There are two sides to every question.
a problem can be seen from more than one angle; English proverb, early 19th century.

Turn about is fair play.
recommending equality of opportunity; English proverb, mid 18th century.

We all love justice—at our neighbour's expense.
American proverb, mid 20th century.

What goes around comes around.
often used as a comment on someone becoming subject to
what they have visited on others; late 20th century, of
US origin.

What's sauce for the goose is sauce for the gander.
originally meaning that what is suitable for a woman is also
suitable for a man, but now sometimes used in wider contexts;
English proverb, late 17th century.

Knowledge

While knowledge is to be sought (The larger the shoreline of knowledge, the longer the shoreline of wonder, *and more simply* Knowledge is power), *we may be betrayed by over-confidence in our prowess:* A little knowledge is a dangerous thing.

The cobbler to his last and the gunner to his linstock.
the gunner's *linstock* was a long pole used to hold a match for firing a cannon, and the saying is a fanciful extension of **let the cobbler stick to his last** below; English proverb, mid 18th century.

Every picture tells a story.
advertisement for Doan's Backache Kidney Pills (early 1900s).

Fools ask questions that wise men cannot answer.
a foolish person may put a question to which there is no simple or easily given answer; English proverb, mid 17th century.

The good Christian should beware of mathematicians, and all those who make empty prophecies. The danger already exists that mathematicians have made a covenant with the Devil to darken the spirit and to confine man in the bonds of Hell.
mistranslation of St Augustine's *De Genesi ad Litteram*, 'Hence, a devout Christian must avoid astrologers and all impious soothsayers, especially when they tell the truth, for fear of leading his soul into error by consorting with demons and entangling himself with the bonds of such association' (the Latin word *mathematicus* means both 'mathematician' and 'astrologer').

I pointed out to you the stars and all you saw was the tip of my finger.
African proverb.

Knowledge and timber shouldn't be much used until they are seasoned.
American proverb, mid 19th century.

Knowledge is power.
English proverb, late 16th century, often with allusion to Francis Bacon *Meditationes Sacrae* (1597), 'Knowledge itself is power.'

The larger the shoreline of knowledge, the longer the shoreline of wonder.
North American proverb, mid 20th century.

Learning is a treasure that follows its owner everywhere.
reflecting on the advantage knowledge has over material possessions; Chinese proverb.

Learning is better than house and land.
reflecting on the difference between knowledge and material, and therefore ephemeral, possessions; English proverb, late 18th century.

Let the cobbler stick to his last.

people should concern themselves only with things they know something about (the cobbler's *last* is a shoemaker's model for shaping or repairing a shoe or boot); English proverb, mid 16th century; compare **The cobbler to his last and the gunner to his linstock** above.

A little knowledge is a dangerous thing.

English proverb, early 18th century; alteration of Alexander Pope *An Essay on Criticism* (1711), 'A little learning is a dangerous thing; Drink deep, or taste not the Pierian spring.'

One half of the world does not know how the other half lives.

often used to comment on a lack of communication between neighbouring groups; English proverb, early 17th century.

Out of the mouths of babes——.

young children may sometimes speak with disconcerting wisdom; English proverb, late 19th century, with allusion to the Bible (Psalms), 'Out of the mouth of very babes and sucklings hast thou ordained strength, because of thine enemies.'

The sea of learning has no end.

Chinese proverb.

Straws tell which way the wind blows.

English proverb, mid 17th century.

There will be trouble if the cobbler starts making pies.

a warning against stepping outside one's area of expertise; modern saying, said to be a Russian proverb.

The truth is out there.

catchphrase from *The X Files* (American television series, 1993–), created by Chris Carter (1957–), in which two special agents repeatedly investigate cases which appear to involve the paranormal, although final proof of extra-terrestrial activity is always lacking.

Walking ten thousand miles; reading ten thousand books.

theoretical knowledge and practical experience are of equal value; Chinese proverb, compare **Walking ten thousand miles is better than reading ten thousand books** at EXPERIENCE.

What's hit is history, what's missed is mystery.

on the importance of securing a dead specimen of a new species; late 19th century saying.

When a pine needle falls in the forest, the eagle sees it, the deer hears it, and the bear smells it.

modern saying, said to be of Native American origin.

When house and land are gone and spent, then learning is most excellent.

contrasting the value of learning with the ephemeral nature of material possessions; English proverb, mid 18th century.

The Law

See also CRIME AND PUNISHMENT, JUSTICE

The legal world is often seen as a perilous one (The more laws, the more thieves and bandits), *although not every saying goes as far as the Scottish proverb:* Home is home, as the Devil said when he found himself in the Court of Session.

The devil makes his Christmas pies of lawyers' tongues and clerks' fingers.

the lawyers' tongues and clerks' fingers stand for the words and actions of the legal profession as welcomed by the Devil; English proverb, late 16th century.

Gray's Inn for walks,
Lincoln's Inn for a wall,
The Inner Temple for a garden,
And the Middle Temple for a hall.

on the four Inns of Court; traditional rhyme, mid 17th century.

Hard cases make bad law.

difficult cases cause the clarity of the law to be obscured by exceptions and strained interpretations; the saying may now also be used to imply that a law framed in response to a particularly distressing case may not be well thought out or well based; English proverb, mid 19th century.

Home is home, as the Devil said when he found himself in the Court of Session.

the *Court of Session* is the supreme civil tribunal of Scotland, established in 1532; Scottish proverbial saying, mid 19th century.

Ignorance of the law is no excuse for breaking it.

English proverb, early 15th century.

A man who is his own lawyer has a fool for his client.

English proverb, early 19th century.

The more laws, the more thieves and bandits.

a rigid and over-detailed code of law is likely to foster rather than prevent lawbreaking; English proverb, late 16th century; the idea is found in the *Tao-te Ching* of Lao Tzu (*c.*604–531 BC), 'The more laws and orders are made prominent, The more thieves and bandits there will be.'

No one should be judge in his own cause.

it is impossible to be impartial where your own interest is involved; English proverb, mid 15th century.

Possession is nine points of the law.

although it does not reflect any specific legal ruling, in early use the satisfaction of ten (sometimes twelve) points was commonly asserted to attest to full entitlement or ownership; possession, represented by nine (or eleven) points is therefore the closest substitute for this; English proverb, early 17th century.

Rules are made to be broken.
English proverb, mid 20th century; the idea expressed by Christopher North in *Blackwood's Magazine* for May 1830, 'Laws were made to be broken.'

 # Leadership
See also MANAGEMENT

While the health of an organization can be judged by that of its leadership (The fish always stinks from the head downwards), there is also an awareness that a successful leader can also at need give loyalty and support to another: A good leader is also a good follower.

As one fern frond dies, another is born to take its place.
Maori proverb, applied particularly to chiefs.

Equality is difficult, but superiority is painful.
on the difficulties of leadership; African proverb.

The fish always stinks from the head downwards.
as the freshness of a dead fish can be judged from the condition of its head, any corruption in a country or organization will be manifested first in its leaders; English proverb, late 16th century.

A good leader is also a good follower.
American proverb, mid 20th century.

He that cannot obey cannot command.
the experience of being under orders teaches one how they
should be given; English proverb, late 15th century.

If the people will lead, then the leaders must follow.
modern saying.

If you are not the lead dog the view never changes.
Canadian saying.

One mountain cannot accommodate two tigers.
there cannot be two leaders; Chinese proverb.

Take me to your leader.
traditional catchphrase from science-fiction stories.

Leisure
See also IDLENESS, WORK

*Leisure is more than idleness in that it provides essential
refreshment:* All work and no play makes Jack a dull boy.

All work and no play makes Jack a dull boy.
warning against a lifestyle without any form of relaxation; English proverb, mid 17th century.

The busiest men have the most leisure.
someone who is habitually busy is likely to make best use of their
time; English proverb, late 19th century.

Have a break, have a Kit-Kat.
advertising slogan for Rowntree's Kit-Kat, from *c*.1955.

Take time to smell the roses.
it is important to spend some time in leisure; modern saying.

The gods do not subtract from a man's allotted span the time spent fishing.
modern saying, sometimes claimed to have originated in an Assyrian tablet.

 Letters

Letters can be a key form of human communication: A love letter sometimes costs more than a three-cent stamp.

Do not close a letter without reading it.
American proverb, mid 20th century.

A love letter sometimes costs more than a three-cent stamp.
American proverb, mid 20th century.

Someone, somewhere, wants a letter from you.
advertising slogan for the British Post Office, 1960s.

Lies

See also DECEPTION, HONESTY, TRUTH

Lies have their own power (A lie can go round the world and back again while the truth is lacing up its boots), *but in the end a falsehood will be exposed:* The liar's candle lasts till evening.

An abomination unto the Lord, but a very present help in time of trouble.

definition of a lie, an amalgamation of lines from the Bible (Proverbs 12:22, 'Lying lips are abomination to the Lord', and Psalms 46:1, 'God is our hope and strength: a very present help in trouble'), often attributed to the American politician Adlai Stevenson (1900–62).

Even a liar tells the truth sometimes.

modern saying.

Half the truth is often a whole lie.

something which is partially true can still convey a completely false impression; English proverb, mid 18th century.

A liar ought to have a good memory.

implying that one lie is likely to lead to the need for another; English proverb, mid 16th century, 1st century AD in Latin.

The liar's candle lasts till evening.
a lie will be exposed sooner or later; Turkish proverb.

A lie can go around the world and back again while the truth is lacing up its boots.
American proverb, late 19th century; a variant is recorded in the words of C. H. Spurgeon in *Gems from Spurgeon* (1859), 'It is well said in the old proverb, "a lie will go round the world while truth is pulling its boots on."'

One seldom meets a lonely lie.
implying that one is likely to lead to the need for another; American proverb, mid 20th century.

To tell a falsehood is like the cut of a sabre, for though the wound may heal the scar will remain.
Persian proverb.

 Life
See also LIFESTYLES

While not necessarily easy (Life isn't all beer and skittles), *the ultimate verdict is positive, if somewhat bleak:* A live dog is better than a dead lion.

Art is long and life is short.
originally from the Greek physician Hippocrates (c.460–357 BC), comparing the difficulties encountered in learning the art of

medicine or healing with the shortness of human life ('Art' is now commonly understood in the proverb in a less specific sense); often quoted in the Latin version *Ars longa, vita brevis* from the rendering by the Roman philosopher and poet Seneca; English proverb, late 14th century.

Be happy while y'er leevin,
For y'er a lang time deid.
Scottish motto for a house.

It's life, Jim, but not as we know it.
late 20th-century saying associated with the television series *Star Trek* (1966–); the precise saying does not occur in the series but is found in the 1987 song 'Star Trekkin'' sung by The Firm.

Life is a sexually transmitted disease.
graffito found on the London Underground.

Life is harder than crossing a field.
Russian proverb.

Life isn't all beer and skittles.
life is not unalloyed pleasure or relaxation; English proverb, mid 19th century.

Life is the best gift; the rest is extra.
African proverb (Swahili).

Life's a bitch, and then you die.
modern saying, late 20th century.

A live dog is better than a dead lion.

often used in the context of a lesser person taking the place of a greater one who has died; English proverb, late 14th century, from the Bible (Ecclesiastes 9:4), 'A living dog is better than a dead lion.'

Man cannot live by bread alone.

a person needs spiritual as well as physical sustenance; English proverb, late 19th century, after the Bible (Matthew 4:4), 'Man shall not live by bread alone, but by every word that proceedeth out of the mouth of God.'

Tout passe, tout casse, tout lasse.

French, meaning 'everything passes, everything perishes, everything palls'.

Lifestyles
See also LIFE

Common wisdom enshrines suggestions for essential principles by which to order our lives, from the simple Do as you would be done by, *to the Middle Eastern advice* If you have two coins, use one to buy bread, the other to buy hyacinths.

Do as you would be done by.

English proverb, late 16th century; in Charles Kingsley's *The Water Babies* (1863), Mrs *Doasyouwouldbedoneby* is the motherly and benevolent figure who is contrasted with her stern sister, Mrs *Bedonebyasyoudid*.

Do unto others as you would they should do unto you.
English proverb, early 10th century; from the Bible (Matthew),
'Therefore all things whatsoever ye would that men should do to
you, do ye even so to them: for this is the law and the prophets.'

Eat, drink and be merry, for tomorrow we die.
a conflation of two biblical sayings, Ecclesiastes 8:15, 'A man
hath no better thing under the sun, than to eat, and to drink, and
to be merry', and Isaiah 22:13, 'Let us eat and drink; for tomorrow we shall die'; English proverb, late 19th century.

**Fear less, hope more; Eat less, chew more; Whine less,
breathe more; Talk less, say more; Love more, and all
good things will be yours.**
Swedish saying.

**If you have two coins, use one to buy bread, the other
to buy hyacinths.**
both the mind and the body should be fed; Middle Eastern
proverb (sometimes roses or lilies are suggested instead).

Make love not war.
student slogan, 1960s.

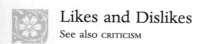

Likes and Dislikes

See also CRITICISM

From One man's meat is another man's poison *to* Tastes differ, *there is an acceptance that there is no consensus of personal preference.*

Every man to his taste.
often used to comment on someone else's choice; English proverb, late 16th century.

One man's meat is another man's poison.
pointing out that what may be necessary to one person is injurious to another; English proverb, late 16th century.

Tastes differ.
different people will like or approve of different things; English proverb, early 19th century.

There is no accounting for tastes.
often used in recognition of a difference in choice between two people; English proverb, late 18th century.

You can't please everyone.
English proverb, late 15th century.

You're going to like this ... not a lot. ... but you'll like it.
catchphrase used by Paul Daniels in his conjuring act, especially on television from 1981 onwards.

Love
See also MARRIAGE, RELATIONSHIPS

Love may be a powerful force (Love makes the world go round), *but it does not necessarily bring ease:* The course of true love never did run smooth.

Can you make me a cambric shirt,
Parsley, sage, rosemary, and thyme,
Without any seam or needlework?
And you shall be a true lover of mine.
traditional song.

The course of true love never did run smooth.
English proverb, late 16th century; originally from Shakespeare *A Midsummer Night's Dream* (1595–6).

It is best to be off with the old love before you are on with the new.
English proverb, early 19th century.

Jove but laughs at lovers' perjury.

English proverb, mid 16th century; from the Roman poet
Tibullus (*c.*50–19 BC) and ultimately from the Greek poet Hesiod
(*c.*700 BC).

Kissing goes by favour.

a kiss is often given as a reward for something done; English
proverb, early 17th century.

Love and a cough cannot be hid.

love can no more be concealed than a cough can be suppressed;
English proverb, early 14th century.

Love begets love.

English proverb, early 16th century.

Love is blind.

Cupid, the god of love, was traditionally portrayed as blind,
shooting his arrows at random, but the saying is generally used
to mean that a person is often unable to see faults in the one they
love; English proverb, late 14th century; compare **L'amour est
aveugle; l'amitié ferme les yeux** at RELATIONSHIPS.

Love laughs at locksmiths.

love is too strong a force to be denied by ordinary barriers;
English proverb, early 19th century, from the title of a play by
George Colman the Younger (1762–1836).

Love makes the world go round.
English proverb, mid 19th century, from a traditional
French song.

Love makes time pass, and time makes love pass.
French proverb.

Love will find a way.
love is a force which cannot be stemmed or denied; English
proverb, early 17th century.

One cannot love and be wise.
English proverb, early 16th century; the statement 'to love
and be wise is scarcely allowed to God' is found in Latin
in the writings of the 1st-century Roman writer
Publilius Syrus.

The quarrel of lovers is the renewal of love.
love can be renewed through reconciliation; English proverb,
early 16th century.

**There are as good fish in the sea as ever came out
of it.**
now often used as a consolation to rejected lovers in the form
'there are plenty more fish in the sea'; English proverb, late 16th
century.

**'Tis better to have loved and lost, than never to have
loved at all.**
English proverb, early 18th century.

When the furze is in bloom, my love's in tune.

with the implication that some furze can always be found in
bloom; English proverb, mid 18th century; compare **When the
gorse is out of bloom, kissing's out of fashion below**.

**When the gorse is out of bloom, kissing's out of
fashion.**

the idea behind the saying is that gorse is always in flower
somewhere (compare **When the furze is in bloom, my love's in
tune** above).

 Loyalty

Loyalty is a key virtue (It's an ill bird that fouls its own
nest) *that is best demonstrated over a long period:* Quickly
come, quickly go.

I'm backing Britain.

slogan coined by workers at the Colt factory, Surbiton, Surrey, in
1968, and subsequently used in a national campaign.

It's an ill bird that fouls its own nest.

a condemnation of a person who brings his own family, home,
or country into disrepute by his words; English proverb, mid
13th century.

Lousy but loyal.

London East End slogan at George V's Jubilee in 1935.

Love me little, love me long.
love of great intensity is unlikely to last; English proverb, early
16th century.

Quickly come, quickly go.
English proverb, late 16th century.

 ## Luck

See CHANCE AND LUCK

WHY KEEP A
DOG AND BARK
YOURSELF

Management

See also EMPLOYMENT, LEADERSHIP

One traditional saying can be seen as an endorsement of the principle of delegation: Why keep a dog and bark yourself?

A committee is a group of the unwilling, chosen from the unfit, to do the unnecessary.
20th-century saying.

The nail that sticks up is certain to be hammered down.
Japanese proverb.

We trained hard...but it seemed that every time we were beginning to form up into teams we would be reorganized. I was to learn later in life that we tend to meet any new situation by reorganizing; and a wonderful method it can be for creating the illusion of progress while producing confusion, inefficiency, and demoralization.
late 20th-century saying, frequently (and wrongly) attributed to the Roman satirist Petronius Arbiter (d. AD 65).

Why keep a dog and bark yourself?
often used to advise against carrying out work which can be done for you by somebody else; English proverb, late 16th century.

You cannot control the winds, but you can adjust the sails.
you may not be able to control matters, but you can respond deftly to them; modern saying.

You can only manage what you can measure.
modern saying.

Manners

See also BEHAVIOUR

While courtesy is seen as an obligation (Manners maketh man), *there is also a note of pragmatism:* There is nothing lost by civility.

Civility costs nothing.
one should behave with at least minimal courtesy; English proverb, early 18th century.

A civil question deserves a civil answer.
English proverb, mid 19th century.

Everyone speaks well of the bridge which carries him over.
someone is naturally well disposed towards a source of help, whether or not it has been beneficial to others; English proverb, late 17th century.

Manners maketh man.
motto of William of Wykeham (1324–1404), bishop of
Winchester and founder of Winchester College; English
proverb, mid 14th century.

Striking manners are bad manners.
American proverb, mid 20th century.

**The test of good manners is being able to put up
pleasantly with bad ones.**
American proverb, mid 20th century.

There is nothing lost by civility.
English proverb, late 19th century.

 Marriage
See also LOVE, MEN AND WOMEN, WEDDINGS

*Despite the assertion that Marriages are made in heaven,
much proverbial wisdom takes a sceptical view of the happiness
offered by the wedded state:* Needles and pins, needles and
pins, when a man marries his trouble begins.

**Better be an old man's darling than a young
man's slave.**
English proverb, mid 16th century.

A DEAF HUSBAND

AND A BLIND WIFE

ARE ALWAYS A

HAPPY COUPLE

Better one house spoiled than two.

said of two wicked or foolish people joined in marriage; English proverb, late 16th century.

Change the name and not the letter, change for the worse and not the better.

it is unlucky for a woman to marry a man whose surname begins with the same letter as her own; English proverb, mid 19th century.

A deaf husband and a blind wife are always a happy couple.

each will remain unaware of drawbacks in the other (the saying is sometimes reversed to a blind husband and a deaf wife); English proverb, late 16th century.

The grey mare is the better horse.

the wife rules, or is more competent than, the husband; English proverb, mid 16th century.

Marriage is a lottery.

referring either to one's choice of partner, or more generally to the element of chance involved in how a marriage will turn out; English proverb, mid 17th century.

Marriages are made in heaven.

often used ironically; English proverb, mid 16th century.

Marry in haste and repent at leisure.

the formula is also applied to rash steps taken in other circumstances; English proverb, mid 16th century; the idea is found in William Congreve's play *The Old Bachelor* (1693), 'Thus grief still treads upon the heels of pleasure: / Married in haste, we may repent at leisure.'

Needles and pins, needles and pins, when a man marries his trouble begins.

traditional saying (originally a nursery rhyme), perhaps reflecting on the pressures of domestic life; English proverb, mid 19th century.

Never marry for money, but marry where money is.

distinguishing between monetary gain as a primary object and a side benefit; English proverb, late 19th century.

There goes more to marriage than four bare legs in a bed.

physical compatibility is not enough for a successful marriage; English proverb, mid 16th century.

Wedlock is a padlock.

English proverb, late 17th century.

A widow is a rudderless boat.

Chinese proverb.

You do not marry the person you love, you love the person you marry.

Indian proverb.

A young man married is a young man marred.
often used as an argument against marrying too young; English
proverb, late 16th century.

Means
See WAYS AND MEANS

Medicine
See also SICKNESS

What drugs can do may be limited (The best doctors are
Dr Diet, Dr Quiet, and Dr Merryman), *and some remedies
may be in our own hands:* Laughter is the best medicine.

**The best doctors are Dr Diet, Dr Quiet, and
Dr Merryman.**
outline of an appropriate regime for someone who is ill; English
proverb, mid 16th century.

Dr Williams' pink pills for pale people.
patent medicine advertisement, from 1890 on.

Good medicine always has a bitter taste.
modern saying, sometimes claimed to be a Japanese proverb.

MEDICINE CAN
PROLONG LIFE,
BUT DEATH WILL
SEIZE THE DOCTOR
TOO

Keep taking the tablets.
supposedly traditional advice from a doctor, especially when little change in the patient's condition is envisaged.

Laughter is the best medicine.
late 20th-century saying; the idea is an ancient one, as in the Bible (Proverbs 17:22), 'A merry heart doeth good like medicine.'

Medicine can prolong life, but death will seize the doctor, too.
American proverb, mid 20th century.

Similia similibus curantur.
Latin, 'Like cures like,' motto of homeopathic medicine attributed to S. Hahnemann (1755–1843), although not found in this form in Hahnemann's writings.

 # Meeting and Parting
See also ABSENCE

While parting may be seen as a regrettable inevitability (The best of friends must part), *meeting is not necessarily welcome:* Talk of the Devil, and he is bound to appear.

The best of friends must part.
no friendship is so close that separation is impossible; English proverb, early 17th century.

Nice to see you—to see you, nice.
catchphrase used by Bruce Forsyth in 'The Generation Game' on
BBC Television, 1973 onwards.

Talk of the Devil, and he is bound to appear.
to speak of the Devil may be to invite his presence;
often abbreviated to 'Talk of the Devil', and used when a
person just spoken of is seen; English proverb, mid
17th century.

Men

See also MEN AND WOMEN

*Proverbial wisdom about men seems to be summed up in the
succinct,* Boys will be boys.

Boys will be boys.
English proverb, early 17th century, often used ironically.

I married my husband for life, not for lunch.
20th-century saying, origin unknown.

The way to a man's heart is through his stomach.
English proverb, early 19th century.

Men and Women

See also MARRIAGE, MEN, WOMEN

A loving partnership between men and women is seen as the natural pattern of life: Every Jack has his Jill.

Every Jack has his Jill.
all lovers have found a mate; English proverb, early 17th century.

A good Jack makes a good Jill.
used of the effect of a husband on his wife; English proverb, early 17th century.

A man is as old as he feels, and a woman as old as she looks.
both parts of the proverb are sometimes used on their own; English proverb, late 19th century.

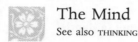

The Mind

See also THINKING

The mind is seen as essential to independent life: Whom the gods would destroy, they first make mad.

A mind enlightened is like heaven; a mind in darkness is hell.
Chinese proverb.

Mind has no sex.

modern saying, ultimately an alteration of the thought of Mary Wollstonecraft (1759–97) in her *A Vindication of the Rights of Women* (1792), 'To give a sex to mind was not very consistent with the principles of a man [Rousseau] who argued so warmly, and so well, for the immortality of the soul.'

A mind is a terrible thing to waste.

motto of the United Negro College Fund.

Our memory is always at fault, never our judgement.

American proverb, mid 20th century.

Whom the gods would destroy, they first make mad.

often used to comment on a foolish action seen as self-destructive in its effect; English proverb, early 17th century; the idea is found in the medieval period, in a scholiastic annotation to Sophocles's *Antigone*, 'Whenever God prepares evil for a man, He first damages his mind, with which he deliberates.'

Misfortunes

See also ADVERSITY, CHANCE AND LUCK

Misfortunes are inevitable (The bread never falls but on its buttered side), *but we should not allow ourselves to be overwhelmed by a sense of our own bad luck:* I cried because I had no shoes, until I met a man who had no feet.

Bad things come in threes.

the belief that an accident or misfortune is likely to be accompanied by two more is traditional, although in this form it is only recorded from the late 20th century.

The bread never falls but on its buttered side.

if something goes wrong, the outcome is likely to be as bad as possible; English proverb, mid 19th century.

Help you to salt, help you to sorrow.

in which salt is regarded as a sign of bad luck (especially if spilt at table); English proverb, mid 17th century.

I cried because I had no shoes, until I met a man who had no feet.

modern saying derived from a Persian original; compare the words of the Persian poet Sadi (c.1213–91) in *The Rose Garden*, 'I never complained at the vicissitudes of fortune ... excepting once, when my feet were bare, and I had not the means of procuring myself shoes. I entered the great mosque at Cufah with a heavy heart when I beheld a man who had no feet. I offered up praise and thanksgiving to God for his bounty, and bore with patience the want of shoes.'

If anything can go wrong, it will.

modern saying reflecting a supposed law of nature, said to have been coined as a maxim in 1949 by George Nichols, as the development of a remark made by a colleague, Captain E. Murphy; the rule is popularly known as 'Murphy's Law'.

It is no use crying over spilt milk.
it is pointless to repine when it is too late to prevent the
misfortune; English proverb, mid 17th century.

It never rains but it pours.
if one thing has gone wrong, worse will follow; English proverb,
early 18th century.

Misfortunes never come singly.
English proverb, early 14th century.

 Mistakes

*Not even the greatest expert can avoid making some mistakes:
we are warned that* Homer sometimes nods, *and* Even
monkeys sometimes fall off a tree.

Even monkeys sometimes fall off a tree.
even the most adept can be careless and make errors; Japanese
proverb.

**He is always right who suspects that he makes
mistakes.**
warning against overconfidence; Spanish proverb.

He who slaps his own face should not cry out.

there is no point in complaining about trouble caused by your own error; Arabic proverb.

Homer sometimes nods.

even the greatest expert may make a mistake (nods here means 'becomes drowsy', implying a momentary lack of attention); English proverb, late fourteenth century, ultimately with allusion to the Roman poet Horace (65–8 BC), 'I'm aggrieved when sometimes even excellent Homer nods.'

If you don't make mistakes you don't make anything.

English proverb, late 19th century; the idea is found in a speech made at the Mansion House in London by the American lawyer and diplomat Edward John Phelps (1822–1900) on 24 January 1889: 'The man who makes no mistakes does not usually make anything.'

A miss is as good as a mile.

if you miss the target, it hardly matters by how much; the syntax has been distorted by abridgement, and the original form was 'an inch in a miss is as good as an ell' (an *ell* being a former measure of length equal to about 1.1 metres); English proverb, early 17th century.

Shome mishtake, shurely?

catchphrase in *Private Eye* magazine, from the 1980s.

There's many a slip 'twixt cup and lip.
much can go wrong between the initiation of a process and its completion, often used as a warning; English proverb, mid 16th century.

To err is human (to forgive divine).
English proverb, late 16th century (in its given form, from Alexander Pope's *An Essay on Criticism* (1711), 'To err is human: to forgive, divine'; compare **To err is human but to really foul things up requires a computer** at COMPUTERS.

Wink at sma' fauts, ye hae great anes yoursel.
avoid criticizing the mistakes of others, as you yourself have great ones; Scottish proverb; the idea is found in the Bible (Matthew 7:3), 'Why beholdest thou the mote that is in thy brother's eye, but considerest not the beam that is in thine own eye?'

Moderation
See also EXCESS, GREED

Moderation is not only a sensible precaution against over-indulgence (Enough is as good as a feast), *it can be positively beneficial in making an effect: Less is more.*

Enough is as good as a feast.
used as a warning against overindulgence, or overdoing something; English proverb, late 14th century.

Enough is enough.

originally used as an expression of content or satisfaction, but now more usually employed as a reprimand, warning someone against persisting in an inappropriate or excessive course of action; English proverb, mid 16th century.

The half is better than the whole.

advising economy or restraint; English proverb, mid 16th century, from the Greek poet Hesiod (fl. *c*.700 BC) *Works and Days* 'the half is greater than the whole.'

Keep no more cats than will catch mice.

recommending efficiency and the ethic of steady work to justify one's place; English proverb, late 17th century.

Less is more.

something simple often has more effect; English proverb, mid 19th century.

Moderation in all things.

English proverb, mid 19th century, from the Greek poet Hesiod (fl. *c*.700 BC) *Works and Days* 'Observe due measure; moderation is best in all things'; compare **There is measure in all things** below.

There is measure in all things.

English proverb, late 14th century; compare **Moderation in all things** above.

Money

See also THRIFT, WEALTH

It is natural to want money (Get the money honestly if you can), *but its power is in the end limited:* Money can't buy happiness.

Bad money drives out good.

money of lower intrinsic value tends to circulate more freely than money of higher intrinsic and equal nominal value, though what is recognized as money of higher value being hoarded; English proverb, early 20th century; known as 'Gresham's law' from Thomas Gresham (d. 1579), English financier and founder of the Royal Exchange.

The best things in life are free.

English proverb, early 20th century, originally from the title of a song (1927) by Buddy De Sylva and Lew Brown.

Cash is king.

modern saying, summarizing the position in a recession.

Get the money honestly if you can.

American proverb, early 19th century; the idea is found in the classical world, in the poetry of Horace (65–8 BC), 'If possible honestly, if not, somehow, make money.'

He that cannot pay, let him pray.

if you have no material resources, prayer is your only resort;
English proverb, early 17th century.

Money can't buy happiness.

English proverb, mid 19th century.

Money has no smell.

English proverb, early 20th century in this form, but originally
deriving from a comment made by the Roman Emperor
Vespasian (AD 9–79), in response to an objection to a tax on
public lavatories; compare **Where there's muck there's
brass** below.

**Money is like sea water. The more you drink, the
thirstier you become.**

possession of wealth creates an addiction to money; modern
saying.

Money isn't everything.

often said in consolation or resignation; English proverb, early
20th century.

Money is power.

English proverb, mid 18th century.

Money is the root of all evil.

English proverb, mid 15th century, deriving from the Bible
(I Timothy 6:10), 'The love of money is the root of all evil';
compare **Idleness is the root of all evil** at IDLENESS.

Money, like manure, does no good till it is spread.

English proverb, early 19th century; the idea is found earlier in the *Essays* of Francis Bacon (1561–1626), 'Money is like muck, not good except it be spread.'

Money makes the mare to go.

referring to money as a source of power; English proverb, late 15th century.

Money talks.

money has influence; English proverb, mid 17th century.

A penny for the guy.

traditional saying, used by children displaying a guy to ask for money towards celebrating Bonfire Night; a *guy* is an effigy representing Guy Fawkes, a leading conspirator in the Gunpowder Plot to blow up James I and his Parliament in 1605, which is traditionally burned on 5 November, the anniversary of the discovery of the plot.

Shrouds have no pockets.

worldly wealth cannot be kept and used after death; English proverb, mid 19th century.

Time is money.

often used to mean that time spent fruitlessly on something represents a real loss of money which could have been earned in that time; English proverb, late 16th century.

Where there's muck there's brass.

dirty or unpleasant activities are also lucrative (brass here means 'money'); English proverb, late 17th century; compare **Money has no smell** above.

You cannot serve God and Mammon.

now generally used of wealth regarded as an evil influence; English proverb, mid 16th century, ultimately from the Bible (Matthew 6:24), 'No man can serve two masters ... Ye cannot serve God and mammon.'

Mourning
See also DEATH, SORROW

Mourning is inevitable and natural (Grief is the price we pay for love), *but overindulgence in it is not a sign of sincere feeling:* A bellowing cow soon forgets her calf.

A bellowing cow soon forgets her calf.

the person who laments most loudly is the one who is soonest comforted; English proverb, late 19th century.

Grief is the price we pay for love.

late 20th-century saying.

Let the dead bury the dead.
often used to mean that the past should be left undisturbed;
English proverb, early 19th century (see Matt. 8:22).

No flowers by request.
an intimation that no flowers are desired at a funeral.

**You can shed tears that she is gone or you can smile
because she has lived.**
preface to the Order of Service at the funeral of Queen Elizabeth
the Queen Mother, 2002.

 Murder

*Traditional sayings emphasize not only that murder cannot be
concealed* (Murder will out), *but also that it is likely to breed
further killing:* Blood will have blood.

Blood will have blood.
killing will provoke further killing; English proverb, mid 15th
century; in this form from Shakespeare *Macbeth* (1606), 'It will
have blood, they say blood will have blood.'

Guns don't kill people; people kill people.
National Rifle Association slogan.

Killing no murder.
English proverb, mid 17th century, originally from the title of a pamphlet by Edward Sexby (d. 1658), 'Killing no murder briefly discourst in three questions', an apology for tyrannicide.

Lizzie Borden took an axe
And gave her mother forty whacks;
When she saw what she had done
She gave her father forty-one!
popular rhyme in circulation after the acquittal of Lizzie Borden, in June 1893, from the charge of murdering her father and step-mother at Fall River, Massachusetts on 4 August 1892.

Murder will out.
the crime of murder can never be successfully concealed; English proverb, early 14th century.

 Music

The world of music may offer great enjoyment, but it is not a shield from reality: we are told from the 17th century that Music helps not the toothache.

Every good boy deserves favour.
traditional mnemonic for the notes (E, G, B, D, F) on the lines of the treble clef stave.

It takes seven years to make a piper.
Scottish proverb.

Music helps not the toothache.
English proverb, mid 17th century.

Play it again, Sam.
popular misquotation of Humphrey Bogart in *Casablanca* (1942),
subsequently used as the title of a play (1969) and film (1972) by
Woody Allen.

Why should the devil have all the best tunes?.
commonly attributed to the English evangelist Rowland Hill
(1744–1833); many hymns are sung to popular secular melodies,
and this practice was especially favoured by the Methodists.

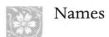

Names

Names enshrine the essence of individual identity: If the cap
fits, wear it.

**The beginning of wisdom is to call things by their
right names.**
modern saying claimed to be a Chinese proverb.

By Tre, Pol, and Pen, you shall know the Cornish men.
traditional saying, referring to the frequency of these elements in
Cornish names; English proverb, mid 16th century.

If the cap fits, wear it.
used with reference to the assumed suitability of a name or
description to a person's behaviour; English proverb, mid 18th
century.

If the shoe fits, wear it.
one has to accept it when a particular comment is shown to
apply to oneself; found mainly in the US; English proverb, late
18th century.

It is not what you call me. It is what I answer to.
African proverb.

Only the camel knows the hundredth name of God.
saying from Arab folklore; in Islam there are ninety-nine names for Allah (referred to as the 'ninety-nine names of God'), in the main taken or derived from the Koran.

Nature
See also THE ENVIRONMENT

Nature is seen as a powerful force beyond our control: You can drive out nature with a pitchfork, but she keeps on coming back.

Nature abhors a vacuum.
English proverb, mid 16th century.

One for the mouse, one for the crow, one to rot, one to grow.
traditionally used when sowing seed, and enumerating the ways in which some of the crop will be lost, leaving the residue to germinate; English proverb, mid 19th century.

You can drive out nature with a pitchfork but she keeps on coming back.
English proverb, mid 16th century, from the Roman poet Horace (65–8 BC) *Epistles*, 'You may drive out nature with a pitchfork, but she will always return.'

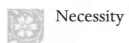

Necessity

Necessity may accustom us to difficult choices (Desperate diseases must have desperate remedies), *but it may also have possible benefits:* Necessity sharpens industry.

Any port in a storm.
when one is in trouble or difficulty, support or shelter from any source is welcome; English proverb, mid 18th century.

Beggars can't be choosers.
someone who is destitute is in no position to criticize what may be offered; English proverb, mid 16th century.

Desperate diseases must have desperate remedies.
in a difficult or dangerous situation it may be necessary to take extreme or risky measures; English proverb, mid 16th century; compare **Exceptional times require exceptional measures** below.

Even a worm will turn.
even a meek person will resist or retaliate if pushed too far; English proverb, mid 16th century.

Exceptional times require exceptional measures.
modern saying; compare **Desperate diseases must have desperate remedies** above.

Hunger drives the wolf out of the wood.
even the fiercest animal will be driven from shelter by acute need; English proverb, late 15th century.

If the mountain will not come to Mahomet, Mahomet must go to the mountain.
used in the context of an apparently insoluble situation. The saying refers to a story of Muhammad recounted by Francis Bacon in his *Essays*, in which the Prophet called a hill to him, and when it did not move, made this remark; English proverb, early 17th century.

Make a virtue of necessity.
one should do with a good grace what is unavoidable; English proverb, late 14th century.

Necessity is the mother of invention.
need is often a spur to the creative process; English proverb, mid 16th century.

Necessity knows no law.
someone in extreme need will disregard rules or prohibitions; English proverb, late 14th century.

Necessity sharpens industry.
American proverb, mid 20th century.

Needs must when the devil drives.

used in recognition of overwhelming force of circumstance;
English proverb, mid 15th century.

When all fruit fails, welcome haws.

often used of someone taking of necessity an older or otherwise
unsuitable lover (*haws*, the red fruit of the hawthorn, are contrasted with fruits generally eaten as food); English proverb, early
18th century.

Who says A must say B.

only recorded in English from North American sources, and
meaning that if a first step is taken; the second will inevitably
follow; English proverb, mid 19th century.

Neighbours

See also FAMILIARITY, FRIENDSHIP

*Common wisdom advises care in not overstepping limits with
one's neighbours, both in terms of territory* (Good fences
make good neighbours) *and personal intimacy* (You should
know a man seven years before you stir his fire).

Good fences make good neighbours.

this reduces the possibility of disputes over adjoining land;
English proverb, mid 17th century.

A hedge between keeps friendship green.

it is wise to have a clear boundary between neighbours; English
proverb.

Love your neighbour, but don't pull down your hedge.
do not let feelings of friendship lead you to act unwisely; English proverb.

A wall between both best preserves friendship.
it is wise to have a clear boundary between neighbours; Spanish proverb.

What a neighbour gets is not lost.
one is likely to benefit from the gain of a neighbour or friend; English proverb, mid 16th century.

You should know a man seven years before you stir his fire.
used as a caution against over-familiarity on slight acquaintance; English proverb, early 19th century.

 # News and Journalism

The traditional view that Bad news travels fast *is countered by an African saying:* One who sees something good must tell of it.

All the news that's fit to print.
motto of the *New York Times*, from 1896; coined by Adolph S. Ochs (1858–1935).

Bad news travels fast.

bad news is more likely to be talked about; English proverb, late 16th century.

Light for all.

slogan of the *Baltimore Sun*.

No news is good news.

often used in consolation or resignation; English proverb, early 17th century.

One who sees something good must tell of it.

African proverb.

Top people take *The Times*.

advertising slogan for the *Times* newspaper, from January 1959.

Watch this space!

further developments are expected and more information will be given later; *space* = an area of a newspaper for a specific purpose, especially for advertising.

Opinion

See also ARGUMENT, THINKING

Independent ideas may be approved (Thought is free), *but too great an affection for one's own views can degenerate into obstinacy:* Those who never retract their opinions, love themselves more than they love truth.

He that complies against his will is of his own opinion still.

English proverb, late 17th century, from Samuel Butler *Hudibras* pt 3 (1680), 'He that complies against his will, Is of his own opinion still.'

So many men, so many opinions.

the greater the number of people involved, the greater the number of different opinions there will be; English proverb, late 14th century, from Terence (*c*.190–159 BC) *Phormio*, 'There are as many opinions as there are people: each has his own correct way.'

Those who never retract their opinions, love themselves more than they love truth.

American proverb, mid 20th century.

Thought is free.

while speech and action can be limited, one's powers of imagination and speculation cannot be regulated; English proverb, late 14th century.

The wish is father to the thought.

one's opinions are influenced by one's wishes; English proverb, late 16th century, from Shakespeare *2 Henry IV* (1597), 'Thy wish was father, Harry, to that thought.'

 # Opportunity

While we may have many opportunities (The world is one's oyster), *we are warned that an opportunity missed will not come again:* He that will not when he may, when he will he shall have nay.

All is fish that comes to the net.

everything can be used to advantage; English proverb, early 16th century.

All is grist that comes to the mill.

all experience or knowledge is useful (*grist* is corn that is ground to make flour); English proverb, mid 17th century.

A bleating sheep loses a bite.

opportunities may be lost through idle chatter; English proverb, late 16th century.

Every crisis provides an opportunity.

often used as encouragement in facing difficult circumstances; modern saying.

Every dog has his day.

everyone, however insignificant, has a moment of strength and power; English proverb, mid 16th century.

IT'S NOT WHAT YOU KNOW, IT'S WHO YOU KNOW

He that will not when he may, when he will he shall have nay.

if an opportunity is not taken when offered, it may well not occur again; English proverb, late 10th century.

If the camel once gets his nose in the tent, his body will soon follow.

an apparently insignificant opening is likely to lead to more serious developments; Arabic proverb.

It is good fishing in troubled waters.

a difficult situation offers opportunities to those prepared to exploit it; English proverb, late 16th century.

It's not what you know, but whom you know.

American proverb, mid 20th century.

Make hay while the sun shines.

one should take advantage of favourable circumstances which may not last; English proverb, mid 16th century.

The mill cannot grind with the water that is past.

an opportunity that has been missed cannot then be used; English proverb, early 17th century.

No time like the present.

often used to urge swift and immediate action; English proverb, mid 16th century.

Opportunities look for you when you are worth finding.

North American proverb, mid 20th century; compare **Opportunity never knocks for persons not worth a rap** below.

Opportunity never knocks for persons not worth a rap.

American proverb, mid 20th century.

Opportunity never knocks twice at any man's door.

a chance once missed will not occur again; English proverb, mid 16th century.

A person who misses his chance, and the monkey who misses his branch, can't be saved.

Indian proverb.

A postern door makes a thief.

referring to the opportunity offered by a back or side entrance; English proverb, mid 15th century.

Strike while the iron is hot.

one should take advantage of opportunity; the allusion was originally to the work of a blacksmith; English proverb, late 14th century.

Take the goods the gods provide.

one should accept and be grateful for unearned benefits; English proverb, late 17th century.

Time and tide wait for no man.

often used as an exhortation to act, in the knowledge that a favourable moment will not last for ever; English proverb, late 14th century.

When one door shuts, another opens.

as one possible course of action is closed off, another opportunity offers; English proverb, late 16th century.

When the cat's away, the mice will play.

many will take advantage of a situation in which rules are not enforced or authority is lacking; English proverb, early 17th century.

The world is one's oyster.

opportunities are unlimited; an *oyster* is seen as both a delicacy and a source of pearls. Perhaps originally with allusion to Shakespeare's *The Merry Wives of Windsor* (1597), 'The world's mine oyster, which I, with sword will open'; English proverb, early 17th century.

Optimism and Pessimism
See also HOPE

Adopting a positive attitude may be recommended (Turn your face to the sun, and the shadows fall behind you), *but we should beware of overconfidence:* Don't halloo till you are out of the wood.

All's for the best in the best of all possible worlds.

English proverb, early 20th century, from Voltaire *Candide* (1759), 'In this best of possible worlds ... all is for the best.'

Another day, another dollar.

a world-weary comment on routine toil to earn a living, originally referring to the custom of paying sailors by the day, so that the longer the voyage, the greater the financial reward; American proverb, mid 20th century.

The darkest hour is just before dawn.

suggesting that the experience of complete despair may mean that matters have reached the lowest point and may shortly improve; English proverb, mid 17th century.

Don't bargain for fish that are still in the water.

Indian proverb; compare **Don't sell the skin till you have caught the bear** below.

Don't count your chickens before they are hatched.

one should not make, or act upon, an assumption (usually favourable) which may turn out to be ill-founded; English proverb, late 16th century; compare **Chickens are counted in the autumn** at AUTUMN.

Don't halloo till you are out of the wood.

you should not exult until danger and difficulty are past (halloo means 'shout in order to attract attention'; English proverb, late 18th century.

Don't sell the skin till you have caught the bear.

do not act upon an assumption of success which may turn out to be ill-founded; English proverb, late 16th century (early versions have *lion* or *beast* in place of *bear*); compare **Don't bargain for fish that are still in the water** above.

Every cloud has a silver lining.
even the gloomiest circumstance has some hopeful element in it;
English proverb, mid 19th century.

God's in his heaven; all's right with the world.
English proverb, from early 16th century in the form 'God is
where he was'; now largely replaced by this poem from Robert
Browning *Pippa Passes* (1841), 'God's in his heaven— All's right
with the world!'

**If ifs and ands were pots and pans, there'd be no work
for tinkers' hands.**
traditional response to an over-optimistic conditional expression,
in which *ands* is the plural form of *and* = 'if'; English proverb,
mid 19th century.

If wishes were horses, beggars would ride.
what one wishes for is often far from reality; English proverb,
early 17th century.

It's an ill wind that blows nobody any good.
good luck may arise from the source of another's misfortune;
English proverb, early 17th century.

The sharper the storm, the sooner it's over.
the more intense something is, the shorter time it is likely to last;
English proverb, late 19th century.

Turn your face to the sun, and the shadows fall behind you.

recommending a positive attitude; modern saying, said to derive from a Maori proverb.

When the axe came into the forest, the trees said 'The handle is one of us!'

relying for safety on a supposed link with a potential aggressor may offer a false hope; Russian proverb.

When things are at their worst they begin to mend.

when a bad situation has reached its worst possible point, the next change must reflect at least a small improvement; English proverb, mid 18th century.

Parents

See also CHILDREN, THE FAMILY

Pride and affection in one's child (Praise the child, and you make love to the mother) *may be associated with ambitions for the child's worldly success:* Parents want their children to become dragons.

A father is a banker provided by nature.
French proverb.

He who takes the child by the hand takes the mother by the heart.
Danish proverb.

It is a wise child that knows its own father.
a child's legal paternity might not reflect an actual blood link;
English proverb, late 16th century.

A mother understands what a child does not say.
Jewish proverb.

My son is my son till he gets him a wife, but my daughter's my daughter all the days of her life.
while a man who establishes his own family relegates former blood ties to second place, a woman's filial role is not affected by her marriage; English proverb, late 17th century.

Parents want their children to become dragons.
parents want their children to be successful; Chinese
proverb.

Praise the child, and you make love to the mother.
English proverb, early 19th century.

**To understand your parents' love, you must raise
children yourself.**
Chinese proverb.

When drinking water, remember the source.
advocating filial piety; Chinese proverb.

Parting
See MEETING AND PARTING

The Past
See also THE FUTURE, HISTORY, THE PRESENT

The past may represent something that cannot now be changed
(The past at least is secure), *or which still has the power to
affect the future:* The past is always ahead of us.

Nostalgia isn't what it used to be.
graffito; taken as the title of a book by Simone Signoret, 1978.

Old sins cast long shadows.
current usage is likely to refer to the wrong done by one
generation affecting its descendants; English proverb, early 20th
century.

**The past always looks better than it was; it's only
pleasant because it isn't here.**
American proverb, late 19th century.

The past at least is secure.
American proverb, early 19th century.

The past is always ahead of us.
the past is a reminder of what has been and what may be; Maori
proverb.

Things past cannot be recalled.
what has already happened cannot be changed; English proverb,
late 15th century.

What's done cannot be undone.
English proverb, mid 15th century.

**You have drunk from wells you did not dig, and been
warmed by fires you did not build.**
the present generation depends on those who have gone before;
modern saying, said to be of Native American origin.

Patience

See also DETERMINATION, HASTE AND DELAY

Not only is patience recommended as in itself the right way to behave (Bear and forbear), it promises ultimate satisfaction: If you sit by the river long enough, you will see the body of your enemy float by.

All commend patience, but none can endure to suffer.
American proverb, mid 20th century.

All things come to those who wait.
often used as an adjuration to patience; English proverb, early 16th century.

Bear and forbear.
recommending patience and tolerance; English proverb, late 16th century.

Don't put the cart before the horse.
don't reverse the proper order of things; English proverb, early 16th century.

First things first.
English proverb, late 19th century.

Hurry no man's cattle.

sometimes used as an injunction to be patient with someone; English proverb, early 19th century.

If you sit by the river long enough, you will see the body of your enemy float by.

advocating patience in the face of wrongs; modern saying, said to derive from a Japanese proverb.

I sit on the shore, and wait for the wind.

what is expected will arrive sooner or later; Russian proverb.

It is a long lane that has no turning.

commonly used as an assertion that an unfavourable situation will eventually change for the better; English proverb, mid 19th century.

The longest way home is the shortest way home.

not trying to take a short cut is often the most effective way; English proverb, mid 17th century.

The man who removes a mountain begins by carrying away small stones.

a major enterprise begins with small but essential tasks; modern saying, claimed to be a Chinese proverb.

Nothing should be done in haste but gripping a flea.

used as a warning against rash action; English proverb, mid 17th century.

One step at a time.

recommending cautious progression along a desired route; English proverb, mid 19th century.

Patience is a virtue.

often used as an exhortation; English proverb, late 14th century.

Rome was not built in a day.

used to warn against trying to achieve too much at once; English proverb, mid 16th century.

Slow but sure.

sure here means 'sure-footed, deliberate'; English proverb, late 17th century.

Softly, softly, catchee monkey.

advocating caution or guile as the best way to achieve an end; English proverb, early 20th century.

There is luck in leisure.

it is often advisable to wait before acting; English proverb, mid 19th century.

Time brings roses.

patience is likely to be rewarded; German proverb.

A watched pot never boils.

to pay too close an attention to the development of a desired event appears to inhibit the result; English proverb, mid 19th century.

We must learn to walk before we can run.

a solid foundation is necessary for faster progress; English proverb, mid 14th century.

What can't be cured must be endured.

there is no point in complaining about what is unavoidable; English proverb, late 16th century.

Where water flows, a channel is formed.

success will come when conditions are right; Chinese proverb.

With time and patience the mulberry leaf becomes satin.

allowing time for a process to complete itself will be rewarded (silkworms feed chiefly on mulberry leaves); English proverb, late 17th century.

 Peace

See also WARFARE

Peace may be desirable, but is perhaps only fully appreciated in contrast to strife: After a storm comes a calm.

After a storm comes a calm.

often used with the implication that a calm situation is only achieved after stress and turmoil; English proverb, late 14th century.

Ban the bomb.
US anti-nuclear slogan, 1953 onwards, adopted by the Campaign
for Nuclear Disarmament.

Nothing can bring you peace but yourself.
American proverb, mid 19th century.

**Peace is the dream of the wise; war is the history
of man.**
saying, recorded from the 19th century.

Pessimism
See OPTIMISM AND PESSIMISM

Politics
See also GOVERNMENT

*Sayings about politics can bring together a wide range of views,
perhaps exemplified in the words,* Politics makes strange
bedfellows.

**Are you now or have you ever been a member of the
Communist Party?**
formal question put to those appearing before the Committee on
UnAmerican Activities during the McCarthy campaign of 1950–4
against alleged Communists in the US government and other
institutions; the allusive form *are you now or have you ever been?*
derives from this.

As Maine goes, so goes the nation.
American political saying relating to presidential elections, *c.*1840.

Democracy is better than tyranny.
an imperfect system is better than a bad one; American proverb.

I am a Marxist—of the Groucho tendency.
slogan found at Nanterre in Paris, 1968.

In politics a man must learn to rise above principle.
American proverb, mid 20th century.

I spy strangers!
the conventional formula demanding the exclusion from the House of Commons of non-members to whose presence attention is thus drawn.

It'll play in Peoria.
catchphrase of the Nixon administration (early 1970s) meaning 'it will be acceptable to middle America', but originating in a standard music hall joke of the 1930s.

Labour isn't working.
on a poster showing a long queue outside an unemployment office; British Conservative Party slogan, 1978.

Lean liberty is better than fat slavery.
asserting that freedom matters more than any material comfort;
English proverb, early 17th century.

Liberté! Égalité! Fraternité!
French, 'Freedom! Equality! Brotherhood!', motto of the French
Revolution, 1789, but of earlier origin.

Meet the challenge—make the change.
Labour Party slogan, 1989.

Mummy, what's that man for?
remark by a small child to its mother; commonly cited as
originally said of a later 19th/early 20th-century politician; the
earliest known instance is a cartoon in *Punch* in 1906 where
it is applied to a man carrying a bag of golf clubs.

Not to be a republican at twenty is proof of
want of heart; to be one at thirty is proof of want
of head.
often used in the form 'Not to be a socialist . . .'; saying attributed
to Georges Clemenceau (1841–1929) and to François Guizot
(1787–1874).

The passion for freedom never dies.
saying, claimed to be a Greek proverb.

The personal is political.
1970s feminist slogan, coined by Carol Hanisch.

A politician is an animal who can sit on a fence and yet keep both ears to the ground.
American saying, mid 20th century.

Politics makes strange bedfellows.
political alliances in a common cause may bring together those of widely differing views; English proverb, mid 19th century.

Power to the people.
slogan of the Black Panther movement, from c.1968 onwards.

A straw vote only shows which way the hot air blows.
American proverb, early 20th century.

Three acres and a cow.
regarded as the requirement for self-sufficiency; late 19th-century political slogan.

The voice of the people is the voice of God.
English version of the Latin *vox populi, vox dei*; English proverb, early 15th century; the Latin form is found in the writings of the English scholar and theologian Alcuin (c.735–804), 'And those people should not be listened to who keep saying the voice of the

people is the voice of God, since the riotousness of the crowd is always very close to madness.'

Vote early and vote often.
American election slogan, already current when quoted by William Porcher Miles in the House of Representatives, 31 March 1858.

Who goes home?
formal question asked by the doorkeeper when the House of Commons adjourns.

 # Possessions

There is considerable emphasis on the idea of ensuring that you keep what you have (What you have, hold), *even if you do not immediately feel that it has a purpose:*
Keep a thing seven years and you'll always find a use for it.

Finders keepers (losers weepers).
English proverb, early 19th century.

Findings keepings.
English proverb, mid 19th century.

If you have nothing, you have nothing to lose.

modern saying, claimed to be an Arabic proverb.

Keep a thing seven years and you'll always find a use for it.

recommending caution and thrift; English proverb, early 17th century.

Light come, light go.

something gained without effort can be lost without much regret; English proverb, late 14th century.

What you have, hold.

with reference to an uncompromising position based on a refusal to make any concession; English proverb, mid 15th century.

What you spend, you have.

the only real possessions one has are those of which one can dispose; English proverb, early 14th century.

You cannot lose what you never had.

used in consolation or resignation; English proverb, late 16th century.

Poverty

See also MONEY, WEALTH

Poverty can be destructive, both in sapping independence
(Empty sacks will never stand upright) *and destroying*
relationships: When poverty comes in at the door, love
flies out of the window.

Both poverty and prosperity come from spending
money—prosperity from spending it wisely.
American proverb, mid 20th century.

Empty sacks will never stand upright.
those in an extremity of need cannot survive; English proverb,
mid 17th century.

Make poverty history.
slogan of a campaign launched in 2005 by a coalition of charities
and other groups to pressure governments to take action to
reduce poverty.

A moneyless man goes fast through the market.
someone without resources is unable to pause to buy anything
(or, in a modern variant, rushes to wherever what they lack may
be found); English proverb, early 18th century.

Poverty comes from God, but not dirt.
American proverb, mid 20th century.

Poverty is a blessing hated by all men.
poverty may shield you from worldly temptations, but it is
unpleasant to experience; Italian proverb.

Poverty is no disgrace, but it's a great inconvenience.
English proverb, late 16th century.

Poverty is not a crime.
English proverb, late 16th century.

**When poverty comes in at the door, love flies out of
the window.**
the strains of living in poverty often destroy a loving relationship;
English proverb, mid 17th century.

 Power

The exercise of power may make someone predatory (Big fish
eat little fish), *but we should remember that even an apparently weak person can be effective:* A mouse may help a lion.

All power to the Soviets.
slogan of workers in Petrograd, 1917.

Better be the head of a dog than the tail of a lion.
it is preferable to be at the head of a small organization than in a
lowly position in a large one; English proverb, late 16th century.

THEY THAT

DANCE MUST

PAY THE

FIDDLER

Big fish eat little fish.

the rich and powerful are likely to prey on those who are less strong, often used with the implication that each predator is in turn victim to a stronger one; English proverb, early 13th century.

He who pays the piper calls the tune.

the person financially responsible for something can control what is done; English proverb, late 19th century.

Kings have long arms.

a king's power reaches a long way; English proverb, mid 16th century.

Might is right.

English proverb, early 14th century.

A mouse may help a lion.

alluding to Aesop's fable of the lion and the rat, in which a rat saved a lion which had been trapped in a net by gnawing through the cords which bound it; English proverb, mid 16th century.

Power corrupts.

English proverb, late 19th century.

Power is like an egg; if you hold it too tightly, it breaks, and if you hold it too loosely, it drops and breaks.

power should be exercised with proper attention, but without repression; African proverb.

Set a beggar on horseback, and he'll ride to the Devil.
a person unused to power will make unwise use of it; English
proverb, late 16th century.

They that dance must pay the fiddler.
you must be prepared to make recompense for the provision of
an essential service; English proverb, mid 17th century.

We have ways of making you talk.
supposedly the characteristic threat of an inquisitor in a 1930s
film, but not traced in this form; 'We have ways of making men
talk' occurs in *Lives of a Bengal Lancer* (1935).

When elephants fight, it is the grass that gets hurt.
the weak are likely to suffer as a result of the conflicts of the
strong and powerful; African proverb (Swahili).

Practicality
See also CIRCUMSTANCE AND SITUATION

*We should be ready to accept the limitations imposed by
circumstances:* Cut your coat according to your cloth.

Cut your coat according to your cloth.
actions taken should suit one's circumstances or resources;
English proverb, mid 16th century.

He who wants a rose must respect the thorn.
someone wanting a desirable object needs to be aware of the dangers it brings with it; Persian proverb; compare **No rose without a thorn** at CIRCUMSTANCE AND SITUATION and **Do not grieve that rose trees have thorns, rather rejoice that thorny bushes bear roses** at SATISFACTION.

Put your trust in God, and keep your powder dry.
often attributed to Oliver Cromwell (1599–1658); English proverb, mid 19th century; compare **Trust in Allah, but tie up your camel** at CAUTION.

You cannot make an omelette without breaking eggs.
often used in the context of a regrettable political necessity which is said to be justified because it will benefit the majority; English proverb, mid 19th century.

 Praise and Flattery

Praise that is well based is worth having (Praise from Sir Hubert is praise indeed)*, but flattery is worthless:* Flattery, like perfume, should be smelled, not swallowed.

Flattery is soft soap, and soft soap is ninety per cent lye.
distinguishing between soundly based compliment and insincere congratulation (*lye* is a strongly alkaline solution, especially of potassium hydroxide, used for washing or cleansing); American proverb, mid 19th century.

Flattery, like perfume, should be smelled, not swallowed.

American proverb, mid 19th century.

Give credit where credit is due.

English proverb, late 18th century.

Imitation is the sincerest form of flattery.

English proverb, early 19th century, from Charles Caleb Colton *Lacon* (1820).

Praise from Sir Hubert is praise indeed.

popular saying, a misquotation of a line from Thomas Morton *A Cure for the Headache* (1797), 'Approbation from Sir Hubert Stanley is praise indeed.'

 # Prejudice and Tolerance

While we should accept the views of others (Live and let live), *real prejudice is both unwelcome and difficult to eradicate:* No tree takes so deep a root as prejudice.

Judge not, that ye be not judged.

used as a warning against overhasty criticism of someone; English proverb, late 15th century, from the Bible (Matthew 7:1).

Live and let live.
often used in the context of coexistence between deeply divided groups; English proverb, early 17th century.

No tree takes so deep a root as prejudice.
emphasizing how difficult it is to eradicate prejudice; American proverb, mid 20th century.

There's none so blind as those who will not see.
used in reference to someone who is unwilling to recognize unwelcome facts; English proverb, mid 16th century.

There's none so deaf as those who will not hear.
used to refer to someone who chooses not to listen to unwelcome information; English proverb, mid 16th century.

 # Preparation and Readiness

Forethought is endorsed (The early bird catches the worm), *but we should not expend too much attention on circumstances that have not yet arisen:* Don't cross the bridge till you come to it.

Be prepared.
motto of the Scout and Guide organizations, deriving from the initials of Robert Baden-Powell (1857–1941), the founder.

HAVE AN
UMBRELLA READY
BEFORE IT RAINS

Dig the well before you are thirsty.

make necessary preparations before you are in need; Japanese proverb.

Don't cross the bridge till you come to it.

warning that you should not concern yourself with possible difficulties unless and until they arise; English proverb, mid 19th century.

Don't throw away the old bucket, until you know whether the new one holds water.

do not get rid of a useful resource until you are sure that its replacement functions properly; Swedish proverb.

The early bird catches the worm.

someone who is energetic and efficient is most likely to be successful; English proverb, mid 17th century; compare **It's the second mouse that gets the cheese** below.

The early man never borrows from the late man.

someone who has made their preparations has no need to turn to someone less efficient; English proverb, mid 17th century.

Forewarned is forearmed.

if one has been warned in advance about a problem one can make preparations for dealing with it; English proverb, early 16th century.

For want of a nail the shoe was lost; for want of a shoe the horse was lost; and for want of a horse the man was lost.

often quoted allusively to imply that one apparently small circumstance can result in a large-scale disaster; English proverb, early 17th century (late 15th century in French).

Have an umbrella ready before it rains.

be sure you are prepared for difficult times; modern saying.

Here's one I made earlier.

catchphrase popularized by the children's television programme Blue Peter, from 1963, as a culmination to directions for making a model out of empty yoghurt pots, coat-hangers, and similar domestic items.

Hope for the best and prepare for the worst.

recommending a balance between optimism and realism; English proverb, mid 16th century.

If you want peace, you must prepare for war.

a country in a state of military preparedness is unlikely to be attacked; English proverb, mid 16th century; the idea is found in the classical world in the *Nicomachaean Ethics* of Aristotle, 'We make war that we may live in peace.'

It's the second mouse that gets the cheese.

modern addition to **The early bird catches the worm** above, suggesting the dangers of being the first to make a venture, and the possible benefits of following directly behind a pioneer; compare **The only free cheese is in a mousetrap** at TEMPTATION.

Measure seven times, cut once.
care taken in preparation will prevent errors (originally referring
to carpentry and needlework); Russian proverb.

No one was ever lost on a straight road.
if you know where you are going you will not make mistakes;
Indian proverb.

No plan survives first contact with the enemy.
modern saying, from the German soldier and statesman Hel-
muth von Moltke (1800–91), 'No plan of operations reaches with
any certainly beyond the first encounter with the enemy's
main force.'

**Prayer to God, and service to the tsar, are never
wasted.**
Russian proverb.

To fail to prepare is to prepare to fail.
modern saying.

The Present

See also THE FUTURE, THE PAST

Although it may seem that what we want never arrives (Jam tomorrow and jam yesterday, but never jam today), *we should not lose sight of the fact that the present is what we have:* Yesterday has gone, tomorrow is yet to be. Today is the miracle.

Better an egg today than a hen tomorrow.
take advantage of what is available now, rather than waiting for possible advantages later; English proverb.

Enjoy the present moment and don't grieve for the future.
American proverb, mid 20th century.

Jam tomorrow and jam yesterday, but never jam today.
English proverb, late 19th century, from Lewis Carroll *Through the Looking-Glass* (1872), 'The rule is, jam to-morrow and jam yesterday—but never jam today!'

Yesterday has gone, tomorrow is yet to be. Today is the miracle.
modern saying.

Yesterday is ashes; tomorrow is wood. Only today does the fire burn brightly.
emphasizing the importance of enjoying and valuing the present rather than dwelling in the past, which cannot be changed, or the

future, which has not yet happened; Canadian saying, said to be of Inuit origin.

Pride

See also SELF-ESTEEM AND SELF-ASSERTION

Pride may shield us from distress (Pride feels no pain), *but the shelter is not likely to last:* Pride goes before a fall.

He that will not stoop for a pin [a penny] will never be worth a point [a pound].

if pride prevents you from taking a small benefit, you will not make further gains; English proverb.

Pride feels no pain.

implying that inordinate self-esteem will not allow the admission that one might be suffering; English proverb, early 17th century.

Pride goes before a fall.

often with the implication that proud and haughty behaviour will contribute to its own downfall; English proverb, late 14th century, often with allusion to the Bible (Proverbs 16:18), 'Pride goeth before destruction, and an haughty spirit before a fall.'

Stupidity and pride grow on the same tree.

pride is likely to blind us to a wise course of action; German proverb.

Problems and Solutions

See also WAYS AND MEANS

A particular situation or course of action is likely to affect what you then do: If you lead your mule to the top of the minaret, then you must lead him down again.

If you lead your mule to the top of the minaret, then you must lead him down again.

if you get yourself into a difficult position, you will have to extricate yourself; Arab proverb.

Jim'll fix it.

catchphrase of a BBC television series (1975–94) starring Jimmy Savile, in which participants had their wishes fulfilled.

Never bid the Devil good morrow until you meet him.

a warning against trying to deal with problems or difficulties before they have actually occurred; English proverb, late 19th century, said to be an old Irish saying.

When all you have is a hammer, everything looks like a nail.

often used to comment on the wholesale application of one solution or method to the solution of any problem; English proverb, late 20th century (chiefly North America).

Why did the chicken cross the road?

traditional puzzle question, to which the answer is, 'to get to the other side'; mid 19th century.

Punctuality

See also TIME

Punctuality shows a proper courtesy (Punctuality is the politeness of princes)*, and also has practical advantages:* First come, first served.

Better late than never.

even if one has missed the first chance of doing something, it is better to attempt it than not to do it at all; English proverb, early 14th century.

Cathedral time is five minutes later than standard time.

order of service leaflet, Christ Church cathedral, Oxford, 1990s.

First come, first served.

English proverb, late 14th century.

Punctuality is the art of guessing correctly how late the other party is going to be.

American proverb, mid 20th century.

Punctuality is the politeness of princes.

English proverb, mid 19th century; the idea is found earlier in French, in a comment by Louis XVIII (1755–1824), 'Punctuality is the politeness of kings.'

Punctuality is the soul of business.

English proverb, mid 19th century.

Punishment

See CRIME AND PUNISHMENT

Quantities and Qualities

From Little fish are sweet *to* One spoonful of tar spoils a barrel of honey, *there is a consensus that a small quantity of something can be potent.*

All that glitters is not gold.

an attractive appearance is not necessarily evidence of intrinsic value; English proverb, early 13th century.

Drops that gather one by one finally become a sea.

Persian proverb.

How long is a piece of string?

traditional saying, used to indicate that something cannot be given a finite measurement.

Little fish are sweet.

small gifts are always acceptable; English proverb, early 19th century.

Many a little makes a mickle.

the proper form of the proverb **Many a mickle makes a muckle** below (*mickle* in Scottish usage means 'a large quantity or amount'); English proverb, mid 13th century.

Many a mickle makes a muckle.

an alteration of the proverb **Many a little makes a mickle**
above; the result is actually nonsensical, since *muckle* is a variant
of *mickle*, and both mean 'a large quantity or amount'.

The more the merrier.

English proverb, late 14th century.

The nearer the bone, the sweeter the meat.

the juiciest meat lies next to the bone, or the meat closest to the
bone is particularly precious because it may represent one's last
scrap of food; English proverb, late 14th century.

Never mind the quality, feel the width.

used as the title of a television comedy series (1967–9) about a
tailoring business in the East End of London, ultimately probably
an inversion of a cloth trade saying.

One spoonful of tar spoils a barrel of honey.

Russian proverb.

Small is beautiful.

title of a book by E. F. Schumacher, 1973.

There is safety in numbers.

now with the implication that a number of people will be
unscathed where an individual might be in danger; English proverb, late 17th century.

Where's the beef?

advertising slogan for Wendy's Hamburgers in a campaign
launched 9 January 1984, and subsequently taken up by the
American politician Walter Mondale in a televised debate with
Gary Hart during the campaign for the US presidential campaign,
11 March 1984: 'When I hear your new ideas I'm reminded of
that ad, "Where's the beef?"'

The whole is more than the sum of the parts.

traditional saying, probably deriving from Aristotle *Metaphysica*,
'Whenever anything which has several parts is such that the
whole is something over and above its parts, and not just the
sum of them, like a heap, then it always has some cause.'

You can count the apples on one tree, but not the trees in one apple.

African proverb.

Rank

The implicit acceptance of the desirability of social rank in It takes three generations to make a gentleman *is questioned by the traditional rhyme from the time of the Peasants' Revolt:* When Adam delved and Eve span, who was then the gentleman?

Everybody loves a lord.
English proverb, mid 19th century.

If two ride on a horse, one must ride behind.
of two people engaged on the same task, one must take a subordinate role; English proverb, late 16th century.

It takes three generations to make a gentleman.
English proverb, early 19th century; the idea that it took three generations before the possession of wealth conferred the status of gentleman occurs from the late 16th century.

When Adam delved and Eve span, who was then the gentleman?
traditional rhyme taken in this form by John Ball as the text of his revolutionary sermon on the outbreak of the Peasants' Revolt, 1381; it appears in the writings of Richard Rolle of Hampole (1290–1349) as, 'When Adam dalfe and Eve spane / Go spire if thou may spede, / Where was than the pride of man / That now merres his mede?'

Where Macgregor sits is the head of the table.

sometimes attributed to 'Rob Roy' MacGregor (other names are used as well as Macgregor); English proverb, mid 19th century.

You may know a gentleman by his horse, his hawk, and his greyhound.

traditional accoutrements of leisure for those of rank; Welsh proverb.

Readiness

See PREPARATION AND READINESS

Reading

See also BOOKS

Reading is not only a valuable activity (The man who reads is the man who leads), *it can provide a bond:* It is a tie between men to have read the same book.

Have you read any good books lately?

catchphrase used by Richard Murdoch in radio comedy series *Much-Binding-in-the-Marsh*, written by Richard Murdoch and Kenneth Horne, started 2 January 1947.

He that runs may read.

meaning very clear and readable; English proverb, late 16th century, originally with allusion to the Bible (Habakkuk 2:2), 'Write the vision, and make it plain upon tables, that he may run that readeth it', reinforced by John Keble's 'Septuagesima' (1827), 'There is a book, who runs may read.'

It is a tie between men to have read the same book.
American proverb, mid 19th century.

The man who reads is the man who leads.
American proverb, mid 20th century.

Rebellion
See REVOLUTION AND REBELLION

Relationships
See also FEELINGS, FRIENDSHIP, LOVE

Proverbial wisdom reflects both on relationships between individuals (There is always one who kisses, and one who turns the cheek), *and the wider link between the individual and society* (I am because we are; we are because I am).

I am because we are; we are because I am.
whatever affects the individual affects the whole community and whatever affects the whole community affects the individual; African proverb.

It is easy to kindle a fire on a familiar hearth.
a relationship which has once existed can be revived; Welsh proverb.

L'amour est aveugle; l'amitié ferme les yeux.
French proverb, meaning that love is blind, while friendship closes its eyes; compare **Love is blind** at LOVE.

There is always one who kisses, and one who turns (or offers) the cheek.
traditional saying, said to be of French origin.

Treat a man as he is, and that is what he remains. Treat a man as he can be, and that is what he becomes.
modern saying, from Goethe *Wilhelm Meisters Lehrjare* (1795–6), 'When we take people, thou wouldst say, merely as they are, we make them worse; when we treat them as if they were what they should be, we improve them as far as they can be improved.'

Religion
See also THE CHRISTIAN CHURCH, THE CLERGY, GOD

Religious practice is seen as a way of life: Laborare est orare [To work is to pray].

The family that prays together stays together.
motto devised by Al Scalpone for the Roman Catholic Family Rosary Crusade, 1947.

Laborare est orare.

Latin, 'To work is to pray,' a traditional motto of the Benedictine order, also found in the form '*Ora, lege, et labora* [Pray, read, and work].'

Man's extremity is God's opportunity.

great distress or danger may prompt a person to turn to God for help; English proverb, early 17th century.

When you pray, move your feet.

advocating works as well as faith; saying, said to be of Quaker origin.

 # Reputation
See also FAME

Not only is a good reputation a positive advantage (When a tiger dies it leaves its skin. When a man dies he leaves his name), *to acquire a bad reputation can be dangerous, since there is ready belief in the idea that there is* No smoke without fire.

De mortuis nil nisi bonum.

Latin, literally the injunction 'Of the dead, speak kindly or not at all'; compare **Never speak ill of the dead** below.

The devil is not so black as he is painted.

someone may not be as bad as their reputation; English proverb, mid 16th century.

A good name is better than a golden girdle.

French proverb.

A good reputation stands still; a bad one runs.

American proverb, mid 20th century.

He that has an ill name is half hanged.

someone with a bad reputation is already half way to being condemned on any charge brought against them; English proverb, late 14th century; compare **Give a dog a bad name and hang him** at GOSSIP.

A man's best reputation for his future is his record of the past.

American proverb, mid 20th century.

Never speak ill of the dead.

English proverb, mid 16th century; see *De mortuis nil nisi bonum* above.

No smoke without fire.

rumour is generally founded on fact; English proverb, late 14th century, earlier in French and Latin.

One may steal a horse, while another may not look over a hedge.

while one person is endlessly indulged, another is treated with suspicion on the slightest evidence; English proverb, mid 16th century.

Speak as you find.
English proverb, late 16th century.

Throw dirt enough, and some will stick.
persistent slander will in the end be believed; English proverb, mid 17th century.

When a tiger dies it leaves its skin. When a man dies he leaves his name.
a person leaves behind more than a body; Japanese proverb.

 ## Responsibility

It is as well to be ready to take responsibility for ourselves, since Don't care was made to care; *however, there is an awareness that there may be a price to be paid:* Take what you want, and pay for it, says God.

Don't care was made to care.
traditional rebuke to someone who has asserted their lack of concern; from the first words of a children's rhyme, 'Don't care was made to care, don't care was hung'; English saying, mid 20th century.

Everybody's business is nobody's business.
when something is of some interest to everyone, no single person takes full responsibility for it; English proverb, early 17th century.

Every herring must hang by its own gill.
everyone is accountable for their own actions; English proverb,
early 17th century.

Take what you want, and pay for it, says God.
traditional saying, sometimes said to be of Spanish origin.

**Those who eat salty fish will have to accept being
thirsty.**
everyone is responsible for the consequences of their own
actions; Chinese proverb.

 Revenge

It is tempting to seek revenge (Revenge is sweet), *but the
unforgiving person may achieve more than they intend:* An eye
for an eye makes the whole world blind.

Don't cut off your nose to spite your face.
warning against spiteful revenge which is likely to result in your
own hurt or loss; English proverb, mid 16th century.

Don't get mad, get even.
late 20th-century saying.

An eye for an eye makes the whole world blind.
modern saying, often attributed to Mahatma Gandhi
(1869–1948); often with allusion to the Bible (Exodus 21:23), 'Life
for life, /Eye for eye, tooth for tooth.'

He laughs last who laughs best.

the most successful person is the one who is finally triumphant; English proverb, early 17th century.

He who laughs last, laughs longest.

early 20th-century saying.

If you want revenge, dig two graves.

pursuit of revenge is likely to be destructive to the pursuer as well as to their object; saying, claimed to be of Chinese or Japanese origin.

Revenge is a dish that can be eaten cold.

vengeance need not be exacted immediately; English proverb, late 19th century.

Revenge is sweet.

English proverb, mid 16th century.

 # Revolution and Rebellion

A revolution may begin with an idea (Every revolution was first a thought in one's man's mind)*, but it will end in violence:* Revolutions are not made with rosewater.

Every revolution was first a thought in one man's mind.

American proverb, mid 19th century.

Revolutions are not made by men in spectacles.

American proverb, late 19th century.

Revolutions are not made with rosewater.

revolutions involve violence and ruthless behaviour; English
proverb, early 19th century.

**Whosoever draws his sword against the prince must
throw away the scabbard.**

anyone who tries to assassinate or depose a monarch must
remain constantly on the defence; English proverb, early 17th
century.

 Rivers

*Rivers may have their own identity, but in the end they come to
same place:* All rivers run into the sea.

All rivers run into the sea.

English proverb, early 16th century; originally with allusion to
the Bible (Ecclesiastes 1:7), 'All the rivers run into the sea; yet the
sea is not full; unto the place from whence the rivers come,
thither they return again.'

Says Tweed to Till—
'What gars ye rin sae still?'
Says Till to Tweed—
'Though ye rin with speed
And I rin slaw,
For ae man that ye droon
I droon twa.'
traditional Scottish rhyme.

 Royalty

The royalty of a sovereign confers a special quality (The king
can do no wrong), *but in lesser figures may not be greatly
regarded:* Camels, fleas, and princes exist everywhere.

Camels, fleas, and princes exist everywhere.
referring to the large numbers of offspring of some rulers; Persian proverb.

The king can do no wrong.
something cannot be wrong if it is done by someone of sovereign
power, who alone is not subject to the law of the land; translation of the Latin legal maxim *rex non potest peccare*; English proverb, mid 17th century.

A king's chaff is worth more than other men's corn.
even minor benefits available to those attending on a sovereign
are more substantial than the best that can be offered by those of
lesser status; English proverb, early 17th century.

THE KING CAN DO NO

WRONG

Satisfaction and Discontent

Satisfaction is most likely to be found by making the best of what is available: Half a loaf is better than no bread.

Acorns were good till bread was found.
until something better is found, what one has will be judged satisfactory; English proverb, late 16th century.

The answer is a lemon.
a *lemon* as the type of something unsatisfactory, perhaps referring to the least valuable symbol in a fruit machine; English proverb, early 20th century.

Better are small fish than an empty dish.
a little is preferable to nothing at all; English proverb, late 17th century.

Do not grieve that rose trees have thorns, rather rejoice that thorny bushes bear roses.
advocating an emphasis on positive aspects; Arab proverb; compare **No rose without a thorn** at CIRCUMSTANCE AND SITUATION, and **He who wants a rose must respect the thorn** at PRACTICALITY.

Go further and fare worse.
it is often wise to take what is on offer; English proverb, mid 16th century.

Half a loaf is better than no bread.
to have part of something is better than having nothing at all;
English proverb, mid 16th century.

Something is better than nothing.
even a possession of intrinsically little value is preferable to being
empty-handed; English proverb, mid 16th century.

What you've never had you've never missed.
English proverb, early 20th century.

 Sayings
See also WORDS

Common wisdom is often enshrined in popular sayings:
Proverbs are the coins of the people.

The devil can quote Scripture for his own ends.
it is possible for someone engaged in wrongdoing to quote
selectively from the Bible in apparent support of their position,
and alluding to the temptation of Christ by the Devil in the Bible
(Matthew); English proverb, late 16th century.

Proverbs are the coins of the people.
Russian proverb.

There is no proverb without a grain of truth.
Russian proverb.

To understand the people acquaint yourself with their proverbs.
Arab proverb.

Traduttore traditore.
Italian, meaning 'Translators, traitors.'

 # Science

A saying such as Science has no enemy but the ignorant *will hold whether 'science' has its original meaning of 'knowledge', or the more specific modern sense.*

Laws of Thermodynamics:
1) You cannot win, you can only break even.
2) You can only break even at absolute zero.
3) You cannot reach absolute zero.
folklore among physicists.

Much science, much sorrow.
suggesting that learning may increase one's awareness of difficult questions; English proverb, early 17th century.

Science has no enemy but the ignorant.
English proverb, mid 16th century, from Latin *Scientia non habet inimicum nisi ignorantem.*

The Sea

Recommendations about seamanship are alive to the dangers of the sea: He that would go to sea for pleasure would go to hell for a pastime.

The good seaman is known in bad weather.
American proverb, mid 18th century.

He that would go to sea for pleasure would go to hell for a pastime.
with reference to the dangers involved in going to sea; English proverb, late 19th century.

If the Bermudas let you pass, you must beware of Hatteras.
traditional saying on the dangers of sailing in the Atlantic, and especially of the waters around Cape Hatteras in North Carolina.

One hand for oneself and one for the ship.
literally, hold on with one hand, and work the ship with the other; English proverb, late 18th century.

The sea wants to be visited.
referring to those who make their living from the sea; Scottish saying.

Secrecy

While it may be desirable to keep information confidential (Don't ask, don't tell, One does not wash one's dirty linen in public), *it is likely to be difficult:* Fields have eyes and woods have ears.

The day has eyes, the night has ears.
there is always someone watching or listening; traditional saying.

Dead men tell no tales.
often used to imply that a person's knowledge of a secret will die with them; English proverb, mid 17th century.

Don't ask, don't tell.
summary of the Clinton administration's compromise policy on homosexuals serving in the armed forces, as described by Sam Nunn (1938–) in May 1993.

Fields have eyes and woods have ears.
one may always be spied on by unseen watchers or listeners; English proverb, early 13th century.

Listeners never hear good of themselves.
English proverb, mid 17th century.

Little pitchers have large ears.
children overhear what is not meant for them (a pitcher's *ears* are its handles); English proverb, mid 16th century.

My lips are sealed.

used to convey that one will not discuss or reveal something; popular version of Stanley Baldwin's speech on the Abyssinian crisis, 10 December 1935, when he told the House of Commons, 'My lips are not yet unsealed. Were these troubles over I would make a case, and I guarantee that not a man would go into the lobby against us.'

Never tell tales out of school.

a warning against indiscretion; English proverb, mid 16th century.

No names, no pack-drill.

if nobody is named as being responsible, nobody can be blamed or punished (*pack-drill* = a military punishment of walking up and down carrying full equipment); English proverb, early 20th century; the expression is now used generally to express an unwillingness to provide detailed information.

One does not wash one's dirty linen in public.

discreditable matters should be dealt with privately; English proverb, early 19th century.

Sch. . . you know who.

advertising slogan for Schweppes mineral drinks, 1960s.

A secret is either too good to keep or too bad not to tell.

American proverb, mid 20th century.

See all your best work go unnoticed.

advertisement for staff for MI5, 2005.

Those who hide can find.

those who have concealed something know where it is to be found; English proverb, early 15th century.

Three may keep a secret, if two of them are dead.

the only way to keep a secret is to tell no-one else; English proverb, mid 16th century.

Walls have ears.

care should be taken for possible eavesdroppers; English proverb, late 16th century.

What is done by night appears by day.

secrets are likely to be revealed; English proverb.

Will the real — please stand up?

catchphrase from an American TV game show (1955–66) in which a panel was asked to identify the 'real' one of three candidates all claiming to be a particular person; after the guesses were made, the compère would request the 'real' candidate to stand up.

You can't hide an awl in a sack.

some things are too conspicuous to hide; Russian proverb.

Self-Esteem and Self-Assertion

See also PRIDE

A slogan such as Because I'm worth it *may assert the value of making clear one's sense of self-worth, but more traditional sayings warn against boasting of one's attributes:* Clever hawks conceal their claws.

Because I'm worth it.

advertising slogan for L'Oreal beauty products, from mid 1980s.

Clever hawks conceal their claws.

it is not necessary to boast of one's abilities; Japanese proverb.

Deny self for self's sake.

the result of self-denial is likely to be self-improvement; American proverb, mid 18th century.

A frog in a well knows nothing of the ocean.

one should be aware of the limitations of one's own experience; Japanese proverb.

Here's tae us; wha's like us?
Gey few, and they're a' deid.

Scottish toast, probably of 19th century origin.

Know thyself.

English proverb, late 14th century; inscribed in Greek on the temple of Apollo at Delphi; Plato, in *Protagoras*, ascribes the saying to the Seven Wise Men of the 6th century BC.

The kumara does not speak of its own sweetness.

one should not praise oneself (a *kumara* is a sweet potato); Maori proverb.

The peacock is always happy because it never looks at its ugly feet.

a person does not see their own faults; Persian proverb.

Self-praise is no recommendation.

a person's own favourable account of themselves is of dubious worth; English proverb, early 19th century.

 ## Self-Interest

Pragmatic advice on watching your own interests (Self-preservation is the first law of nature) *may be set against reflections on fulfilling one's one responsibilities:* If every man would sweep his own doorstep the city would soon be clean.

Every man for himself and God for us all.

ultimately God is concerned for humankind while individuals are concerned only for themselves; English proverb, mid 16th century.

Every man for himself, and the Devil take the hindmost.

each person must look out for their own interests, and the weakest is likely to come to disaster; English proverb, early 16th century.

Every man is the architect of his own fortune.

each person is ultimately responsible for what happens to them; English proverb, mid 16th century.

Hear all, see all, say nowt, tak' all, keep all, gie nowt, and if tha ever does owt for nowt do it for thysen.

now associated with Yorkshire, and caricaturing supposedly traditional Yorkshire attributes, in the picture of someone who is shrewd, taciturn, grasping, and selfish; English proverb, early 15th century.

If every man would sweep his own doorstep the city would soon be clean.

if everyone fulfils their own responsibilities, what is necessary will be done; English proverb, early 17th century.

If you want a thing done well, do it yourself.

no-one else has so much interest in your own welfare; English proverb, mid 17th century.

If you would be well served, serve yourself.

no-one else has so much interest in your own welfare; English proverb, mid 17th century.

Near is my kirtle, but nearer my smock.

used as a justification for putting one's own interests first (a *kirtle* is a woman's skirt or gown, and a *smock* is an undergarment); English proverb, mid 15th century.

Near is my shirt, but nearer my skin.

a justification of self-interest; English proverb, late 16th century.

A satisfied person does not know the hungry person.

African proverb.

Self-interest is the rule, self-sacrifice the exception.

American proverb, mid 20th century.

Self-preservation is the first law of nature.

the instinct for self-preservation is inbuilt and instinctive; English proverb, mid 17th century.

Sex

See also LOVE, MARRIAGE

A question such as Did the earth move for you? *suggests a less bleak view of sex than the dismissive view that* Dirty water will quench fire.

Did the earth move for you?

supposedly said to one's partner after sexual intercourse, after Ernest Hemingway *For Whom the Bell Tolls* (1940), 'But did thee feel the earth move.'

Dirty water will quench fire.
mainly used to mean that a man's sexual needs can be satisfied by
any woman, however ugly or immoral; English proverb, mid
16th century.

Post coitum omne animal triste.
Latin, 'After coition every animal is sad.'

Why buy a cow when milk is so cheap?
putting forward an argument for choosing the least troublesome
alternative; frequently used as an argument against marriage;
English proverb, mid 17th century.

 Sickness
See also HEALTH, MEDICINE

*While sickness should be avoided, ailments are not necessarily
fatal:* A creaking door hangs longest.

**Cough and sneezes spread diseases. Trap the germs in
your handkerchief.**
Second World War health slogan (1942).

A creaking door hangs longest.
someone who is apparently in poor health may well outlive the
ostensibly stronger; English proverb, late 17th century.

Feed a cold and starve a fever.

probably intended as two separate admonitions, but sometimes interpreted to mean that if you feed a cold you will have to starve a fever later; English proverb, mid 19th century.

Sickness arrives on horseback, and departs on foot.

illness comes on quickly, but regaining health is a slower process; Dutch proverb.

 Silence

See also SPEECH

Silence can be impressive in itself (Silence is a still noise) *as well as a guard against idle talk:* A shut mouth catches no flies.

A shut mouth catches no flies.

a warning against the dangers of idle talk; English proverb, late 16th century.

Silence is a still noise.

American proverb, late 19th century.

Silence means consent.

English proverb, late 14th century; translation of a Latin tag, '*Qui tacet consentire videtur* [He who is silent seems to consent]', said to have been spoken by Thomas More (1478–1535) when asked at his trial why he was silent on being asked to acknowledge the king's supremacy over the Church. The principle is not accepted in modern English law.

Speech is silver, but silence is golden.

discretion can be more valuable than the most eloquent words; English proverb, mid 19th century; compare **Who knows most, speaks least** at SPEECH.

Speech sows, silence reaps.

once an argument has been put, it is wise to give time for the words to have an effect; saying, said to be a Persian proverb.

A still tongue makes a wise head.

a person who is not given to idle talk, and who listens to others, is likely to be wise; English proverb, mid 16th century.

 # Similarity and Difference

Similarity may be a bond (Birds of a feather flock together), *or may promote rivalry:* Two swords cannot fit in one scabbard.

All cats are grey in the dark.

darkness obscures inessential differences; English proverb, mid 16th century.

Birds of a feather flock together.

people of the same (usually unscrupulous) character tend to associate; English proverb, mid 16th century.

Comparisons are odious.

often used to suggest that to compare two different things or persons is unhelpful or misleading; English proverb, mid 15th century.

East is east, and west is west.

an assertion of ineradicable racial and cultural differences; English proverb, late 19th century, from Kipling 'The Ballad of East and West' (1892), 'Oh, East is East, and West is West, and never the twain shall meet, Till Earth and Sky stand presently at God's great Judgement Seat; But there is neither East nor West, Border, nor Breed, nor Birth, When two strong men stand face to face, tho' they come from the ends of the earth!'

Extremes meet.

opposite extremes have much in common; English proverb, mid 18th century.

From the sweetest wine, the tartest vinegar.

the strongest hate comes from former love; English proverb, late 16th century.

Like breeds like.

a particular kind of event may well be the genesis of a similar occurrence; English proverb, mid 16th century.

Like will to like.

those of similar nature and inclination are drawn together; English proverb, late 14th century.

One nail drives out another.

like will counter like; English proverb, mid 13th century.

Two of a trade never agree.
close association with someone makes disagreement over policy
and principles more likely; English proverb, early 17th century.

Two swords do not fit in one scabbard.
Indian proverb.

When Greek meets Greek, then comes the tug of war.
when two people of a similar kind are opposed, there is a
struggle for supremacy; English proverb, late 17th century, from
Nathaniel Lee *The Rival Queens* (1677), 'When Greeks joined
Greeks, then was the tug of war!'

Situation
See CIRCUMSTANCE AND SITUATION

Sleep
See also DREAMS

Sleep is a source of essential refreshment (One hour's sleep
before midnight is worth two after), *but overindulgence in it
is a bad sign:* Some sleep five hours; nature requires seven,
laziness nine, and wickedness eleven.

The beginning of health is sleep.
Irish proverb.

The morning knows more than the evening.
the mind is clearer after sleep; Russian proverb.

**One hour's sleep before midnight is worth
two after.**
English proverb, mid 17th century.

**Six hours' sleep for a man, seven for a woman, and
eight for a fool.**
implying that the more sleep a person needs, the less vigorous
and effective they are likely to be; English proverb, early 17th
century.

**Some sleep five hours; nature requires seven, laziness
nine, and wickedness eleven.**
American proverb, mid 20th century.

We never sleep.
motto of the American detective agency founded by Allan
Pinkerton (c.1855).

 # Smoking

*Sayings about smoking trace a changing attitude to the habit,
culminating in the warning* Smoking can seriously damage
your health.

**Coffee without tobacco is like a Jew without
a rabbi.**
Moroccan proverb.

Happiness is a cigar called Hamlet.
advertising slogan for Hamlet cigars, UK.

More doctors recommend Camels than any other cigarette.
advertising slogan for Camel cigarettes.

Smoking can seriously damage your health.
government health warning now required by British law to be
printed on cigarette packets; in the form 'Smoking can damage
your health' from early 1970s.

You're never alone with a Strand.
advertising slogan for Strand cigarettes, 1960; the image of
loneliness was so strongly conveyed by the solitary smoker that
sales were adversely affected.

 # Solitude

While you may be hampered by companionship (He travels
the fastest who travels alone), *there are risks in solitude:*
The lone sheep is in danger of the wolf.

Better alone than in bad company.
American proverb, late 17th century.

He travels the fastest who travels alone.
implying that single-minded pursuit of an objective is more
easily achieved by someone without family commitments; English proverb, late 19th century; from Kipling 'The Winners'
(1890), 'Down to Gehenna or up to the Throne, He travels the
fastest who travels alone.'

The lone sheep is in danger of the wolf.
stressing the importance of mutual support; English proverb, late
16th century.

Solutions
See PROBLEMS AND SOLUTIONS

Sorrow
See also MOURNING, SUFFERING

*Grief is inevitable, but we may find ways of dealing with it—
perhaps by seeking the support of others:* Misery loves
company.

He that conceals his grief, finds no remedy for it.
trying to hide distress means that you do not recover from it;
proverb, said to be of Turkish origin.

Misery loves company.
English proverb, late 16th century, now predominantly current in the United States.

Wednesday's child is full of woe.
traditional rhyme, mid 19th century (compare qualities associated with birth on other days at entries under BEAUTY, GIFTS, TRAVEL, and WORK).

You cannot prevent the birds of sorrow from flying overhead, but you can prevent them from building nests in your hair.
sorrow may be unavoidable, but one can respond to it in different ways; Chinese proverb.

 # Speech

While conversation is endorsed by the slogan It's good to talk, *there is a traditional consensus that concision in speech is desirable:* Length begets loathing.

Brevity is the soul of wit.
English proverb, early 17th century, from Shakespeare *Henry IV, Part 2* (1597).

How now, brown cow?
a traditional elocution exercise.

If I listen, I have the advantage; if I speak, others have it.

a warning against rushing into speech; Arabic proverb.

It's good to talk.

advertising slogan for British Telecom from 1994.

Length begets loathing.

in reference to verbosity; English proverb, mid 18th century.

Listen a thousand times, and speak once.

warning against making a hasty response; Turkish proverb.

Unaccustomed as I am...

clichéistic opening words by a public speaker.

Who knows most, speaks least.

English proverb, mid 17th century.

 Sports and Games

The saying Nice guys finish last *might be applied to the results of a number of games.*

Anyone for tennis?

said to be a typical entrance or exit line given to a young man in a superficial drawing-room comedy.

Chess is a sea where a gnat may drink and an elephant may bathe.

the game may be played at many levels; modern saying, said to derive from an Indian proverb.

Drive for show, and putt for dough.

Golf saying meaning that matches are won in the final strokes on the green, and not by the opening drive from the tee.

Nice guys finish last.

modern saying, from a casual remark by the American coach Leo Durocher (1906–91), 'I called off his players' names as they came marching up the steps behind him ... All nice guys. They'll finish last. Nice guys. Finish last.'

 # Spring

See also AUTUMN, SUMMER, WINTER

Individual months have their own character (March comes in like a lion, and goes out like a lamb), *but spring as a season depends on progression:* April showers bring forth May flowers.

April and May are the keys to the whole year.

good weather in April and May lays an essential foundation for the rest of the year; German proverb.

April showers bring forth May flowers.

English proverb.

A cold April the barn will fill.
cold weather in April is likely to mean a good harvest later in the
year; traditional saying.

**March borrowed from April three days, and they
were ill.**
English proverb.

March comes in like a lion, and goes out like a lamb.
English proverb.

May chickens come cheeping.
English proverb.

On the first of March, the crows begin to search.
English proverb.

A peck of March dust is worth a king's ransom.
English proverb.

Rain in spring is as precious as oil.
Chinese proverb.

So many mists in March, so many frosts in May.
English proverb.

Spring is sooner recognized by plants than by men.
Chinese proverb.

Strength and Weakness

Individuals may be specially gifted with strength (Only an elephant can bear an elephant's load), *but there may be an interrelationship between the strong and the weak:* The caribou feeds the wolf, but it is the wolf that keeps the caribou strong.

The caribou feeds the wolf, but it is the wolf that keeps the caribou strong.
stressing the interrelationship between predator and prey; Inuit proverb.

An elephant does not die of one broken rib.
a strong person will not be brought down by a minor injury; African proverb.

Every tub must stand on its own bottom.
it is necessary to support oneself by one's own efforts; English proverb, mid 16th century.

If you don't like the heat, get out of the kitchen.
if you choose to work in a particular sphere you must also deal with its pressures; English proverb, mid 20th century, from a comment associated with the American statesman Harry S. Truman (though attributed by him to his 'military jester' Harry Vaughan, 1893–1981), 'If you can't stand the heat, get out of the kitchen.'

It is the pace that kills.

used as a warning against working under extreme pressure;
English proverb, mid 19th century.

Only an elephant can bear an elephant's load.

heavy responsibilities require significant strength; Indian proverb
(Marathi).

Only the eagle can gaze at the sun.

only a strong person can undertake a demanding task; English
proverb; late 16th century.

**A reed before the wind lives on, while mighty
oaks fall.**

something which bends to the force of the wind is less likely to
be broken than something which tries to withstand it; English
proverb, late 14th century.

Strength through joy.

German Labour Front slogan from 1933, coined by Robert Ley
(1890–1945).

The weakest go to the wall.

usually said to derive from the installation of seating (around the
walls) in the churches of the late Middle Ages; English proverb,
early 16th century.

What does not kill you makes you stronger.

an encouragement in difficult circumstances; modern saying.

You are the weakest link . . . goodbye.

catchphrase used by Anne Robinson on the television game
show *The Weakest Link* (2000–); compare **A chain is no
stronger than its weakest link** at COOPERATION.

Success and Failure

See also WINNING AND LOSING

Success and failure are both part of life (You win a few, you
lose a few), *and it is wise to remember that notable and sudden
success is likely to be transient:* Up like a rocket, down like
a stick.

The bigger they are, the harder they fall.

English proverb, early 20th century, commonly attributed in its
current form to the boxer Robert Fitzsimmons, prior to a
fight, *c.*1900.

Do not laugh at the fallen; there may be slippery
places ahead.

it is wise to remember when seeing someone in trouble that you
too may have difficulties; African proverb.

From clogs to clogs is only three generations.

the *clog*, a shoe with a thick wooden sole, was worn by manual
workers in the north of England. The implication is that the
energy and ability required to raise a person's material status
from poverty is often not continued to the third generation, and
that the success is therefore not sustained; English proverb, late
19th century, said to be a Lancashire proverb.

From shirtsleeves to shirtsleeves in three generations.

wealth gained in one generation will be lost by the third; English proverb, early 20th century. The saying is often attributed to the Scottish-born American industrialist and philanthropist Andrew Carnegie (1835–1919) but is not found in his writings.

From the sublime to the ridiculous is only one step.

English proverb, late 19th century; the idea is found earlier in the writings of Thomas Paine *The Age of Reason* pt 2 (1795), 'The sublime and the ridiculous are often so nearly related, that it is difficult to class them separately. One step above the sublime, makes the ridiculous; and one step above the ridiculous, makes the sublime again.' A similar comment is found in a comment of Napoleon's after the 1812 retreat from Moscow, 'There is only one step from the sublime to the ridiculous.'

He who fails to plan, plans to fail.

modern saying.

He who leaves succeeds.

moving away from home territory leads to success; Italian proverb.

Let them laugh that win.

triumphant laughter should be withheld until success is assured; English proverb, mid 16th century.

Nothing succeeds like success.

someone already regarded as successful is likely to attract more support; English proverb, mid 19th century.

The only place where success comes before work is in a dictionary.

modern saying.

The race is not to the swift, nor the battle to the strong.

the person with the most apparent advantages will not necessarily be successful; English proverb, mid 17th century; often with allusion to the Bible (Ecclesiastes 9:11).

A rising tide lifts all boats.

usually taken to mean that a prosperous society benefits everybody; in America the expression was particularly associated with John Fitzgerald Kennedy (1917–63); English proverb, mid 20th century.

Rooster today, feather duster tomorrow.

one who is currently successful may subsequently find that circumstances change dramatically; Australian saying.

Success has many fathers, while failure is an orphan.

once something is seen to succeed many people will claim to have initiated it, while responsibility for failure is likely to be disclaimed; English proverb, mid 20th century; the idea is found in the diary (for 9 September 1942) of Mussolini's son-in-law Count Galeazzo Ciano (1903–44), 'Victory has a hundred fathers, but no-one wants to recognise defeat as his own.'

Up like a rocket, down like a stick.
sudden marked success is likely to be followed by equally sudden
failure; English proverb, late 19th century; the simile is found
earlier in Thomas Paine's (1737–1809) comment on Edmund
Burke's losing the parliamentary debate on the French Revolution to Charles James Fox, 'As he rose like a rocket, he fell like
the stick.'

**When an elephant is in trouble, even a frog can
kick him.**
the weak can attack the strong when they are in difficulty; Indian
proverb.

You win a few, you lose a few.
one has to accept failure as well as success, and used as an
expression of consolation or resignation; English proverb, mid
20th century.

 # Suffering
See also MOURNING, SORROW, SYMPATHY

Suffering may ennoble (Crosses are ladders that lead to heaven), *but the slogan* Beauty without cruelty *reminds us that we
have no right to inflict it to satisfy our own wants.*

Beauty without cruelty.
slogan for Animal Rights.

Crosses are ladders that lead to heaven.

the way to heaven is through suffering; crosses refers either to
the crucifix, or more generally to troubles or misfortunes; English proverb, early 17th century.

Ee, it was agony, Ivy.

catchphrase from *Ray's a Laugh* (BBC radio programme,
1949–61), written by Ted Ray.

No cross, no crown.

cross is here used punningly, as in **Crosses are ladders that lead
to heaven** above; English proverb, early 17th century.

Summer

See also AUTUMN, SPRING, WINTER

Summer may see the longest days of the year (Barnaby bright,
Barnaby bright, the longest day and the shortest night),
but it does not necessarily imply good weather: A dripping
June sets all in tune.

**Barnaby bright, Barnaby bright, the longest day and
the shortest night.**

in the Old Style calendar St Barnabas' Day, 11 June, was
reckoned the longest day of the year; English proverb, mid 17th
century.

A cherry year, a merry year; a plum year, a dumb year.

recording the tradition that a good crop of cherries is a promising sign for the year; English proverb, late 17th century.

A dripping June sets all in tune.

English proverb.

One swallow does not make a summer.

English proverb.

Saint Swithin's day, if thou be fair, for forty days it will remain; Saint Swithin's day, if thou bring rain, for forty days it will remain.

Saint Swithin's day is 15 July, and the tradition may have its origin in the heavy rain said to have occurred when his relics were to be transferred to a shrine in Winchester cathedral; English proverb, early 17th century.

Summer is the mother of the poor.

for someone living in poverty, summer is easier than cold weather; Italian proverb.

A swarm in May is worth a load of hay; a swarm in June is worth a silver spoon; but a swarm in July is not worth a fly.

traditional beekeepers' saying, meaning that the later in the summer it is, the less time there will be for bees to collect pollen from flowers in blossom; English proverb, mid 17th century.

Surprise

A saying such as You could have knocked me down with a feather *suggests a lack of awareness that* The unexpected always happens.

The age of miracles is past.

often used ironically, or as a comment on failure; English proverb, late 16th century.

Nobody expects the Spanish Inquisition.

from the script of an episode of *Monty Python's Flying Circus* (BBC TV programme, 1970), 'Nobody expects the Spanish Inquisition! Our chief weapon is surprise—surprise and fear. . .fear and surprise. . .our two weapons are fear and surprise—and ruthless efficiency. . . .'

The unexpected always happens.

warning against an overconfident belief that something cannot occur; English proverb, late 19th century.

Wonders will never cease.

often used ironically to comment on an unusual circumstance; English proverb, late 18th century.

You could have knocked me down with a feather.

expressing great surprise; English saying, mid 19th century.

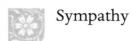

Sympathy

While we cannot necessarily depend on unstinting sympathy (Laugh and the world laughs with you, weep and you weep alone), *to seek for it is natural:* One kind word warms three winter months.

God makes the back to the burden.
an assertion that nothing is truly insupportable used in resignation or consolation; English proverb, early 19th century.

God tempers the wind to the shorn lamb.
God so arranges it that bad luck does not unduly plague the weak or unfortunate; English proverb, mid 17th century.

Laugh and the world laughs with you, weep and you weep alone.
English proverb, late 19th century; in this form from the poem 'Solitude' by the American poet Ella Wheeler Wilcox (1855–1919), 'Laugh and the world laughs with you; Weep, and you weep alone'; ultimately echoing the Bible (Romans 16:15), 'Rejoice with them that do rejoice, and weep with them that weep', and Horace (*c.*65–8) *Ars Poetica*, 'Men's faces laugh on those who laugh, and correspondingly weep on those who weep.

Nothing so bad but it might have been worse.
used in resignation or consolation; English proverb, late 19th century.

GOD MAKES THE
BACK TO THE
BURDEN

One kind word warms three winter months.
Japanese proverb.

Pity is akin to love.
English proverb, early 17th century.

The rock in the water does not know the pain of the rock in the sun.
awareness of your own suffering prevents you from understanding the pain of those in different circumstances; Hawaiian proverb.

Shared joy is double joy, and shared sorrow is double sorrow.
proverb, said to be of German origin.

The tears of the stranger are only water.
sympathy for grief may be limited to those whom we already know; Russian proverb.

Teaching

See also EDUCATION

Teaching is important (Who teaches me for a day is my father for a lifetime), *but it may have its limitations:* Tell me and I'll forget. Show me and I'll remember. Involve me and I'll be changed forever.

He teaches ill who teaches all.
English proverb, early 17th century.

He that teaches himself has a fool for a master.
English proverb, early 17th century.

Nobody forgets a good teacher.
Teacher Training Agency slogan, late 20th century.

Tell me and I'll forget. Show me and I'll remember. Involve me and I'll be changed forever.
Japanese proverb.

Who teaches me for a day is my father for a lifetime.
Chinese proverb; compare **Give a man a fish, and you feed him for a day; show him how to catch fish, and you feed him for a lifetime** at CHARITY.

Technology

See also CHANGE, COMPUTING, SCIENCE

Technology may provide us with solutions (You press the button, we do the rest), *but it can also constrict us:* Science finds, industry applies, man conforms.

The camera never lies.
20th-century saying.

Let your fingers do the walking.
1960s advertisement for the Bell system Telephone Directory Yellow Pages.

Science finds, industry applies, man conforms.
subtitle of guidebook to 1933 Chicago World's Fair.

Vorsprung durch Technik.
German, 'Progress through technology', advertising slogan for Audi motors, from 1986.

You press the button, we do the rest.
advertising slogan to launch the Kodak camera 1888, coined by George Eastman (1854–1932).

Temptation

What is forbidden is particularly attractive (Naughty but nice)*; however, the attraction is likely to conceal danger:* The only free cheese is in a mousetrap.

The bleating of the lamb excites the tiger.
of a prey staked out to attract a predator; Indian proverb; used by Kipling in *Stalky & Co.* (1899) in the form 'the bleating of the kid. . .'

Fish follow the bait.
English proverb, 17th century.

The fish will soon be caught that nibbles at every bait.
English proverb, 16th century.

Naughty but nice.
advertising slogan for cream cakes in the first half of the 1980s; earlier, the title of a 1939 film.

The only free cheese is in a mousetrap.
Russian proverb; compare **It's the second mouse that gets the cheese** at PREPARATION AND READINESS.

Stolen fruit are sweet.
The knowledge that something is forbidden makes it more attractive; English proverb, early 17th century.

Stolen waters are sweet.
something which has been obtained secretly or illicitly seems particularly attractive; English proverb, late 14th century.

There's no such thing as a free lunch.

colloquial axiom in American economics from the mid 20th
century, much associated with the economist Milton Friedman
(1912–2006), but not coined by him.

 # Thinking

See also HYPOTHESIS AND FACT, OPINION

Thought may or may not be productive (the boast I have a
cunning plan *was rarely promising), but we should exercise
the faculty:* To question and ask is a moment's shame, but
to question and not ask is a lifetime's shame.

Elementary, my dear Watson.

remark attributed to Sherlock Holmes, but not found in this
form in any book by Arthur Conan Doyle; first found in P. G.
Wodehouse *Psmith Journalist* (1915).

Great minds think alike.

English proverb, early 17th century, now often used ironically.

I have a cunning plan.

Baldrick's habitual overoptimistic promise, originally in *Black-
adder II* (1987 television series, written by Richard Curtis and
Ben Elton).

Perish the thought!

saying used, often ironically, to show that one finds a suggestion
or idea completely ridiculous; the phrase probably derives from
'Perish that thought!' in Colley Cibber's *Richard III* (1700).

There is one thing stronger than all the armies in the world; and that is an idea whose time has come.

mid 20th-century saying; the idea is found in Victor Hugo *Histoire d'un Crime* (written 1851–2, published 1877), 'A stand can be made against invasion by an army; no stand can be made against invasion by an idea.'

To question and ask is a moment's shame, but to question and not ask is a lifetime's shame.

Japanese proverb.

Two heads are better than one.

it is advisable to discuss a problem with another person; English proverb, late 14th century.

 Thoroughness

See also DETERMINATION

Even if you are putting yourself at risk, thoroughness is to be recommended: Might as well be hanged for a sheep as for a lamb.

Do not spoil the ship for a ha'porth of tar.

used generally to warn against risking loss or failure through unwillingness to allow relatively trivial expenditure; *ship* is a dialectal pronunciation of *sheep*, and the original literal sense was 'do not allow sheep to die for the lack of a trifling amount of tar', *tar* being used to protect sores and wounds on sheep from flies; English proverb, early 17th century.

In for a penny, in for a pound.
If one is to be involved at all, it may as well be fully; English proverb, late 17th century.

Nothing venture, nothing gain.
a later variant of **Nothing venture, nothing have** below; English proverb, early 17th century.

Nothing venture, nothing have.
one must be prepared to take some risks to gain a desired end; English proverb, late 14th century.

One might as well be hanged for a sheep as a lamb.
if one is going to incur a severe penalty it may as well be for something substantial; English proverb, late 17th century.

Thrift and Extravagance
See also DEBT AND BORROWING, MONEY, POVERTY, WEALTH

Thrift is not only desirable itself, but is likely to be rewarded (A penny saved is a penny earned)*; however, it may be easier to admire than to practise it:* Most people consider thrift a fine virtue in ancestors.

Bang goes sixpence.
ironic commentary on regretted expenditure, deriving from a cartoon in *Punch* of 5 December 1868, featuring a miserly Scotsman. The caption read, 'a had na' been the-erre abune Twa Hoours when—Bang—went Saxpence!'

Make do and mend.
wartime slogan, 1940s.

Most people consider thrift a fine virtue in ancestors.
American proverb, mid 20th century.

A penny saved is a penny earned.
used as an exhortation to thrift; English proverb, mid 17th century.

Penny wise and pound foolish.
too much concern with saving small sums may result in larger loss if necessary expenditure on maintenance and safety has been withheld; English proverb, early 17th century.

Spare at the spigot, and let out the bung-hole.
referring to the practice of being overcareful on the one hand, and carelessly generous on the other. A *spigot* is a peg or pin used to regulate the flow of liquid through a tap on a cask, and a *bung-hole* is a hole through which a cask is filled or emptied, and which is closed by a bung; English proverb, mid 17th century.

Spare well and have to spend.
the person who is thrifty and careful with their resources can use them lavishly when the occasion offers; English proverb, mid 16th century.

Stretch your arm no further than your sleeve will reach.
you should not spend more than you can afford; English proverb, mid 16th century.

Take care of the pence and the pounds will take care of themselves.

thrift and small savings will grow to substantial wealth; English proverb, mid 18th century.

Thrift is a great revenue.

care with expenditure is one of the best ways of providing an income for oneself; English proverb, mid 17th century.

Wilful waste makes woeful want.

deliberate misuse of resources is likely to lead to severe shortage; English proverb, early 18th century.

 # Time

See also TRANSIENCE

Time is seen not only as a powerful force (Time works wonders)*, but as one which is beyond any control:* An inch of gold cannot buy time.

Be the day weary or be the day long, at last it ringeth to evensong.

even the most difficult time will come to an end; English proverb, early 16th century.

Even a stopped clock is right twice a day.

modern humorous saying.

Give us back our eleven days.

slogan protesting against the adoption of the Gregorian Calendar in 1752, which meant that 14 September followed immediately after 2 September.

TIME WILL TELL

An inch of gold cannot buy time.
time cannot be bought with money; Chinese proverb.

A long time ago in a galaxy far, far away ...
advertising copy for the film *Star Wars* (1977).

Man fears Time, but Time fears the Pyramids.
Egyptian proverb.

The morning daylight appears plainer when you put out your candle.
American proverb.

Never is a long time.
often used to indicate that circumstances may ultimately change; English proverb, late 14th century.

Spring forward, fall back.
a reminder that clocks are moved *forward* in the spring, and *back* in the fall (autumn).

There is a time for everything.
there is always a suitable time to do something; English proverb, late 14th century, from the Bible (Ecclesiastes 3:1), 'To every thing there is a season, and a time to every purpose under heaven.'

Time is a great healer.
initial pain is felt less keenly with the passage of time; English proverb, late 14th century.

Time will tell.

the true nature of something is likely to emerge over a period of time, and conversely it is only after time has passed that something can be regarded as settled; English proverb, mid 16th century.

Time works wonders.

often used to suggest that with the passage of time something initially unknown and unwelcome will become familiar and acceptable; English proverb, late 16th century.

Tolerance

See PREJUDICE AND TOLERANCE

Town

See THE COUNTRY AND THE TOWN

Towns and Cities

See also BRITISH TOWNS AND REGIONS

Individual cities may be seen as a spiritual as well as geographical centre: All roads lead to Rome.

All roads lead to Rome.

English proverb, late 14th century, earlier in Latin.

From Madrid to heaven, and in heaven a little window from which to look down on Madrid.

Spanish saying.

Isfahan is half the world.

Isfahan was the capital of Persia from 1598 until 1722; Persian proverb.

Next year in Jerusalem!

traditionally the concluding words of the Jewish Passover service, expressing the hope of the Diaspora that Jews dispersed throughout the world would once more be reunited.

See Naples and die.

implying that after seeing Naples, one could have nothing left on earth to wish for; Goethe noted it as an Italian proverb in his diary in 1787.

Transience

See also OPPORTUNITY, TIME

Awareness of transience may be used as a comfort (And this, too, shall pass away) *or as a warning: Sic transit gloria mundi.*

And this, too, shall pass away.

traditional saying said to be true for all times and situations; the story is told by Edward Fitzgerald in *Polonius* (1852), 'The Sultan asked for a signet motto, that should hold good for Adversity or Prosperity, Solomon gave him—"This also shall pass away."'

Sic transit gloria mundi.
Latin, 'Thus passes the glory of the world', said during the coronation of a new Pope, while flax is burned (used at the coronation of Alexander V in Pisa, 7 July 1409, but earlier in origin).

Time flies.
English proverb, late 14th century, from Virgil (70–19 BC) *Georgics* '*Sed fugit interea, fugit inreparabile tempus* [But meanwhile it is flying, irretrievable time is flying.'

Travel
See also COUNTRIES AND PEOPLES

Travel may provide us with many different experiences (Every two miles the water changes, every twelve miles the speech), *but we are also warned:* Go abroad and you'll hear news of home.

Been there, done that, got the T-shirt.
evoking a jaded tourist as the image of someone who is bored by too much sightseeing.

Clunk, click, every trip.
road safety campaign promoting the use of seatbelts, 1971.

Come with me to the Casbah.
often attributed to the actor Charles Boyer in the film *Algiers* (1938), but not found there.

Every two miles the water changes, every twelve miles the speech.
commenting on the changes experienced by travellers (the number of miles varies); Indian proverb.

Go abroad and you'll hear news of home.
information about one's immediate vicinity may have become more widely publicized; English proverb, late 17th century.

Have gun, will travel.
supposedly characteristic statement of a hired gunman in a western; popularized as the title of an American television series (1957–64).

The heaviest baggage for the traveller is an empty purse.
travelling is difficult without the money to pay for it; German proverb.

Here be dragons.
alluding to a traditional indication of early map-makers that a region was unexplored and potentially dangerous.

If it's Tuesday, this must be Belgium.
late 20th-century saying, from the title of a 1969 film written by David Shaw.

If you don't know where you are going, any road will do.
modern saying, originally with allusion to Lewis Carroll.

Is your journey really necessary?
1939 slogan, coined to discourage Civil Servants from going home for Christmas.

Let the train take the strain.
British Rail slogan, 1970 onwards.

Put a tiger in your tank.
advertising slogan for Esso petrol, 1964.

Roads are made by walking.
Spanish proverb.

Thursday's child has far to go.
line from a traditional rhyme (compare qualities associated with birth on other days at entries under BEAUTY, GIFTS, SORROW, and WORK).

Travel broadens the mind.
English proverb, early 20th century.

The traveller discards his sense of shame.
people will behave in a strange country as they will not behave in their own; Japanese proverb.

Travelling is learning.
African proverb.

Travelling is one way of lengthening life, at least in appearance.
American proverb, mid 20th century.

A wise man will climb Mount Fuji once, but only a fool will climb it twice.
Japanese proverb.

Treachery
See TRUST AND TREACHERY

Trees

The oak, the ash, and the elm may have particular attributes, but any tree can link the past with the future: Trees planted by the ancestors provide shade for their descendants.

The best time to plant a tree was twenty years ago. The second best is now.
even if you regret not having already planted a tree, it is still worth doing so; modern saying.

Beware of an oak, it draws the stroke; avoid an ash, it counts the flash; creep under the thorn, it can save you from harm.
recording traditional beliefs on where to shelter from lightning during a thunderstorm; English proverb, late 19th century.

Every elm has its man.

perhaps referring to the readiness of the tree to drop its branches on the unwary (elm wood was also traditionally used for coffins); English proverb, early 20th century.

In the woods it rains twice.

after a rainstorm, water continues to drip from overhead branches; German proverb.

One generation plants the trees; another sits in their shade.

Chinese proverb.

To plant a tree is to plant hope.

modern saying.

A seed hidden in the heart of an apple is an orchard invisible.

Welsh proverb; compare **All the flowers of tomorrow are in the seeds of today** at GARDENS.

Trees planted by the ancestors provide shade for their descendants.

Chinese proverb; a comparable idea is found in the western classical world, in the writings of Caecilius Statius (d. after 166 BC) *Synephebi*, 'He plants the trees to serve another age.'

When the oak is before the ash, then you will only get a splash; When the ash is before the oak, then you will get a soak.

a traditional way of predicting whether the summer will be wet or dry on the basis of whether the oak or the ash is first to come into leaf in the spring; English proverb, mid 19th century.

Trust and Treachery

The traditional warning Promises, like pie-crust, are made to be broken, *current since the 17th century, emphasizes the shrewdness of the Russian proverb,* Test before you trust.

Confidence is a plant of slow growth.
English proverb.

Fear the Greeks bearing gifts.
English proverb, late 19th century; originally from Virgil (70–19 BC) *Aeneid, 'Equo ne credite, Teucri, Quidquid id est, timeo Danaos et dona ferentes* [Do not trust the horse, Trojans. Whatever it is, I fear the Greeks even when they bring gifts.]'

Please to remember the Fifth of November,
Gunpowder Treason and Plot.
We know no reason why gunpowder treason
Should ever be forgot.
traditional rhyme on the Gunpowder Plot (1605).

Promises, like pie-crust, are made to be broken.
English proverb, late 17th century.

Test before you trust.
Russian proverb.

Would you buy a used car from this man?

campaign slogan directed against Richard Nixon.

You cannot run with the hare and hunt with the hounds.

you must take one of two opposing sides; English proverb, mid 15th century.

Truth

See also HONESTY, LIES

Telling the truth is an obligation (Tell the truth and shame the devil), *but an admixture of tact may be advisable:* When you shoot an arrow of truth, dip its point in honey.

Believe it or not.

title of syndicated newspaper feature (from 1918), written by Robert L. Ripley.

Fact is stranger than fiction.

English proverb, mid 19th century; compare **Truth is stranger than fiction** below.

Many a true word is spoken in jest.

an apparent joke may often include a shrewd comment, or what is spoken of as unlikely or improbable may in the future turn out to be true; English proverb, late 14th century.

An old error is always more popular than a new truth.
German proverb.

Se non è vero, è molto ben trovato.
Italian, 'If it is not true, it is a happy invention'; common saying
from the 16th century.

Tell the truth and shame the devil.
by telling the truth one is taking the right course however
embarrassing or difficult it may be; English proverb, mid 16th
century; compare **Truth makes the Devil blush** below.

Truth is stranger than fiction.
implying that no invention can be as remarkable as what may
actually happen; English proverb, early 19th century, from Byron
Don Juan (1819–24), ''Tis strange—but true; for truth is always
strange; Stranger than fiction'; compare **Fact is stranger than
fiction** above.

Truth lies at the bottom of a well.
sometimes used to imply that the truth of a situation can be hard
to find; English proverb, mid 16th century.

Truth makes the Devil blush.
English proverb, mid 20th century; compare **Tell the truth and
shame the devil** above.

Truth will out.
in the end what has really happened will become apparent;
English proverb, mid 15th century.

What everybody says must be true.

sometimes used ironically to assert that popular gossip is often inaccurate; English proverb, late 14th century.

When you shoot an arrow of truth, dip its point in honey.

advocating tact; Arab proverb.

Value

A sense of values is worth having: If you pay peanuts, you get monkeys, *and conversely* Gold may be bought too dear.

Everything has a price, but jade is priceless.
modern saying said to derive from a Chinese proverb extolling the value of jade.

Gold may be bought too dear.
wealth may be acquired at too great a price; English proverb, mid 16th century.

I am not rich enough to buy cheap goods.
a warning against practising false economies; modern saying.

If you pay peanuts, you get monkeys.
a poor rate of pay will attract only poorly qualified and incompetent staff (*peanuts* here means 'a small sum of money'); English proverb, mid 20th century.

It is a poor dog that's not worth whistling for.
a dog is of no value if the owner will not even go to the trouble of whistling for it; English proverb, mid 16th century.

Little things please little minds.
English proverb, late 16th century.

Nothing comes from nothing.
English proverb, late 14th century.

Nothing for nothing.
summarizing the attitude that nothing will be offered unless a
return is assured; English proverb, early 18th century.

What can a monkey know of the taste of ginger?
ginger as the type of a rare and expensive delicacy; Indian
proverb.

Worth a guinea a box.
advertising slogan for Beecham's pills, from *c.*1859, from the
chance remark of a lady purchaser.

The worth of a thing is what it will bring.
the real value of something can only be measured by what
another person is willing to pay for it; English proverb, mid 16th
century.

 Virtue
See also GOOD AND EVIL

Virtue should be pursued for its own sake (Virtue is its own
reward), *although it will not necessarily evoke gratitude in
others:* No good deed goes unpunished.

The good die young.
English proverb, late 17th century, often used ironically; compare **Whom the gods love die young** at YOUTH.

Good men are scarce.
English proverb, early 17th century.

He lives long who lives well.

the reputation derived from living a good and moral life will mean that one's name will last; English proverb, mid 16th century.

No good deed goes unpunished.

modern humorous saying, sometimes attributed to Oscar Wilde but not traced in his writings.

See no evil, hear no evil, speak no evil.

conventionally represented by 'the three wise monkeys' covering their eyes, ears, and mouth respectively with their hands, and used particularly to imply a deliberate refusal to notice something that is wrong; English proverb, early 20th century.

Virtue is its own reward.

the satisfaction of knowing that one has observed appropriate moral standards should be all that is sought; English proverb, early 16th century.

Warfare

See also THE ARMED FORCES, PEACE

War is seen as likely to cause more than physical injury and death: When war is declared, Truth is the first casualty.

A bayonet is a weapon with a worker at each end.
British pacifist slogan, 1940.

A bigger bang for a bigger buck.
Charles E. Wilson's defence policy, in *Newsweek* 22 March 1954.

Hey, hey, LBJ, how many kids have you killed today?
anti-Vietnam marching slogan.

Remember the Alamo!
Texan battle-cry at the battle of San Jacinto, 1836, referring to the defence of a Franciscan mission in the Texan War of Independence, in which all of the defenders were killed.

War will cease when men refuse to fight.
pacifist slogan, from *c*.1936, often in the form 'Wars will cease when...'

When war is declared, Truth is the first casualty.
epigraph to Arthur Ponsonby's *Falsehood in Wartime* (1928),
perhaps deriving from Samuel Johnson in *The Idler* 11
November 1758, 'Among the calamities of war may be jointly
numbered the diminution of the love of truth, by the falsehoods
which interest dictates and credulity encourages'; attributed also
to Hiram Johnson, speaking in the US Senate, 1918, but not
recorded in his speech.

 ## Ways and Means

When choosing the right tool (Honey catches more flies than
vinegar), *it is as well to be aware of what is really essential:* It
hardly matters if it is a white cat or a black cat that catches
the mice.

Catching's before hanging.
an essential step must be taken before the consequences can
ensue; English proverb, early 19th century.

Eat the mangoes. Do not count the trees.
concentrate on the task in hand; Indian proverb.

The end justifies the means.
English proverb, late 16th century.

Even if the sky falls down, there is a hole to escape.
there is often a way out of disaster; modern saying, said to be a
Korean proverb.

Fight fire with fire.

one should counter like with like; English proverb, mid 19th century.

Fire is a good servant, but a bad master.

acknowledging that fire is both essential for living and potentially destructive; English proverb, early 17th century.

First catch your hare.

referring to the first essential step that must be taken before a process can begin; English proverb, early 19th century, often attributed to the English cook Hannah Glasse (fl. 1747), but her directions for making hare soup are, 'Take your hare when it is cased' (*cased* here meaning 'skinned').

Give a man enough rope, and he will hang himself.

often used to mean that someone given enough licence or freedom will defeat themselves through their own mistakes; English proverb, mid 17th century.

The hammer shatters glass, but forges steel.

modern saying, said to be of Russian origin.

Honey catches more flies than vinegar.

soft or ingratiating words achieve more than sharpness; English proverb, mid 17th century.

If you can't beat them, join them.

often used in consolation or resignation; English proverb, mid 20th century.

It hardly matters if it is a white cat or a black cat that catches the mice.

Chinese proverb.

It is good to make a bridge of gold to a flying enemy.

it is wiser to give passage to an enemy in flight, who may be desperate, than to bring them to bay; English proverb, late 16th century.

An old poacher makes the best gamekeeper.

someone who has formerly taken part in wrongdoing knows best how to counter it in others; English proverb, late 14th century.

One size does not fit all.

an assertion of individual requirements; earlier versions are based on the metaphor of different size shoes for different feet; English proverb, early 17th century.

The paths are many, but the goal is the same.

Indian proverb, deriving from Sanskrit.

The pen is mightier than the sword.

written words may often have more lasting force than military strength; English proverb, mid 17th century; compare **What is written with a pen cannot be cut out with an axe** at WRITING.

Set a thief to catch a thief.

used to imply that the person best placed to catch someone out in dishonest practices is one whose own nature tends that way; English proverb, mid 17th century.

A short cut is often a wrong cut.

a warning against trying to cut corners; Danish proverb.

There are more ways of killing a cat than choking it with cream.

there are more ways of achieving an end than giving an opponent a glut of what they most want; English proverb, mid 19th century.

There are more ways of killing a dog than choking it with butter.

there are more ways of achieving an end than giving an opponent a glut of what they most want; English proverb, mid 19th century.

There are more ways of killing a dog than hanging it.

there are more ways than one of achieving an end; English proverb, late 17th century.

There is more than one way to skin a cat.

English proverb, mid 19th century.

There is nothing like leather.

referring to the toughness and durability of leather (the saying comes from one of Aesop's fables, in which a leatherworker contributed this opinion to a discussion on how to fortify a city); English proverb, late 17th century.

What matters is what works.

late 20th-century saying.

Weakness

See STRENGTH AND WEAKNESS

Wealth

See also MONEY, THRIFT

Possession of wealth confers status (Money makes a man), *and may be self-renewing:* Money makes money.

A diamond is forever.
advertising slogan for De Beers Consolidated Mines, 1940s onwards.

Few have too much, and fewer too little.
too much wealth is not necessarily a good thing; Danish proverb.

If you really want to make a million, found a new religion.
previously attributed to L. Ron Hubbard (1911–86) in B. Corydon and L. Ron Hubbard Jr. *L. Ron Hubbard* (1987), but attribution subsequently rejected by L. Ron Hubbard Jr., who also dissociated himself from this book.

Money makes a man.
possession of wealth confers status; English proverb, early 16th century.

Money makes money.

implying that those who are already wealthy are likely to become more so; English proverb, late 16th century.

The rich man gets his ice in the summer, and the poor man gets his in the winter.

contrasting luxury with hardship through apparent equality; English proverb, early 20th century.

 # The Weather

Traditional sayings about weather are likely to be predictive (North wind doth blow, we shall have snow, Rain before seven, fine before eleven), *but a more modern saying focuses on how to respond to such changes:* There is no such thing as bad weather, only the wrong clothes.

As the day lengthens, so the cold strengthens.

recording the tradition that the coldest weather arrives when days begin to grow lighter; English proverb, early 17th century.

Green Christmas, white Easter.

mild weather at Christmas may mean snow at Easter; German proverb.

Long foretold, long last; short notice, soon past.
if there is a long gap between the signs that the weather will
change and the change itself, then the predicted weather will last
a long time. If the intervening period is a short one, then the
predicted weather will be of correspondingly short duration;
English proverb, mid 19th century.

Nine months of winter and three months of hell.
on the long cold winters and hot summers supposedly typical of
the Castilian climate; Spanish saying.

North wind doth blow, we shall have snow.
traditional weather rhyme, deriving from a nursery rhyme of the
early 19th century.

Rain before seven, fine before eleven.
English proverb, mid 19th century.

Rain, rain, go away, come again another day.
traditional rhyme, mid 17th century.

**Red sky at night, shepherd's delight, Red sky in the
morning, shepherd's warning.**
good and bad weather respectively is presaged by a red sky at
sunset and dawn; English proverb, late 14th century.

**Robin Hood could brave all weathers but a thaw
wind.**
a *thaw wind* is a cold wind which accompanies the breaking up of
frost; English proverb, mid 19th century.

NORTH WIND DOTH BLOW, WE SHALL HAVE SNOW

So much sun as shines on Shrove Tuesday, so it shines all Lent.

traditional prediction.

There is no such thing as bad weather, only the wrong clothes.

late 20th-century saying.

A warm January, a cold May.

mild weather in January means there will be cold weather in May; Welsh proverb.

When the wind is in the east, 'tis good for neither man nor beast.

referring to the traditional bitterness of the east wind; English proverb, early 17th century.

Winter thunder, summer hunger.

thunderstorms in winter are taken as presage of a poor harvest; English proverb.

 # Weddings

See also MARRIAGE

The day chosen for one's wedding may turn out to be important: Marry in May, rue for aye, *but* Happy is the bride the sun shines on.

Always a bridesmaid, never a bride.

recording the belief that to be a bridesmaid too often is unlucky for one's own chances of marriage; English proverb, late 19th century.

Happy is the bride the sun shines on.
English proverb, mid 17th century.

Marry in May, rue for aye.
English proverb, late 17th century.

Now you will feel no rain, for each of you will be shelter for the other. Now you will feel no cold, for each of you will be warmth for the other.
from the saying known as the 'Apache Blessing'.

One wedding brings another.
English proverb, mid 17th century.

 # Winning and Losing
See also SUCCESS AND FAILURE

There is a consensus that winning and losing are both a part of the pattern of life: What you lose on the swings, you gain on the roundabouts.

All your base are belong to us.
deriving from the poor English translation of the Japanese video game Zero Wing, released 1989; late 20th-century saying.

Heads I win, tails you lose.
I win in any event; *heads* and *tails* the obverse and reverse images on a coin; English proverb, late 17th century.

What you lose on the swings, you gain on the roundabouts.

one's losses and gains tend to cancel one another out; English proverb, early 20th century.

You can't win them all.

used as an expression of consolation or resignation; English proverb, mid 20th century.

 Winter

See also AUTUMN, SPRING, SUMMER, THE WEATHER

Sayings about winter reflect both weather lore (February fill dyke, be it black or white), and traditional activities for the season: On Saint Thomas the Divine, kill all turkeys, geese and swine.

Candlemas day, put beans in the clay, put candles and candlesticks away.

recording the tradition that the feast of Candlemas, on 2 February, was the time for planting beans; English proverb, late 17th century.

February fill dyke, be it black or white.

February is a month likely to bring rain (black) or snow (white); English proverb, mid 16th century.

The fire is winter's fruit.
Arabic proverb.

If Candlemas day be sunny and bright, winter will have another flight; if Candlemas day be cloudy with rain, winter is gone and won't come again.
English proverb, late 17th century.

If in February there be no rain, 'tis neither good for hay nor grain.
a drought in February will be damaging to crops later in the year; English proverb, early 18th century.

If Saint Paul's day be fair and clear, it will betide a happy year.
the feast of the conversion of St Paul is 25 January; English proverb, late 16th century.

On Saint Thomas the Divine kill all turkeys, geese and swine.
21 December, the traditional feast-day in the Western Church of St Thomas the Apostle, taken as marking the season at which domestic animals not kept through the winter were to be slaughtered; English proverb, mid 18th century.

The winter does not go without looking backward.
there is likely to be bad weather towards the end of winter; Finnish proverb.

**Winter either bites with its teeth or lashes
with its tail.**

bad weather is expected at either the beginning or the end of
winter; Montenegrin proverb.

Winter is summer's heir.

the warmth of summer naturally gives way to the cold of winter;
English proverb.

Winter never rots in the sky.

the arrival of winter is not delayed; English proverb, early 17th
century.

 # Women

See also MEN AND WOMEN

Traditional views on what is appropriate for women (A whistling woman and a crowing hen, is good for neither God
nor men) *contrast with more radical assessments of a woman's
place in the world:* Women hold up half the sky.

Burn your bra.

feminist slogan, 1970s.

Far-fetched and dear-bought is good for ladies.

expensive or exotic articles are suitable for women; English
proverb, mid 14th century.

WOMEN HOLD

UP HALF THE

SKY

The female of the species is more deadly than the male.

English proverb, early 20th century, from the title of a poem (1919) by Rudyard Kipling.

The hand that rocks the cradle rules the world.

referring to the strength of a woman's indirect influence on the male world; English proverb, mid 19th century.

Hell hath no fury like a woman scorned.

a woman whose love has turned to hate is the most savage of creatures; a fury here may be either one of the avenging deities of classical mythology, or more generally someone in a state of frenzied rage; English proverb, late 17th century.

Long and lazy, little and loud; fat and fulsome, pretty and proud.

categorizing supposed physical and temperamental characteristics in women; English proverb, late 16th century.

Silence is a woman's best garment.

often used as recommending a traditionally submissive and discreet role for women; English proverb, mid 16th century.

Votes for women.

slogan of the women's suffrage movement, adopted when it proved impossible to use a banner with the longer slogan 'Will the Liberal Party Give Votes for Women?' made by Emmeline Pankhurst, Christabel Pankhurst, and Annie Kenney.

A whistling woman and a crowing hen are neither fit for God nor men.

both the woman and the hen are considered unnatural, and therefore unlucky; English proverb, early 18th century.

A woman, a dog, and a walnut tree, the more you beat them the better they be.

the walnut tree was beaten firstly to bring down the fruit, and then to break down long shoots and encourage short fruit-bearing ones; English proverb, late 16th century.

A woman and a ship ever want mending.

both women and ships require constant attention and expenditure; English proverb, late 16th century.

A woman's place is in the home.

reflecting the traditional view of a woman's role; English proverb, mid 19th century.

Women hold up half the sky.

women should be considered equal in status to men; Chinese proverb.

Words

See also NAMES, SAYINGS, SPEECH, WORDS AND DEEDS, WRITING

There are contrasting views on the power of a word: we are told that The swiftest horse cannot overtake the word once spoken, *but on the other hand,* Hard words break no bones.

All words are pegs to hang ideas on.
American proverb, late 19th century.

Elephants are contagious.
Surrealist 'proverb'.

Hard words break no bones.
the damage done by verbal attack is limited; English proverb, late 17th century.

I before e, except after c.
traditional spelling rule, 19th century.

If you take hyphens seriously you will go mad.
said to be from a style book in use with Oxford University Press, New York; perhaps apocryphal.

The quick brown fox jumps over the lazy dog.
traditional sentence used by keyboarders to ensure that all letters of the alphabet are functioning.

Sticks and stones may break my bones, but words will never hurt me.

verbal attack does no real injury; English proverb, late 19th century.

The swiftest horse cannot overtake the word once spoken.

Chinese proverb; compare Horace (65–8) *Epistles*, 'And once sent out, a word takes wing beyond recall.'

 Words and Deeds

See also ACTION AND INACTION, WORDS

There is a consensus in favour of action (Example is better than precept), *but we are warned that it is also wise to keep a guard on the tongue:* Don't add insult to injury.

Actions speak louder than words.

real feeling is expressed not by what someone says but by what they do; English proverb, early 17th century.

Brag is a good dog, but Holdfast is better.

perseverance is a better quality than ostentation; English proverb, early 18th century.

Don't add insult to injury.

recommendation not to treat a person one has hurt with contempt as well; American proverb, mid 18th century.

Example is better than precept.

English proverb, early 15th century.

Fine words butter no parsnips.

nothing is ever achieved by fine words alone (*butter* was the traditional garnish for parsnips); English proverb, mid 17th century.

One picture is worth ten thousand words.

English proverb, early 20th century.

An ounce of practice is worth a pound of precept.

a small amount of practical assistance is worth more than a great deal of advice; English proverb, late 16th century.

Practise what you preach.

you should follow the advice you give to others; English proverb, late 14th century.

Stabs heal, but bad words never.

words can inflict more lasting wounds than any physical hurt; Spanish proverb.

Talk is cheap.

it is easier to say than to do something; English proverb, mid 19th century.

Talk will not cook rice.

modern saying, said to be a Chinese proverb.

Threatened men live long.
threats are often not put into effect, and those who express resentment are actually much less dangerous than those who conceal animosity; English proverb, mid 16th century.

Vision without action is a daydream, Action without vision is a nightmare.
recommending a balance between idealism and reality; modern saying, said to derive from a Japanese proverb.

Words are sweet, but they never take the place of food.
African proverb.

Work
See also EMPLOYMENT, IDLENESS, LEISURE

Industry is traditionally commended (Practice makes perfect), *but it should be properly rewarded:* The labourer is worthy of his hire.

Arbeit macht frei.
German, 'Work liberates', words inscribed on the gates of Dachau concentration camp, 1933, and subsequently on those of Auschwitz.

The better the day, the better the deed.
frequently used to justify working on a Sunday or Holy Day; English proverb, early 17th century.

Every man to his trade.

one should operate within one's own area of expertise; English
proverb, late 16th century.

Fools and bairns should never see half-done work.

the unwise and the inexperienced may judge the quality of a
finished article from its rough unfinished state; English proverb,
early 18th century.

**From beavers, bees should learn to mend their ways.
A bee works; a beaver works and plays.**

American proverb, mid 20th century.

The labourer is worthy of his hire.

someone should be properly recompensed for effort; English
proverb, late 14th century, from the Bible (Luke 10:7).

Like master, like man.

English proverb, mid 16th century; *man* here means 'servant'.

One volunteer is worth two pressed men.

a *pressed man* was someone forcibly enlisted by the press gang, a
body of men which in the 18th and 19th centuries was employed
to enlist men forcibly into service in the army or navy; English
proverb, early 18th century.

Practice makes perfect.

often used as an encouragement; English proverb, mid 16th
century.

Saturday's child works hard for a living.

first line of a traditional rhyme, mid 19th century (compare qualities associated with birth on other days at entries under BEAUTY, GIFTS, SORROW, and TRAVEL).

A short horse is soon curried.

a slight task is soon completed (literally, that it does not take long to rub down a short horse with a curry-comb); English proverb, mid 14th century.

Too many cooks spoil the broth.

the involvement of too many people is likely to mean that something is done badly; English proverb, late 16th century.

Trifles make perfection, but perfection is no trifle.

American proverb, mid 20th century, from a comment attributed to the painter Michelangelo (1475–1564).

Two boys are half a boy, and three boys are no boy at all.

the more boys there are present, the less work will be done; English proverb, mid 20th century.

Where bees are, there is honey.

industrious work is necessary to create riches; English proverb, early 17th century.

Work expands so as to fill the time available.

English proverb, mid 20th century, from C. Northcote Parkinson *Parkinson's Law* (1958), 'Work expands so as to fill the time available for its completion.'

 Worry

Worry is not only exhausting (Care killed the cat, It is not work that kills, but worry), *but ultimately pointless:* Worry is like a rocking chair: both give you something to do, but neither get you anywhere.

Care killed the cat.

the meaning of *care* has shifted somewhat from 'worry, grief' to 'care, caution'; English proverb, late 16th century.

Do not meet troubles half way.

warning against anxiety about something that has not yet happened; English proverb, late 19th century.

It is not work that kills, but worry.

direct effort is less stressful than constant concern; English proverb, late 19th century.

Sufficient unto the day is the evil thereof.

dealing with unpleasant matters should be left until it becomes necessary; English proverb, mid 18th century, with allusion to the Bible (Matthew 6:34).

Worry is interest paid on trouble before it falls due.
American proverb, early 20th century.

Worry is like a rocking chair: both give you something to do, but neither gets you anywhere.
American proverb, mid 20th century.

 Writing
See also BOOKS, WORDS

Not only is writing powerful (What is written with a pen cannot be cut out with an axe), *it is likely to reveal the essential nature of the writer:* Writing is a picture of the writer's heart.

The art of writing is the art of applying the seat of the pants to the seat of the chair.
American proverb, mid 20th century.

He who would write and can't write can surely review.
American proverb, mid 19th century.

Paper bleeds little.
Spanish proverb,

Paper is patient.

paper allows the writer to put down what they choose; German proverb.

What is written with a pen cannot be cut out with an axe.

words are more powerful than violence; Russian proverb; compare **The pen is mightier than the sword** at WAYS AND MEANS.

Writing is a picture of the writer's heart.

Chinese proverb.

Youth

See also AGE, CHILDREN

To be young is often to overestimate one's powers (Young folks think old folks to be fools, but old folks know young folks to be fools), *but even the irresponsible young may grow up to more serious ways:* Wanton kittens make sober cats.

All dancing girls are nineteen years old.

Japanese proverb.

Never send a boy to do a man's job.

someone who is young and inexperienced should not be given too much responsibility; English proverb, mid 20th century.

The old net is cast aside while the new net goes fishing.

the future belongs to the young; Maori proverb.

Soon ripe, soon rotten.

a warning against precocity, meaning that notably early achievement is unlikely to be long-lasting; English proverb, late 14th century (earlier in Latin).

Wanton kittens make sober cats.

someone who in youth is light-minded and lascivious may be soberly behaved in later life; English proverb, early 18th century.

Whom the gods love die young.

the happiest fate is to die before health and strength are lost;
English proverb, mid 16th century; the idea is found in the classical world in Menander (342–*c.*292 BC) *Dis Exapaton*, 'Whom the
gods love dies young'; compare also **The good die young** at
VIRTUE.

**Young folks think old folks to be fools, but old folks
know young folks to be fools.**

asserting the value of the experience of life which comes with
age over youth and inexperience; English proverb, late 16th
century.

Youth must be served.

some indulgence should be given to the wishes and enthusiasms
of youth; English proverb, early 19th century.

YOUTH MUST BE
SERVED

Keyword Index

Each context line represents the opening words of a proverb (initial 'a' and 'the' being omitted). The proverb will be found in alphabetical sequence in the given section.

adventures Adventures are to the adventurous DANGER

adventurous Adventures are to the adventurous DANGER

adversity Adversity is the foundation of virtue ADVERSITY
Adversity makes strange ADVERSITY
dose of adversity is often ADVERSITY

advertise Don't advertise what you can't ADVERTISING
It pays to advertise ADVERTISING

advice Ask advice, but use ADVICE
Never give advice ADVICE

afraid Be afraid. Be very afraid FEAR

Africa Always something new out of Africa CHANGE

after After dinner rest a while EATING
After meat, mustard EATING
And they all lived happily ever after ENDING

again Not guilty, but don't do it again GUILT

Agamemnon Brave men lived before Agamemnon FAME

age age of miracles is past SURPRISE
For the unlearned, old age is winter AGE

agony Ee, it was agony, Ivy SUFFERING

agree Birds in their little nests agree ARGUMENT
Two of a trade never agree SIMILARITY AND DIFFERENCE

ahead He who can see three days ahead FORESIGHT
If you want to get ahead DRESS
past is always ahead of us PAST

aircraft One of our aircraft is missing ARMED FORCES

Alamo Remember the Alamo WARFARE

alcohol Alcohol will preserve anything DRINK

alibis Corruption will find a dozen alibis CORRUPTION

alike Great minds think alike THINKING

all All cats are grey in the dark SIMILARITY AND DIFFERENCE
All is fish that comes to the net OPPORTUNITY
All power to the Soviets POWER
All roads lead to Rome TOWNS AND CITIES
All that glitters is not gold QUANTITIES AND QUALITIES
All things are possible with God GOD
All things come to those who wait PATIENCE
All's for the best OPTIMISM AND PESSIMISM
He teaches ill who teaches all TEACHING
Hear all, see all, say nowt SELF-INTEREST
Light for all NEWS AND JOURNALISM
Moderation in all things MODERATION
One size does not fit all WAYS AND MEANS
There is measure in all things MODERATION

Allah Trust in Allah, but tie up your camel CAUTION

alone Better alone than in bad company SOLITUDE
He travels the fastest who travels alone SOLITUDE

He who travels fast, travels
alone COOPERATION
live by bread alone LIFE
We are not alone HUMAN RACE
You're never alone with a
Strand SMOKING

always Always in a hurry, always
behind HASTE AND DELAY
always a priest CLERGY
Once a —, always a —
CHARACTER

am I am because we
are RELATIONSHIPS

America America is a tune
COUNTRIES AND PEOPLES

American American Express? . . .
That'll do DEBT AND BORROWING

Americans Good Americans
when they die COUNTRIES
AND PEOPLES

amour L'amour est
aveugle RELATIONSHIPS

ancestors Trees planted by the
ancestors TREES

angels How many angels can dance
on HYPOTHESIS
AND FACT

anger Anger improves
nothing ANGER

angry He that will be angry ANGER
hungry man is an angry
man FOOD
When angry count a
hundred ANGER

animal Cet animal est très
méchant CHARACTER
politician is an animal who can
sit POLITICS

animals It takes forty dumb
animals DRESS

another Another day, another
dollar OPTIMISM AND PESSIMISM

One wedding brings
another WEDDINGS
Tomorrow is another
day FUTURE

answer answer is a lemon
SATISFACTION AND DISCONTENT
answer lies in the soil GARDENS
civil question deserves a civil
answer MANNERS
soft answer turneth away
wrath ANGER

anvil church is an anvil CHRISTIAN
CHURCH

anyone Anyone for tennis? SPORTS
AND GAMES

ape ape's an ape, a varlet's a
varlet CHARACTER

apology Apology is only
egoism APOLOGY AND EXCUSES

appearance Merit in
appearance APPEARANCE

appearances Appearances are
deceptive APPEARANCE

appetite Appetite comes with
eating EXPERIENCE

apple apple a day keeps the
doctor away HEALTH
apple never falls far from the
tree FAMILY
apple-pie without some
cheese FOOD
rotten apple injures its
neighbour CORRUPTION
seed hidden in the heart of an
apple TREES

apples Small choice in rotten
apples CHOICE
You can count the apples
on one tree QUANTITIES AND
QUALITIES

April April and May are keys to the
whole year SPRING

April showers bring forth May flowers SPRING

cold April the barn will fill SPRING

March borrowed from April three days SPRING

Arbeit Arbeit macht frei WORK

Arcadia Et in Arcadia ego DEATH

arch arch never sleeps ARCHITECTURE

architect Every man is the architect of his own SELF-INTEREST

ardua Per ardua ad astra ACHIEVEMENT

are Are you now or have you ever been POLITICS

I am because we are RELATIONSHIPS

argue Do not argue against the sun ARGUMENT

argument only thing a heated argument ever ARGUMENT

arguments more arguments you win, the less ARGUMENT

arm Stretch your arm no further than THRIFT

arms Kings have long arms POWER

army army knows how to gain a victory ARMED FORCES

army of stags led by a lion ARMED FORCES

singing army and a ARMED FORCES

around What goes around comes around JUSTICE

arrow single arrow is easily broken COOPERATION

When you shoot an arrow of truth TRUTH

art Art is long and life is short LIFE

art of being a parent CHILDREN

art of writing is the art of applying WRITING

arts All arts are brothers COOPERATION

ash When the oak is before the ash TREES

ashes Yesterday is ashes; tomorrow is wood PRESENT

ask Ask a silly question and you get FOOLS

Ask advice, but use ADVICE

Don't ask, don't tell SECRECY

To question and ask is a moment's shame THINKING

asked Never give advice unless asked ADVICE

assistant Assistant heads must roll BROADCASTING

attack Attack is the best form of defence COURAGE

aunt Vodka is an aunt of wine DRINK

Australia Advance Australia COUNTRIES AND PEOPLES

Australians Australians wouldn't give COUNTRIES AND PEOPLES

autumn Chickens are counted in the autumn AUTUMN

autumns All autumns do not fill granaries AUTUMN

away Rain, rain, go away WEATHER

awl You can't hide an awl in a sack SECRECY

axe Lizzie Borden took an axe MURDER

When the axe came into the forest OPTIMISM AND PESSIMISM

B Who says A must say B NECESSITY

babes Out of the mouths of babes— KNOWLEDGE

baby Burn, baby, burn DEFIANCE

back God makes the back to the
burden   SYMPATHY
Spring forward, fall back   TIME
What is got under the
Devil's back   GOOD AND
EVIL

backing I'm backing
Britain   LOYALTY

bad bad custom is like a good
cake   CUSTOM AND HABIT
bad excuse is better than
APOLOGY AND EXCUSES
Bad money drives out
good   MONEY
Bad news travels fast   NEWS AND
JOURNALISM
bad penny always turns
up   CHARACTER
Bad things come in
threes   MISFORTUNES
bad workman blames his
tools   APOLOGY AND
EXCUSES
Better alone than in bad
company   SOLITUDE
Give a dog a bad name and
hang   GOSSIP
good seaman is known in bad
weather   SEA
Hard cases make bad law   LAW
He that cannot abide a bad
market   BUSINESS
Nothing so bad but it might have
been   SYMPATHY
Stabs heal, but bad words never
WORDS AND DEEDS
Striking manners are bad
manners   MANNERS
There is no such thing as bad
weather   WEATHER

baggage heaviest baggage for the
traveller   TRAVEL

bairns Fools and bairns should
never see   WORK

bait Fish follow the
bait   TEMPTATION

bake As you bake, so shall you
brew   CAUSES AND CONSEQUENCES

ban Ban the bomb   PEACE

bandits more laws, the more
thieves and bandits   LAW

bang Bang goes sixpence   THRIFT
bigger bang for a bigger
buck   WARFARE

banker father is a banker provided
by nature   PARENTS

bargain Don't bargain for fish that
are still   OPTIMISM AND PESSIMISM
It takes two to make a
bargain   COOPERATION

bark Dogs bark, but the caravan
goes   FUTILITY
Do not judge a tree by its
bark   APPEARANCE
Why keep a dog and bark
yourself   MANAGEMENT

barking barking dog never
bites   ACTION AND INACTION

barn cold April the barn will
fill   SPRING

Barnaby Barnaby bright, Barnaby
bright   SUMMER

barrel One spoonful of tar spoils a
barrel   QUANTITIES AND QUALITIES

base All your base are belong to
us   WINNING AND LOSING

basket Don't put all your eggs in
one basket   CAUTION
Each of us at a handle of the
basket   COOPERATION
With your food
basket   COOPERATION

battle race is not to the swift, nor
the battle   SUCCESS AND FAILURE

bayonet bayonet is a weapon with a worker WARFARE

be Be afraid. Be very afraid FEAR
Be what you would seem BEHAVIOUR
What must be, must be FATE

beans Candlemas day, put beans in the clay WINTER

bear Bear and forbear PATIENCE

beards It is merry in hall when beards wag all HOSPITALITY

bears bulls make money, the bears make BUYING AND SELLING

beat If you can't beat them, join them WAYS AND MEANS

beats It beats as it sweeps as it cleans HOUSEWORK

beautiful Black is beautiful BEAUTY
It is the beautiful bird BEAUTY
Small is beautiful QUANTITIES AND QUALITIES

beauty Beauty draws with a single hair BEAUTY
Beauty is a good letter BEAUTY
Beauty is in the eye of the beholder BEAUTY
Beauty is only skin deep BEAUTY
Beauty is power BEAUTY
Beauty without cruelty SUFFERING

beavers From beavers, bees should learn WORK

bed As you make your bed CAUSES AND CONSEQUENCES
Early to bed and early to rise HEALTH

bedfellows Adversity makes strange bedfellows ADVERSITY
Politics makes strange bedfellows POLITICS

bee bee sucks honey where the spider CHARACTER

beef Where's the beef QUANTITIES AND QUALITIES

been Been there, done that, got the T-shirt TRAVEL

beer he that drinks beer, thinks beer DRUNKENNESS
I'm only here for the beer DRINK
Life isn't all beer and skittles LIFE
Turkeys, heresy, hops, and beer CHANGE

bees From beavers, bees should learn WORK
Where bees are, there is honey WORK

before Dig the well before you are thirsty PREPARATION AND READINESS
Have an umbrella ready before it rains PREPARATION AND READINESS
I before e, except after c WORDS

beforehand Pay beforehand was never well BUSINESS

begets Love begets love LOVE

beggar Set a beggar on horseback POWER
Sue a beggar and catch a louse FUTILITY

beggars Beggars can't be choosers NECESSITY
If wishes were horses, beggars OPTIMISM AND PESSIMISM

beginning Beginning is easy BEGINNING
beginning of health is sleep SLEEP
beginning of wisdom is to call things NAMES
good beginning makes a good BEGINNING
In my end is my beginning ENDING

begins longest journey begins with a single BEGINNING

begun sooner begun, the sooner done BEGINNING

Well begun is half done BEGINNING

behaviour Good behaviour is the last BEHAVIOUR

behind Always in a hurry, always behind HASTE AND DELAY

Behind an able man ACHIEVEMENT

beholder Beauty is in the eye of the beholder BEAUTY

Belgium If it's Tuesday, this must be Belgium TRAVEL

believe Believe it or not TRUTH

Believe nothing of what you hear BELIEF

eyes believe themselves CERTAINTY AND DOUBT

Ohhh, I don't believe it BELIEF

believer believer is a songless bird BELIEF

believing Believing has a core of unbelieving BELIEF

Seeing is believing BELIEF

bellowing bellowing cow soon forgets her calf MOURNING

belong All your base are belong to us WINNING AND LOSING

I belong by blood relationship FAMILY

ben Se non è vero, è molto ben trovato TRUTH

bent As the twig is bent EDUCATION

Bermudas If the Bermudas let you pass SEA

best All's for the best OPTIMISM AND PESSIMISM

best doctors are Dr Quiet, Dr Diet MEDICINE

best fish swim near the bottom DETERMINATION

best of friends must part MEETING AND PARTING

best of men are but men at best HUMAN RACE

best place for criticism CRITICISM

best things in life are free MONEY

best time to plant a tree was TREES

Corruption of the best EXCELLENCE

East, west, home's best HOME

Experience is the best teacher EXPERIENCE

Good to forgive, best to forget FORGIVENESS

Honesty is the best policy HONESTY

Hope for the best and prepare for PREPARATION AND READINESS

Laughter is the best medicine MEDICINE

Life is the best gift LIFE

Of soup and love, the first is best FOOD

See all your best work go unnoticed SECRECY

Why should the devil have all the best MUSIC

better Be sure you can better your condition CHANGE

Better a dinner of herbs FEELINGS

Better an egg today than a hen tomorrow PRESENT

Better be an old man's darling MARRIAGE

Better be envied than pitied ENVY

Better be idle than ill doing IDLENESS

Better be safe than sorry CAUTION

Better be the head of a dog POWER

Better late than
never PUNCTUALITY
Better one house spoiled than
two MARRIAGE
better the day, the better the
deed WORK
Better the devil you
know FAMILIARITY
Better to light one candle ACTION
AND INACTION
Better to wear out than to
rust IDLENESS
Better wed over the
mixen FAMILIARITY
Democracy is better than
tyranny POLITICS
Example is better than precept
WORDS AND DEEDS
Half a loaf is better than no
bread SATISFACTION AND
DISCONTENT
half is better than the
whole MODERATION
It is better to give than to
receive GENEROSITY
It is better to travel
hopefully HOPE
less you know, the better you
sleep IGNORANCE
past always looks better PAST
Prevention is better than
cure FORESIGHT
Something is better than
nothing SATISFACTION AND
DISCONTENT
'Tis better to have loved and
lost LOVE
To change, and change for the
better CHANGE
Two heads are better than
one THINKING

between Between two stools one
falls INDECISION
hedge between keeps friendship
green NEIGHBOURS
wall between both best
preserves NEIGHBOURS
beware Beware of an oak,
it draws the
stroke TREES
Beware of the man of one
book BOOKS
beyond Beyond mountains there
are more DETERMINATION
big Big fish eat little fish POWER
No fist is big enough to hide the
sky GOVERNMENT
bigger bigger bang for a bigger
buck WARFARE
bigger they are, the harder they
fall SUCCESS AND FAILURE
Fear makes the wolf
bigger FEAR
bind Safe bind, safe find CAUTION
bird believer is a songless
bird BELIEF
bird in the hand is worth
two CAUTION
bird never flew on one
wing GENEROSITY
early bird catches the worm
PREPARATION AND READINESS
However high a bird may
soar ENVIRONMENT
It is the beautiful bird
that BEAUTY
It's an ill bird that fouls its own
nest LOYALTY
birds Birds in their little
nests ARGUMENT
Birds of a feather flock together
SIMILARITY AND DIFFERENCE

Birds of prey do not sing   BIRDS

Fine feathers make fine
birds   DRESS

Inside the forest there are many
birds   ABILITY

Little birds that can
sing   COOPERATION

There are no birds in last year's
nest   CHANGE

You cannot catch old
birds   EXPERIENCE

You cannot prevent the birds of
sorrow   SORROW

bishops bishops are made
men   CLERGY

bitch Life's a bitch, and then you
die   LIFE

bite bleating sheep loses a
bite   OPPORTUNITY

Dead men don't bite   ENEMIES

bites barking dog never bites
ACTION AND INACTION

bitten Once bitten by a
snake   CAUTION

Once bitten, twice
shy   EXPERIENCE

bitter Good medicine always has a
bitter taste   MEDICINE

Sour, sweet, bitter,
pungent   FATE

black Black is beautiful   BEAUTY

devil is not so black as he is
painted   REPUTATION

February fill dyke, be it black or
white   WINTER

blacks Two blacks don't make a
white   GOOD AND EVIL

blame Common fame is seldom to
blame   FAME

blames One who cannot dance
blames   DANCE

bleating bleating of the lamb
excites the
tiger   TEMPTATION

bleating sheep loses a
bite   OPPORTUNITY

bleeds Paper bleeds little   WRITING

blessed Blessed are the dead
that the rain   DEATH

Blessed is he who expects
nothing   HOPE

blessing Poverty is a blessing hated
by all   POVERTY

blessings Blessings brighten as they
take   HAPPINESS

blind Blind chance sweeps   CHANCE
AND LUCK

blind man's wife needs no
paint   APPEARANCE

deaf husband and a blind
wife   MARRIAGE

Love is blind   LOVE

Nothing so bold as a blind
mare   IGNORANCE

There's none so blind as those
PREJUDICE AND TOLERANCE

When the blind lead the
blind   IGNORANCE

blood Blood is thicker than
water   FAMILY

blood of the martyrs is the seed
CHRISTIAN CHURCH

Blood will have blood   MURDER

Blood will tell   FAMILY

I belong by blood
relationship   FAMILY

You cannot get blood from a
stone   FUTILITY

bloody bloody war and a sickly
season   ARMED FORCES

bloom When the furze is in
bloom   LOVE

When the gorse is out of bloom   LOVE

blow Blow your own horn, even if   ADVERTISING

North wind doth blow   WEATHER

blows It's an ill wind that blows nobody   OPTIMISM AND PESSIMISM

Straws tell which way the wind blows   KNOWLEDGE

blue Blue and green should never be   DRESS

Blue are the hills that are far   FAMILIARITY

Light the blue touch paper   DANGER

blush Truth makes the Devil blush   TRUTH

boat widow is a rudderless boat   MARRIAGE

boats rising tide lifts all boats   SUCCESS AND FAILURE

body Christ has no body now on earth   CHRISTIAN CHURCH

larger the body, the bigger the heart   BODY

boils pot boils, friendship lives   HOSPITALITY

watched pot never boils   PATIENCE

bold Nothing so bold as a blind mare   IGNORANCE

bomb Ban the bomb   PEACE

bond Englishman's word is his bond   COUNTRIES AND PEOPLES

bone Charity is not a bone   CHARITY

dog that will fetch a bone   GOSSIP

nearer the bone, the sweeter the meat   QUANTITIES AND QUALITIES

What's bred in the bone   CHARACTER

While two dogs are fighting for a bone   ARGUMENT

bones Hard words break no bones   WORDS

Sticks and stones may break my bones   WORDS

bonum De mortuis nil nisi *bonum*   REPUTATION

book Beware of the man of one book   BOOKS

book is like a garden   BOOKS

great book is a great evil   BOOKS

You can't tell a book by its cover   APPEARANCE

books Have you read any good books   READING

Borden Lizzie Borden took an axe   MURDER

born child that is born on the Sabbath   CHILDREN

Every Turk is born a soldier   COUNTRIES AND PEOPLES

If you're born to be hanged   FATE

It is better to be born lucky   CHANCE AND LUCK

man who is born in a stable   CHARACTER

Nobody is born learned   CLERGY

Yorkshire born and Yorkshire bred   BRITISH TOWNS AND REGIONS

borrowed March borrowed from April three days   SPRING

borrower Neither a borrower, nor a lender be   DEBT AND BORROWING

borrowing He that goes a-borrowing   DEBT AND BORROWING

borrows early man never borrows from the late   PREPARATION AND READINESS

bottles You can't put new wine in old bottles   CHANGE

bottom best fish swim near the bottom   DETERMINATION

bride Always a bridesmaid, never a bride WEDDINGS
Happy is the bride the sun shines on WEDDINGS

bridesmaid Always a bridesmaid, never a bride WEDDINGS

bridge Don't cross the bridge till you come to it PREPARATION AND READINESS
Everyone speaks well of the bridge MANNERS
It is good to make a bridge of gold WAYS AND MEANS
London Bridge is broken down BRITISH TOWNS AND REGIONS

bright Barnaby bright, Barnaby bright SUMMER
future's bright, the future's Orange FUTURE

brighten Blessings brighten as they take HAPPINESS

bring worth of a thing is what it will bring VALUE

Britain I'm backing Britain LOYALTY

broadens Travel broadens the mind TRAVEL

broke If it ain't broke ACTION AND INACTION

broken Although the branch is broken off CIRCUMSTANCE AND SITUATION
elephant does not die of one broken rib STRENGTH AND WEAKNESS
London Bridge is broken down BRITISH TOWNS AND REGIONS
Rules are made to be broken LAW
single arrow is easily broken COOPERATION

brooms New brooms sweep clean CHANGE

broth Too many cooks spoil the broth WORK

brother Am I not a man and a brother HUMAN RACE
My brother and I against my cousin FAMILY

brothers All arts are brothers COOPERATION

brown How now, brown cow SPEECH
quick brown fox jumps over the lazy dog WORDS

buck bigger bang for a bigger buck WARFARE

bucket Dig the well before you are thirsty PREPARATION AND READINESS

bug It's not a bug, it's a feature COMPUTING

build Fools build houses and wise men FOOLS
It is easier to build two ARCHITECTURE

building Building and marrying of children ARCHITECTURE
In settling an island, the first building ARCHITECTURE
No good building without ARCHITECTURE

built Rome was not built in a day PATIENCE

bull Bull markets climb a wall of worry BUSINESS

bulls bulls make money, the bears make BUYING AND SELLING

bully bully is always a coward COURAGE

bumping Education doesn't come by bumping EDUCATION

burden God makes the back to the burden SYMPATHY

burn Burn, baby, burn DEFIANCE
  Burn your bra WOMEN
  Hot water does not burn
  down FUTILITY
burnt burnt child dreads the
  fire EXPERIENCE
  If you play with fire you get
  burnt DANGER
bury Let the dead bury their
  dead MOURNING
bush Good wine needs no
  bush ADVERTISING
  Poke a bush, a snake
  comes CAUTION
busiest busiest men have the most
  leisure LEISURE
  Tomorrow is often the busiest
  day FUTURE
business Business before
  pleasure BUSINESS
  Business goes where it is
  invited BUSINESS
  Business is like a car BUSINESS
  Business is war BUSINESS
  Business neglected BUSINESS
  Everybody's business is
  nobody's RESPONSIBILITY
  Punctuality is the soul of
  business PUNCTUALITY
butter Fine words butter no
  parsnips WORDS AND DEEDS
  more butter, the worse
  cheese FOOD
buttered bread never falls but on its
  buttered side MISFORTUNES
button You press the button, we do
  the rest TECHNOLOGY
buy Buy in the cheapest market
  BUYING AND SELLING
  inch of gold cannot buy
  time TIME
  One white foot, buy him HORSES

Stop me and buy one FOOD
Why buy a cow when milk is so
cheap SEX
Would you buy a used car
from this man TRUST AND
TREACHERY
You buy land, you buy stones
  BUYING AND SELLING
buyer buyer has need of a
  hundred eyes BUYING AND
  SELLING
  Let the buyer beware BUYING AND
  SELLING
cabbage Twice-cooked cabbage is
  death FOOD
Caesar *Aut Caesar, aut
  nihil* AMBITION
caff ace caff with quite a nice
  museum HOSPITALITY
cake bad custom is like a good
  cake CUSTOM AND HABIT
  You cannot have your
  cake ACHIEVEMENT
calf bellowing cow soon forgets her
  calf MOURNING
call beginning of wisdom is to call
  things NAMES
  Call on God, but row
  away CAUTION
  Do not call a wolf to help
  you ENEMIES
  It is not what you call me NAMES
calls He who pays the piper calls the
  tune POWER
calm After a storm comes a
  calm PEACE
  In a calm sea every
  man ACHIEVEMENT
  It is the calm and silent
  water DANGER
cambric Can you make me a
  cambric shirt LOVE

camel He who steals an egg will
steal a camel HONESTY
Only the camel knows the
hundredth NAMES
Trust in Allah, but tie up your
camel CAUTION

camels Camels, fleas, and
princes ROYALTY
More doctors recommend
Camels SMOKING

camera camera never
lies TECHNOLOGY

candle Better to light one candle
ACTION AND INACTION
liar's candle lasts till evening LIES

Candlemas Candlemas day,
beans in the clay WINTER
If Candlemas day be sunny and
bright WINTER

canem Cave canem DOGS

cap If the cap fits, wear it NAMES

car Business is like a car BUSINESS
Would you buy a used car from
this man TRUST AND TREACHERY

caravan Dogs bark, but the caravan
goes FUTILITY

carborundum Nil carborundum
illegitimi DETERMINATION

carcase Where the carcase
is GREED

cards Lucky at cards, unlucky in
love CHANCE AND LUCK

care Care, and not fine
stables HORSES
Care killed the cat WORRY
Don't care was made to
care RESPONSIBILITY
Take care of the pence and the
pounds THRIFT

careful If you can't be good, be
careful CAUTION
Let's be careful CAUTION

careless Careless talk costs
lives GOSSIP

cares Children are certain
cares FAMILY

caribou caribou feeds the wolf
STRENGTH AND WEAKNESS

carpenter carpenter is known by his
chips APPEARANCE

carry You cannot carry two
watermelons FUTILITY

cart Don't put the cart before the
horse PATIENCE

Casbah Come with me to the
Casbah TRAVEL

cases Circumstances alter
cases CIRCUMSTANCE AND
SITUATION
Hard cases make bad law LAW

cash Cash is king MONEY

castle Englishman's home is his
castle HOME

cat Care killed the cat WORRY
cat always lands on its feet CATS
cat has nine lives CATS
cat in gloves catches no
mice CAUTION
cat may look at a king CATS
cat would eat fish INDECISION
cat, the rat, and Lovell the
dog GOVERNMENT
It hardly matters if it is a white cat
or WAYS AND MEANS
There are more ways of killing a
cat WAYS AND MEANS
There is more than one way to
skin a cat WAYS AND MEANS
Touch not the cat but a
glove CATS
When the cat's away, the mice
will OPPORTUNITY

catch First catch your hare WAYS
AND MEANS

Set a thief to catch a thief WAYS
AND MEANS

Sue a beggar and catch a
louse FUTILITY

catchee Softlee, softlee, catchee
monkey PATIENCE

catches Honey catches more
flies than vinegar WAYS
AND MEANS

catching Catching's before
hanging WAYS AND MEANS

cathedral Cathedral time is five
minutes later PUNCTUALITY

cats All cats are grey in the
dark SIMILARITY AND
DIFFERENCE

Keep no more cats than will catch
mice MODERATION

Wanton kittens make sober
cats YOUTH

cattle Hurry no man's
cattle PATIENCE

caught fish will soon be caught that
nibbles TEMPTATION

cause need not the cause CHARITY

caution Caution is the parent of
safety CAUTION

cave Cave canem DOGS

cease War will cease when men
refuse to fight WARFARE

certain Nothing is certain but
death CERTAINTY AND DOUBT

Nothing is certain but the
unforeseen FORESIGHT

chaff king's chaff is worth
more ROYALTY

chain chain is no stronger than its
weakest COOPERATION

challenge Meet the challenge—
make the change POLITICS

chance Blind chance sweeps
CHANCE AND LUCK

Moses took a chance CHANCE
AND LUCK

person who misses his
chance OPPORTUNITY

chances You have two chances
CHANCE AND LUCK

change change is as good as a
rest CHANGE

Change the name and not the
letter MARRIAGE

leopard does not change his
spots CHANGE

Meet the challenge—make the
change POLITICS

Times change and we with
time CHANGE

To change, and change for the
better CHANGE

changes Every two miles the water
changes TRAVEL

When the music
changes CHANGE

wise man changes his
mind FOOLS

channel Where water flows, a
channel PATIENCE

character Character is what we
are CHARACTER

Like a fence, character
cannot CHARACTER

charity Charity begins at
home CHARITY

Charity covers a multitude of
sins FORGIVENESS

Charity is not a bone CHARITY

Charity sees the need CHARITY

roots of charity are always
green CHARITY

charm third time is the charm
CHANCE AND LUCK

chase stern chase is a long
chase DETERMINATION

cheap It is as cheap sitting ACTION AND INACTION
Pile it high, sell it cheap BUSINESS
Talk is cheap WORDS AND DEEDS
Why buy a cow when milk is so cheap SEX

cheapest Buy in the cheapest market BUYING AND SELLING

cheats Cheats never prosper DECEPTION

cheeping May chickens come cheeping SPRING

cheese apple-pie without some cheese FOOD
more butter, the worse cheese FOOD
only free cheese is in a mousetrap TEMPTATION

cherries He who likes cherries ACHIEVEMENT

cherry cherry year, a merry year SUMMER

chess Chess is a sea where a gnat may drink SPORTS AND GAMES

Chester More than one yew bow in Chester DANGER

chewing So much chewing gum for the eyes BROADCASTING

chicken Kill the chicken to scare CAUSES AND CONSEQUENCES
Why did the chicken cross the road PROBLEMS AND SOLUTIONS

chickens Chickens are counted in the autumn AUTUMN
Curses, like chickens, come home FEELINGS
Don't count your chickens before OPTIMISM AND PESSIMISM
howlin' coyote ain't stealin' no chickens HONESTY

May chickens come cheeping SPRING

child burnt child dreads the fire EXPERIENCE
child is the father of the man CHARACTER
child of a frog is a frog FAMILY
child that is born on the Sabbath CHILDREN
Friday's child is loving and giving GENEROSITY
Give me a child for the first seven EDUCATION
He who takes the child by the hand PARENTS
It is a wise child that knows PARENTS
It takes a village to raise a child CHILDREN
Monday's child is fair of face BEAUTY
mother understands what the child PARENTS
Praise the child, and you make love to PARENTS
Saturday's child works hard for a living WORK
Thursday's child has far to go TRAVEL
Wednesday's child is full of woe SORROW

children Building and marrying of children ARCHITECTURE
Children and fools tell the truth HONESTY
Children are certain cares FAMILY
Children: one is one CHILDREN
Children should be seen and not CHILDREN
Heaven protects children, sailors DANGER

Little children, little
sorrows CHILDREN
Parents want their children to
become PARENTS
Women and children
first DANGER

chimneys It is easier to build two
chimneys ARCHITECTURE

chips carpenter is known by his
chips APPEARANCE

choice He that has a choice CHOICE
obvious choice is usually CHOICE

choose Never choose your women
or linen APPEARANCE
Of two evils choose the
less CHOICE

choosers Beggars can't be
choosers NECESSITY

Christ Christ has no body now on
earth CHRISTIAN CHURCH

Christian good Christian should
beware KNOWLEDGE

Christians Christians to the
lions CHRISTIAN CHURCH

Christmas Christmas comes but
once a year CHRISTMAS
Christmas is coming, and the
goose CHRISTMAS
devil makes his Christmas
pies LAW
dog is for life, not just for
Christmas DOGS
Green Christmas, white
Easter WEATHER
On the first day of
Christmas CHRISTMAS
Only — shopping days to
Christmas CHRISTMAS

church church is an anvil
CHRISTIAN CHURCH
church is God between four
walls CHRISTIAN CHURCH

He is a good dog who goes to
church BEHAVIOUR
nearer the church CHRISTIAN
CHURCH
Where God builds a church
GOOD AND EVIL
You can't build a church with
CHRISTIAN CHURCH

churchyard green Yule makes a fat
churchyard CHRISTMAS

cigar Happiness is a cigar called
Hamlet SMOKING

circle nature of of God is a
circle GOD
wheel has come full circle
CIRCUMSTANCE AND SITUATION

circumspice Si monumentum
requiris, circumspice
ARCHITECTURE

circumstances Circumstances
alter cases CIRCUMSTANCE AND
SITUATION
New circumstances, new
controls CIRCUMSTANCE AND
SITUATION

civil civil question deserves a civil
answer MANNERS

civility Civility costs
nothing MANNERS
There is nothing lost by
civility MANNERS

claws conceal their claws
SELF-ESTEEM AND SELF-ASSERTION

clay Candlemas day, put beans in
the clay WINTER
Sow corn in clay GARDENS

clean clean conscience is a good
pillow CONSCIENCE
New brooms sweep
clean CHANGE

cleanliness Cleanliness is next to
godliness BEHAVIOUR

cleans It beats as it sweeps as it cleans HOUSEWORK

clergymen Clergymen's sons always CLERGY

clever Clever hawks conceal their claws SELF-ESTEEM AND SELF-ASSERTION

click Clunk, click, every trip TRAVEL

climbers Hasty climbers have sudden falls AMBITION

climbs higher the monkey climbs AMBITION

clock Even a stopped clock is right twice a day TIME

clogs From clogs to clogs is only three SUCCESS AND FAILURE

close Do not close a letter without reading it LETTERS

closest Even your closest friends won't HEALTH

cloth Cut your coat according to your cloth PRACTICALITY

clothes Clothes make the man DRESS

cloud Every cloud has a silver lining OPTIMISM AND PESSIMISM

clout Ne'er cast a clout till May be out DRESS

clunk Clunk, click, every trip TRAVEL

clutch drowning man will clutch at a straw HOPE

coat Cut your coat according to your cloth PRACTICALITY

cobbler cobbler to his last and the gunner KNOWLEDGE
Let the cobbler stick to his last KNOWLEDGE
There will be trouble if the cobbler KNOWLEDGE

cock Every cock will crow upon his own HOME
There's many a good cock CHARACTER

coffee Coffee without tobacco SMOKING

coincidence It is a striking coincidence that COUNTRIES AND PEOPLES

coins If you have two coins LIFESTYLES
Proverbs are the coins of the people SAYINGS

coitum Post coitum omne animal triste SEX

cold As the day lengthens, so the cold WEATHER
cold April the barn will fill SPRING
Cold hands, warm heart BODY
Feed a cold and starve a fever SICKNESS
warm January, a cold May WEATHER

colour good horse cannot be of a bad colour APPEARANCE

comb Experience is the comb EXPERIENCE

come Come with me to the Casbah TRAVEL
Easy come, easy go EFFORT
Light come, light go POSSESSIONS
Quickly come, quickly go LOYALTY

comes Tomorrow never comes FUTURE
What goes around comes around JUSTICE

comfort Oh, the comfort— the inexpressible comfort FRIENDSHIP

comfortably Are you sitting comfortably? BEGINNING

Talk will not cook rice WORDS
AND DEEDS
cooks All are not cooks
who COOKING
Too many cooks spoil the
broth WORK
cooperation If you don't believe in
cooperation COOPERATION
If you think cooperation
is COOPERATION
core Believing has a core of
unbelieving BELIEF
corn Sow corn in clay GARDENS
Cornwall There are more saints in
Cornwall BRITISH TOWNS AND
REGIONS
corrupt Evil communications
corrupt BEHAVIOUR
corruption Corruption of the
best EXCELLENCE
Corruption will find a dozen
alibis CORRUPTION
corrupts Power corrupts POWER
costs Careless talk costs
lives GOSSIP
Civility costs nothing MANNERS
love letter sometimes costs
more LETTERS
cough Love and a cough LOVE
coughs Coughs and sneezes spread
diseases SICKNESS
could It could be you CHANCE
AND LUCK
councils Councils of war never
fight INDECISION
counsel fool may give a wise man
counsel ADVICE
Night brings counsel ADVICE
count Don't count your chickens
before OPTIMISM AND PESSIMISM
Eat the mangoes. Do not count
the trees WAYS AND MEANS

When angry count a
hundred ANGER
You can count the apples on one
tree QUANTITIES AND QUALITIES
counted Chickens are counted in
the autumn AUTUMN
country everyday story of
country folk COUNTRY AND
THE TOWN
God made the country COUNTRY
AND THE TOWN
Happy is the country HISTORY
If you have not lived in the
country COUNTRY AND
THE TOWN
You can take the boy out of the
country COUNTRY AND THE TOWN
Your King and Country need
you ARMED FORCES
courage Courage is fear
that COURAGE
Courage without
conduct COURAGE
course course of true love never did
run smooth LOVE
courses Horses for courses ABILITY
cousin My brother and I against my
cousin FAMILY
cover Duck and cover CAUTION
You can't tell a book by its
cover APPEARANCE
cow bellowing cow soon forgets her
calf MOURNING
Better a good cow CHARACTER
How now, brown cow SPEECH
It is idle to swallow the
cow DETERMINATION
Three acres and a cow POLITICS
Why buy a cow when milk is so
cheap SEX
coward bully is always a
coward COURAGE

cowards Cowards may die many times FEAR

cowl cowl does not make the monk APPEARANCE

coyote howlin' coyote ain't stealin' no chickens HONESTY

cradle hand that rocks the cradle rules WOMEN

creaking creaking door hangs longest SICKNESS

credit Conscience gets a lot of credit CONSCIENCE

Give credit where credit is due PRAISE AND FLATTERY

Crediton Kirton was a borough town BRITISH TOWNS AND REGIONS

cried I cried because I had no shoes MISFORTUNES

crime Crime doesn't pay CRIME AND PUNISHMENT

Crime leaves a trail like CRIME AND PUNISHMENT

Crime must be concealed CRIME AND PUNISHMENT

Poverty is not a crime POVERTY

crisis Every crisis provides an opportunity OPPORTUNITY

criticism best place for criticism CRITICISM

Criticism is something CRITICISM

crooked God writes straight with crooked lines CAUSES AND CONSEQUENCES

crop Good seed makes a bad crop CAUSES AND CONSEQUENCES

cross Don't cross the bridge till you come to it PREPARATION AND READINESS

No cross, no crown SUFFERING

Why did the chicken cross the road PROBLEMS AND SOLUTIONS

crosses Crosses are ladders that lead to heaven SUFFERING

crossing Life is harder than crossing a field LIFE

crow Every cock will crow upon his own HOME

One for the mouse, one for the crow NATURE

crowing whistling woman and a crowing hen WOMEN

crown No cross, no crown SUFFERING

crowns end crowns the work ENDING

crows On the first of March, crows begin SPRING

cruelty Beauty without cruelty SUFFERING

cry Don't cry before you're hurt COURAGE

Much cry and little wool EFFORT

Sing before breakfast, cry FEELINGS

crying It is no use crying over spilt milk MISFORTUNES

culture man without culture is like APPEARANCE

cunning I have a cunning plan THINKING

cup Full cup, steady hand CAUTION

last drop makes the cup run over EXCESS

There's many a slip 'twixt cup and lip MISTAKES

Cupar He that will to Cupar DETERMINATION

curantur Similia similibus curantur MEDICINE

cure drunkard's cure is drink again DRUNKENNESS

No cure, no pay BUSINESS

Prevention is better than cure FORESIGHT

cured What can't be cured must be endured PATIENCE

curried short horse is soon curried WORK

curses Curses, like chickens, come home FEELINGS

custom bad custom is like a good cake CUSTOM AND HABIT

Custom is mummified by habit CUSTOM AND HABIT

customer customer is always right BUSINESS

cut Cut your coat according to your cloth PRACTICALITY

Don't cut off your nose to spite REVENGE

Measure seven times, cut once PREPARATION AND READINESS

short cut is often a wrong cut WAYS AND MEANS

slice off a cut loaf isn't missed IGNORANCE

daddy Daddy, what did you do in the Great War ARMED FORCES

dance One who cannot dance blames DANCE

They that dance must pay the fiddler POWER

We're fools whether we dance or DANCE

dancer When you go to dance, take heed DANCE

dances He that lives in hope dances to an ill tune HOPE

dancing All dancing girls are nineteen YOUTH

You need more than dancing shoes DANCE

danger common danger causes common action DANGER

lone sheep is in danger from the wolf SOLITUDE

Out of debt, out of danger DEBT AND BORROWING

post of honour is the post of danger DANGER

dangerous Delays are dangerous HASTE AND DELAY

little knowledge is a dangerous thing KNOWLEDGE

dares Who dares wins DANGER

dark All cats are grey in the dark SIMILARITY AND DIFFERENCE

It is dark at the foot of the lighthouse IGNORANCE

It was a dark and stormy night BEGINNING

darkest darkest hour is just before dawn OPTIMISM AND PESSIMISM

darkness An inch ahead is darkness FUTURE

darling Better be an old man's darling MARRIAGE

daughter Like mother, like daughter FAMILY

dawn darkest hour is just before dawn OPTIMISM AND PESSIMISM

day Action this day ACTION AND INACTION

Another day, another dollar OPTIMISM AND PESSIMISM

apple a day keeps the doctor away HEALTH

As the day lengthens, so the cold WEATHER

Be the day weary or be the day long TIME

better the day, the better the deed WORK

day has eyes, the night has ears SECRECY

Every dog has his day OPPORTUNITY

first day of Christmas CHRISTMAS

Not a day without a line ART

Rome was not built in a
day PATIENCE

Sufficient unto the day is the
evil WORRY

Tomorrow is another
day FUTURE

Tomorrow is often the busiest
day FUTURE

What is done by night appears by
day SECRECY

Who teaches me for a day is my
father TEACHING

daydream Vision without action is a
daydream WORDS AND DEEDS

daylight morning daylight appears
plainer TIME

days Give us back our eleven
days TIME

He who can see three days
ahead FORESIGHT

March borrowed from April three
days SPRING

Treat your guest as a guest for
two days HOSPITALITY

dead Better red than dead CHOICE

Blessed are the dead that the
rain DEATH

Dead men don't bite ENEMIES

Dead men tell no tales SECRECY

It's ill waiting for dead men's
shoes AMBITION

Let the dead bury their
dead MOURNING

live dog is better than a dead
lion LIFE

Never speak ill of the
dead REPUTATION

Stone-dead hath no fellow DEATH

To dream of the dead is a sign of
rain DREAMS

deadly female of the species is more
deadly WOMEN

deaf deaf husband and a blind
wife MARRIAGE

There's none so deaf as those
PREJUDICE AND TOLERANCE

dear Experience keeps a dear
school EXPERIENCE

Far-fetched and
dear-bought WOMEN

Gold may be bought too
dear VALUE

death Death is nature's
way DEATH

Death is the great leveller DEATH

Death pays all debts DEATH

Life without a friend, is
death FRIENDSHIP

Nothing is certain but death
CERTAINTY AND DOUBT

They offered death CHOICE

Twice-cooked cabbage is
death FOOD

debt man in debt is caught in a
net DEBT AND BORROWING

national debt, if it is not
excessive DEBT AND
BORROWING

Out of debt, out of danger DEBT
AND BORROWING

debts Death pays all debts DEATH

deceit Deceit is a lie DECEPTION

deceptive Appearances are
deceptive APPEARANCE

declared When war is declared,
Truth is the first WARFARE

deed better the day, the better the
deed WORK

No good deed goes
unpunished VIRTUE

deep Still waters run
deep CHARACTER

deepest Where the river is deepest CHARACTER

defence Attack is the best form of defence COURAGE

deferred Hope deferred makes the heart sick HOPE

defiled He that touches pitch shall be defiled GOOD AND EVIL

delayed Justice delayed is justice denied JUSTICE

delays Delays are dangerous HASTE AND DELAY

Delhi Delhi is far away CAUTION

delight Red sky at night, shepherd's delight WEATHER

delved When Adam delved and Eve span RANK

democracy Democracy is better than tyranny POLITICS

denied Justice delayed is justice denied JUSTICE

deny Deny self for self's sake SELF-ESTEEM AND SELF-ASSERTION

deserve None but the brave deserve the fair COURAGE

desperate Desperate diseases must have NECESSITY

destroy Whom the gods would destroy MIND

determined determined fellow can do more with DETERMINATION

Devil Better the Devil you know FAMILIARITY

Devil can quote Scripture SAYINGS

Devil finds work for idle hands IDLENESS

Devil is not so black as he is painted REPUTATION

Devil looks after his own CHANCE AND LUCK

Devil makes his Christmas pies LAW

Devil was sick, the Devil a saint GRATITUDE

Devil's children have the Devil's luck CHANCE AND LUCK

Every man for himself, and the Devil SELF-INTEREST

Give the Devil his due JUSTICE

God sends meat, but the Devil COOKING

good painter can draw a devil ART

Haste is from the Devil HASTE AND DELAY

He who sups with the Devil CAUTION

Home is home, as the Devil said LAW

idle brain is the Devil's workshop IDLENESS

It is easier to raise the Devil BEGINNING

Needs must when the Devil drives NECESSITY

Never bid the Devil good morrow PROBLEMS AND SOLUTIONS

Talk of the Devil MEETING AND PARTING

Tell the truth and shame the Devil TRUTH

Truth makes the Devil blush TRUTH

What is got under the Devil's back GOOD AND EVIL

Why should the Devil have all the best MUSIC

Young saint, old devil HUMAN RACE

dew guest is like the morning dew HOSPITALITY

diamond Diamond cuts
diamond   CHARACTER
diamond is forever   WEALTH

die Cowards may die many
times   FEAR
Don't die of ignorance   HEALTH
Eat, drink and be merry, for
tomorrow   LIFESTYLES
elephant does not die of one
broken rib   STRENGTH AND
WEAKNESS
Good Americans when they die
COUNTRIES AND PEOPLES
good die young   VIRTUE
Life's a bitch, and then you
die   LIFE
More die of food than
famine   HEALTH
Old habits die hard   CUSTOM
AND HABIT
Old soldiers never die   ARMED
FORCES
See Naples and die   TOWNS AND
CITIES
Whom the gods love die
young   YOUTH
You can only die once   DEATH
You'll die facing the
monument   CRIME AND
PUNISHMENT
Young men may die, but old
men   DEATH

dies Call no man happy till he
dies   HAPPINESS
When an elder dies, it is as
if   AGE
When a tiger dies it leaves its
skin   REPUTATION

diet best doctors are Dr Quiet,
Dr Diet   MEDICINE

differ Tastes differ   LIKES AND
DISLIKES

different Different strokes for
different folks   CHOICE

difficult difficult is done at
once   ACHIEVEMENT
Equality is difficult, but
superiority   LEADERSHIP

difficulty England's difficulty
is Ireland's   COUNTRIES AND
PEOPLES

dig Dig for victory   GARDENS
Dig the well before you are
thirsty   PREPARATION AND
READINESS
If you want revenge, dig two
graves   REVENGE

digging When you are in a hole,
stop digging   APOLOGY AND
EXCUSES

diligence Diligence is the mother
of   CHANCE AND LUCK

dinner After dinner rest a
while   EATING
better the salad, the worse the
dinner   COOKING
No dinner without bread   FOOD

dirt Throw dirt enough, and some
will stick   REPUTATION
We must eat a peck of
dirt   EATING

dirty Dirty water will
quench fire   SEX
One does not wash one's dirty
linen   SECRECY
You dirty rat   CHARACTER

discretion Discretion is the better
part   CAUTION

disease Life is a sexually transmitted
disease   LIFE

diseases Coughs and sneezes spread
diseases   SICKNESS
Desperate diseases must
have   NECESSITY

disgrace Poverty is no
disgrace POVERTY

dish Better are small fish than an
empty dish SATISFACTION AND
DISCONTENT
Revenge is a dish that can be
eaten REVENGE

disillusion Absence is the mother of
disillusion ABSENCE

disposes Man proposes, God
disposes FATE

distance Distance lends
enchantment APPEARANCE

divide Divide and
rule GOVERNMENT

divided United we stand, divided
we COOPERATION

divine To err is human (to forgive
divine) MISTAKES

do Do as I say, not as I
do BEHAVIOUR
Do as you would be done
by LIFESTYLES
Do unto others as you would
they LIFESTYLES
Make do and mend THRIFT
Not guilty, but don't do it
again GUILT
You never know what you can
do COURAGE

doctor apple a day keeps the
doctor away HEALTH
Dr Williams' pink pills for pale
people MEDICINE

doctors best doctors are Dr Quiet,
Dr Diet MEDICINE
More doctors recommend
Camels SMOKING

doers Evil doers are evil
dreaders CONSCIENCE

does Does she ... or doesn't she
CERTAINTY AND DOUBT

dog barking dog never bites
ACTION AND INACTION
Better be the head of a
dog POWER
Brag is a good dog, but
Holdfast WORDS AND DEEDS
cat, the rat, and Lovell the
dog GOVERNMENT
Dog does not eat
dog COOPERATION
dog is a lion in his own
house DOGS
dog is for life, not just for
Christmas DOGS
dog that will fetch a bone GOSSIP
Every dog has his
day OPPORTUNITY
Feed a dog for three days CATS
Give a dog a bad name and
hang GOSSIP
He is a good dog who goes to
church BEHAVIOUR
If you are not the lead
dog LEADERSHIP
It is a poor dog that's not
worth VALUE
It is easy to find a stick to beat a
dog APOLOGY AND EXCUSES
live dog is better than a dead
lion LIFE
Love me, love my dog DOGS
quick brown fox jumps over the
lazy dog WORDS
There are more ways of
killing a dog WAYS AND
MEANS
Why keep a dog and bark
yourself MANAGEMENT
woman, a dog, and a walnut
tree WOMEN
You can't teach an old dog new
tricks CUSTOM AND HABIT

dogged It's dogged as does it DETERMINATION

dogs Dogs bark, but the caravan goes FUTILITY
If you lie down with dogs FAMILIARITY
Let sleeping dogs lie CAUTION
While two dogs are fighting ARGUMENT

dollar Another day, another dollar OPTIMISM AND PESSIMISM

done Do as you would be done by SELF-INTEREST
If you want a thing done well SELF-INTEREST
If you want something done ACTION AND INACTION
Whatever man has done ACHIEVEMENT
What's done cannot be undone PAST

don't Don't ask, don't tell SECRECY
Don't care was made to care RESPONSIBILITY

door creaking door hangs longest SICKNESS
door must be either shut or open CHOICE
golden key can open any door CORRUPTION
postern door makes a thief OPPORTUNITY
Teachers open the door EDUCATION
When one door shuts, another opens OPPORTUNITY
When poverty comes in at the door POVERTY

dose dose of adversity is often ADVERSITY

double Shared joy is double joy SYMPATHY

doubt When in doubt, do nowt ACTION AND INACTION

dough Drive for show, and putt for dough SPORTS AND GAMES

down Up like a rocket, down like a stick SUCCESS AND FAILURE
What goes up must come down FATE

dragons Dragons beget dragons FAMILY
Here be dragons TRAVEL

drama We won't make a drama out of CAUTION

draw good painter can draw a devil ART

draws Whosoever draws his sword against REVOLUTION AND REBELLION

dreaders Evil doers are evil dreaders CONSCIENCE

dream Dream of a funeral DREAMS
Peace is the dream of the wise PEACE
To dream of the dead is a sign of rain DREAMS
You cannot dream yourself into CHARACTER

dreams Dreams go by contraries DREAMS
Dreams retain the infirmities of DREAMS
God sleeps in the stone, dreams HUMAN RACE
Morning dreams come true DREAMS

drink Don't ask a man to drink and drive DRINK
drunkard's cure is drink again DRUNKENNESS
Eat, drink and be merry, for tomorrow LIFESTYLES

When you drink water, remember GRATITUDE

drinka Drinka Pinta Milka HEALTH

drinking When drinking water, remember the PARENTS

drinks he that drinks beer, thinks beer DRUNKENNESS

dripping dripping June sets all in tune SUMMER

drive Don't ask a man to drink and drive DRINK
Drive for show, and putt for dough SPORTS AND GAMES

drives Needs must when the devil drives NECESSITY
One nail drives out another SIMILARITY AND DIFFERENCE

drop last drop makes the cup run over EXCESS

dropping Constant dropping wears away DETERMINATION

drops Drops that gather one by one QUANTITIES AND QUALITIES

drowning drowning man will clutch at a straw HOPE

drunk You have drunk from wells you did not PAST

drunkard drunkard's cure is drink again DRUNKENNESS

druv Sussex won't be druv BRITISH TOWNS AND REGIONS

dry Sow dry and set wet GARDENS

duck Duck and cover CAUTION

due Give credit where credit is due PRAISE AND FLATTERY
Give the Devil his due JUSTICE

dumb It takes forty dumb animals DRESS

duster Rooster today, feather duster tomorrow SUCCESS AND FAILURE

duty first duty of a soldier ARMED FORCES

dyke February fill dyke, be it black or white WINTER

eagle Only the eagle can gaze at the sun STRENGTH AND WEAKNESS

eagles Eagles don't catch flies CHARACTER

earlier Here's one I made earlier PREPARATION AND READINESS

early Don't hurry—start early HASTE AND DELAY
early bird catches the worm PREPARATION AND READINESS
early man never borrows from the late PREPARATION AND READINESS
Early to bed and early to rise HEALTH
Vote early and vote often POLITICS

earned penny saved is a penny earned THRIFT

ears day has eyes, the night has ears SECRECY
Fields have eyes and woods have ears SECRECY
Little pitchers have large ears SECRECY
Walls have ears SECRECY

earth Did the earth move for you SEX
earth is man's only friend ENVIRONMENT
earth laughs at him who ENVIRONMENT
Touch the earth lightly ENVIRONMENT

We do not inherit the
earth ENVIRONMENT
easier It is easier to build two
chimneys ARCHITECTURE
It is easier to raise the
Devil BEGINNING
east East is east, and west is
west SIMILARITY AND DIFFERENCE
East, west, home's best HOME
When the wind is in the
east WEATHER
Easter Green Christmas, white
Easter WEATHER
easy Beginning is easy BEGINNING
Easy come, easy go EFFORT
It is easy to be generous
with GENEROSITY
It is easy to be wise after the
event FORESIGHT
It is easy to find a stick to beat a
dog APOLOGY AND EXCUSES
eat Dog does not eat
dog COOPERATION
Eat, drink and be merry, for
tomorrow LIFESTYLES
Eat leeks in March and ramsons in
May HEALTH
Eat the mangoes. Do not
count the trees WAYS AND
MEANS
Eat to live, not live to eat EATING
Fear less, hope more; Eat
less LIFESTYLES
If you won't work you shan't
eat IDLENESS
We must eat a peck of
dirt EATING
You are what you eat EATING
eaten Revenge is a dish that can be
eaten REVENGE
eating Appetite comes with
eating EXPERIENCE

proof of the pudding is in the
eating HYPOTHESIS AND FACT
eats way one eats is the way one
works EATING
education Education doesn't come
by bumping EDUCATION
Genius without
education EDUCATION
Never let your
education EDUCATION
ee Ee, it was agony, Ivy SUFFERING
egg As good be an addled
egg IDLENESS
Better an egg today than a hen
tomorrow PRESENT
Go to work on an egg EATING
He who steals an egg will steal a
camel HONESTY
Power is like an egg POWER
same fire that hardens the
egg CHARACTER
eggs Don't put all your eggs in one
basket CAUTION
There is reason in the roasting of
eggs CAUSES AND CONSEQUENCES
You can't unscramble scrambled
eggs FUTILITY
egoism Apology is only
egoism APOLOGY AND EXCUSES
elder When an elder dies, it is
as if AGE
elementary Elementary, my dear
Watson THINKING
elephant elephant does not die of
one broken rib STRENGTH AND
WEAKNESS
When an elephant is in
trouble SUCCESS AND FAILURE
elephants Elephants are
contagious WORDS
When elephants fight, it is the
grass POWER

eleven Give us back our eleven days TIME

Rain before seven, fine before eleven WEATHER

elm Every elm has its man TREES

emperor mountains are high, and the emperor GOVERNMENT

empty Better are small fish than an empty dish SATISFACTION AND DISCONTENT

Empty sacks will never stand upright POVERTY

Empty vessels make the most sound FOOLS

enchantment Distance lends enchantment APPEARANCE

end All good things must come to an end ENDING

end crowns the work ENDING

End good, all good ENDING

end justifies the means WAYS AND MEANS

Everything has an end ENDING

He who wills the end DETERMINATION

In my end is my beginning ENDING

sea of learning has no end KNOWLEDGE

endured What can't be cured must be endured PATIENCE

enemy Action is worry's worst enemy ACTION AND INACTION

enemy of my enemy is my friend ENEMIES

Love your enemy ENEMIES

Man is the enemy of IGNORANCE

Science has no enemy but the ignorant SCIENCE

There is no little enemy ENEMIES

England England is the paradise of women COUNTRIES AND PEOPLES

England's difficulty is Ireland's COUNTRIES AND PEOPLES

Englishman Englishman's home is his castle HOME

Englishman's word is his bond COUNTRIES AND PEOPLES

enjoy Enjoy the present moment PRESENT

enjoyable Idleness is never enjoyable IDLENESS

enlightened mind enlightened is like heaven MIND

enough Enough is as good as a feast MODERATION

Enough is enough MODERATION

envied Better be envied than pitied ENVY

envy Envy feeds on the living ENVY

If envy were a fever ENVY

equality Equality is difficult, but superiority LEADERSHIP

err To err is human but to really COMPUTING

To err is human (to forgive divine) MISTAKES

error old error is always more popular TRUTH

Essex Essex stiles, Kentish miles BRITISH TOWNS AND REGIONS

eternal Hope springs eternal HOPE

eve When Adam delved and Eve span RANK

even Don't get mad, get even REVENGE

evening liar's candle lasts till evening LIES

morning knows no more than the evening SLEEP

---

event It is easy to be wise after the event FORESIGHT

events Coming events cast their shadow FUTURE

ever Are you now or have you ever been POLITICS

Nothing is for ever CHANGE

every Every man to his taste LIKES AND DISLIKES

Every painter paints himself ART

everybody Everybody's business is nobody's RESPONSIBILITY

What everybody says must be true TRUTH

everyday everyday story of country folk COUNTRY AND THE TOWN

everything Everything has an end ENDING

Money isn't everything MONEY

There is a time for everything TIME

evidence What the soldier said isn't evidence GOSSIP

evil Don't be evil COMPUTING

Evil communications corrupt BEHAVIOUR

Evil doers are evil dreaders CONSCIENCE

great book is a great evil BOOKS

Money is the root of all evil MONEY

Never do evil that good may come BEHAVIOUR

See no evil, hear no evil, speak no evil VIRTUE

Sufficient unto the day is the evil WORRY

evils Of two evils choose the less CHOICE

example Example is better than precept WORDS AND DEEDS

exception exception proves the rule HYPOTHESIS AND FACT

There is an exception to every rule HYPOTHESIS AND FACT

exceptional Exceptional times require NECESSITY

excessive national debt, if it is not excessive DEBT AND BORROWING

exchange fair exchange is no robbery JUSTICE

excuse bad excuse is better than APOLOGY AND EXCUSES

Excuse (or pardon) my French APOLOGY AND EXCUSES

Ignorance of the law is no excuse LAW

excuses Don't make excuses APOLOGY AND EXCUSES

He who excuses himself, accuses APOLOGY AND EXCUSES

exercise Those who do not find time for exercise HEALTH

expands Work expands so as to fill the time WORK

expect What can you expect from a pig CHARACTER

expects Blessed is he who expects nothing HOPE

experience Experience is the best teacher EXPERIENCE

Experience is the comb EXPERIENCE

Experience is the father EXPERIENCE

Experience keeps a dear school EXPERIENCE

Some folks speak from experience EXPERIENCE

express American Express? ... That'll do DEBT AND BORROWING

extremes Extremes meet
SIMILARITY AND DIFFERENCE

extremity Man's extremity is God's
opportunity RELIGION

eye Beauty is in the eye of the
beholder BEAUTY

eye for an eye makes REVENGE

eye of a master does more
work EMPLOYMENT

Keep one eye on the
frying-pan COOKING

Please your eye and
plague BEAUTY

What the eye doesn't see, the
heart IGNORANCE

eyes buyer has need of a
hundred eyes BUYING
AND SELLING

day has eyes, the night has
ears SECRECY

eyes are the window of the
soul BODY

eyes believe themselves
CERTAINTY AND DOUBT

Fields have eyes and woods have
ears SECRECY

Four eyes see more than
two COOPERATION

Hawks will not pick out hawks'
eyes COOPERATION

So much chewing gum for the
eyes BROADCASTING

fable History is a fable HISTORY

face He who slaps his own
face MISTAKES

Monday's child is fair of
face BEAUTY

Turn your face to the sun
OPTIMISM AND PESSIMISM

fact Fact is stranger than
fiction TRUTH

facts Facts are stubborn
things HYPOTHESIS
AND FACT

fail He who fails to plan, plans to
fail SUCCESS AND FAILURE

To fail to prepare is to prepare to
fail PREPARATION AND READINESS

fails He who fails to plan, plans to
fail SUCCESS AND FAILURE

When all fruit fails, welcome
haws NECESSITY

failure Success has many
fathers, while failure SUCCESS AND
FAILURE

faint Faint heart never won fair
lady COURAGE

fair All's fair in love and
war JUSTICE

Faint heart never won fair
lady COURAGE

fair exchange is no
robbery JUSTICE

Fair play's a jewel JUSTICE

fair skin hides seven
defects APPEARANCE

Give and take is fair play JUSTICE

Monday's child is fair of
face BEAUTY

None but the brave deserve the
fair COURAGE

Saint Swithin's day, if thou be
fair SUMMER

Turn about is fair play JUSTICE

faith Faith will move
mountains BELIEF

fall bigger they are, the harder they
fall SUCCESS AND FAILURE

Even monkeys sometimes fall
off a tree MISTAKES

Fall seven times, stand up
eight DETERMINATION

Pride goes before a fall PRIDE

Spring forward, fall back TIME

fallen Do not laugh at the fallen SUCCESS AND FAILURE

falling Falling leaves have to return HOME

falls apple never falls far from the tree FAMILY

As a tree falls, so shall it lie DEATH

Between two stools one falls INDECISION

Hasty climbers have sudden falls AMBITION

If the sky falls we shall catch larks EFFORT

falsehood To tell a falsehood is like the cut of LIES

fame Common fame is seldom to blame FAME

familiarity Familiarity breeds contempt FAMILIARITY

family family that prays together stays RELIGION

large family, quick help FAMILY

famine More die of food than famine HEALTH

far Delhi is far away CAUTION

Far-fetched and dear-bought WOMEN

God is high above, and the tsar GOVERNMENT

long time ago in a galaxy far, far away TIME

Thursday's child has far to go TRAVEL

fast Bad news travels fast NEWS AND JOURNALISM

He who travels fast, travels alone COOPERATION

moneyless man goes fast through POVERTY

fastest He travels the fastest who travels alone SOLITUDE

fat green Yule makes a fat churchyard CHRISTMAS

opera isn't over till the fat lady sings ENDING

Pigs get fat, but hogs get GREED

fatal Indecision is fatal INDECISION

fate Fate can be taken by the horns FATE

father child is the father of the man CHARACTER

father is a banker provided by nature PARENTS

Like father, like son FAMILY

Who teaches me for a day is my father TEACHING

wish is father to the thought OPINION

fathers Success has many fathers, while failure SUCCESS AND FAILURE

fault fault confessed is half redressed FORGIVENESS

Our memory is always at fault MIND

faults Wink at sma' fauts, ye hae great anes MISTAKES

favour Every good boy deserves favour MUSIC

Kissing goes by favour LOVE

fear Courage is fear that COURAGE

Do right and fear no man CONSCIENCE

Fear less, hope more; Eat less LIFESTYLES

Fear makes the wolf bigger FEAR

Fear the Greeks bearing gifts TRUST AND TREACHERY

feast After the feast, comes the reckoning CAUSES AND CONSEQUENCES
company makes the feast HOSPITALITY
Enough is as good as a feast MODERATION

feather Birds of a feather flock together SIMILARITY AND DIFFERENCE
Rooster today, feather duster tomorrow SUCCESS AND FAILURE

feathers Fine feathers make fine birds DRESS

feature It's not a bug, it's a feature COMPUTING

February February fill dyke, be it black or white WINTER

fed wolves are well fed and the sheep DANGER

feed Feed a cold and starve a fever SICKNESS
Feed a dog for three days CATS
Give a man a fish, and you feed CHARITY

feeding Feeding a snake with milk CHARACTER

feeds Envy feeds on the living ENVY

feel Never mind the quality, feel the width QUANTITIES AND QUALITIES

feet cat always lands on its feet CATS
When you pray, move your feet RELIGION

fellow Stone-dead hath no fellow DEATH

female female of the species is more deadly WOMEN

fence fence between makes love more CAUSES AND CONSEQUENCES

Like a fence, character cannot CHARACTER

fences Good fences make good neighbours NEIGHBOURS

fern As one fern frond dies, another LEADERSHIP

fever Feed a cold and starve a fever SICKNESS
If envy were a fever ENVY

few Few have too much, and fewer too little WEALTH
You win a few, you lose a few SUCCESS AND FAILURE

fiction Fact is stranger than fiction TRUTH
History is fiction HISTORY
Truth is stranger than fiction TRUTH

fiddler They that dance must pay the fiddler POWER

field Life is harder than crossing a field LIFE

fields Fields have eyes and woods have ears SECRECY

fifth Please to remember the Fifth TRUST AND TREACHERY

fight Councils of war never fight INDECISION
Fight fire with fire WAYS AND MEANS
War will cease when men refuse to fight WARFARE
When elephants fight POWER

fighting While two dogs are fighting ARGUMENT

fights He who fights and runs away CAUTION

fill Work expands so as to fill the time WORK

find Safe bind, safe find CAUTION
Seek and ye shall find ACTION AND INACTION

Speak as you find REPUTATION
Those who hide can find SECRECY
finders Finders keepers (losers weepers) POSSESSIONS
Seekers are finders ACHIEVEMENT
findings Findings keepings POSSESSIONS
fine Fine feathers make fine birds DRESS
Fine words butter no parsnips WORDS AND DEEDS
Rain before seven, fine before eleven WEATHER
finger Whose finger do you want CHOICE
fingers Fingers were made before forks EATING
Let your fingers do the walking TECHNOLOGY
finish I've started so I'll finish BEGINNING
fire burnt child dreads the fire EXPERIENCE
Dirty water will quench fire SEX
Fight fire with fire WAYS AND MEANS
Fire is a good servant, but a bad master WAYS AND MEANS
fire is winter's fruit WINTER
If you play with fire you get burnt DANGER
It is easy to kindle a fire RELATIONSHIPS
No smoke without fire REPUTATION
same fire that hardens CHARACTER
fired No manager ever got fired COMPUTING
first First catch your hare WAYS AND MEANS

first day a guest, the second day HOSPITALITY
First impressions are BEGINNING
First things first PATIENCE
First thoughts are best INDECISION
Give me a child for the first seven EDUCATION
If at first you don't succeed DETERMINATION
In settling an island, the first building ARCHITECTURE
It is the first step BEGINNING
No plan survives first contact PREPARATION AND READINESS
On the first day of Christmas CHRISTMAS
On the first of March, crows begin SPRING
There is always a first time BEGINNING
Women and children first DANGER
fish All is fish that comes to the net OPPORTUNITY
best fish swim near the bottom DETERMINATION
Better are small fish than an empty dish SATISFACTION AND DISCONTENT
Big fish eat little fish POWER
cat would eat fish INDECISION
Don't bargain for fish that are still OPTIMISM AND PESSIMISM
fish always stinks from the head LEADERSHIP
Fish and guests stink after three days HOSPITALITY
Fish follow the bait TEMPTATION
fish will soon be caught that nibbles TEMPTATION

Fish, to taste good, must swim COOKING

Give a man a fish, and you feed CHARITY

Keep your own fish-guts CHARITY

Little fish are sweet QUANTITIES AND QUALITIES

There are as good fish in the sea LOVE

Those who eat salty fish RESPONSIBILITY

fishing It is good fishing in troubled waters OPPORTUNITY

fist No fist is big enough to hide the sky GOVERNMENT

fit One size does not fit all WAYS AND MEANS

fits If the cap fits, wear it NAMES

If the shoe fits, wear it NAMES

five Cathedral time is five minutes later PUNCTUALITY

fix If it ain't broke, don't fix it ACTION AND INACTION

Jim'll fix it PROBLEMS AND SOLUTIONS

flag Trade follows the flag BUSINESS

flagpole Let's run it up the flagpole ADVERTISING

flattery Flattery is soft soap PRAISE AND FLATTERY

Flattery, like perfume PRAISE AND FLATTERY

Imitation is the sincerest form of flattery PRAISE AND FLATTERY

fleas fleas, and princes ROYALTY

flee guilty flee when no man pursueth GUILT

flew bird never flew on one wing GENEROSITY

flexible Access—your flexible friend DEBT AND BORROWING

flies Eagles don't catch flies CHARACTER

Honey catches more flies than vinegar WAYS AND MEANS

shut mouth catches no flies SILENCE

Time flies TRANSIENCE

flight While heron is a bird of a single flight BIRDS

floats No matter how long a log floats CHANGE

flock Birds of a feather flock together SIMILARITY AND DIFFERENCE

There is no good flock without DOGS

flow Do not push the river, it will flow FUTILITY

flowers All the flowers of tomorrow FLOWERS

April showers bring forth May flowers SPRING

No flowers by request MOURNING

Say it with flowers FLOWERS

flows Where water flows, a channel PATIENCE

fly Pigs may fly BELIEF

foe willing foe and sea room ARMED FORCES

fold Do not fold, spindle or COMPUTING

folk everyday story of country folk COUNTRY AND THE TOWN

There's nowt so queer as folk HUMAN RACE

folks Different strokes for different folks CHOICE

Young folks think old folks to be fools YOUTH

follow Fish follow the bait TEMPTATION

follower good leader is also a good follower LEADERSHIP

follows He that follows freits FUTURE

Learning is a treasure that follows KNOWLEDGE

fonder Absence makes the heart grow fonder ABSENCE

food Food without hospitality is medicine HOSPITALITY

More die of food than famine HEALTH

With your food basket COOPERATION

Your food is your medicine HEALTH

fool fool and his money are soon parted FOOLS

fool at forty is a fool indeed AGE

fool may give a wise man ADVICE

Fool me once, shame on you DECEPTION

He that teaches himself has a fool for TEACHING

man who is his own lawyer has a fool LAW

There's no fool like an old fool AGE

foolish Penny wise and pound foolish THRIFT

fools Children and fools tell the truth HONESTY

Fools and bairns should never see WORK

Fools ask questions that wise men KNOWLEDGE

Fools build houses and wise men FOOLS

Fools for luck CHANCE AND LUCK

Fortune favours fools FOOLS

We're fools whether we dance or DANCE

Young folks think old folks to be fools YOUTH

foot It is dark at the foot of the lighthouse IGNORANCE

No foot, no horse HORSES

One white foot, buy him HORSES

for Mummy, what's that man for? POLITICS

forbear Bear and forbear PATIENCE

forearmed Forewarned is forearmed PREPARATION AND READINESS

foresight If a man's foresight were as good FORESIGHT

forest Inside the forest there are many birds ABILITY

When a pine needle falls in the forest KNOWLEDGE

When the axe came into the forest OPTIMISM AND PESSIMISM

foretold Long foretold, long last WEATHER

forever diamond is forever WEALTH

forewarned Forewarned is forearmed PREPARATION AND READINESS

forget Good to forgive, best to forget FORGIVENESS

Tell me and I'll forget. Show me and TEACHING

forgets bellowing cow soon forgets her calf MOURNING

Nobody forgets a good teacher TEACHING

river that forgets its source GRATITUDE

forgive Good to forgive, best to forget FORGIVENESS

To err is human (to forgive divine) MISTAKES

To know all is to forgive
all FORGIVENESS

forgiving Forgiving the
unrepentant FORGIVENESS

forks Fingers were made before
forks EATING

Fortran If you can't do it in
Fortran COMPUTING

fortune Fortune favours
fools FOOLS

Fortune favours the
brave COURAGE

great fortune depends on luck
CHANCE AND LUCK

forty fool at forty is a fool
indeed AGE

It takes forty dumb
animals DRESS

Life begins at forty AGE

forward Spring forward, fall
back TIME

fouls It's an ill bird that fouls its
own nest LOYALTY

foundation Adversity is the
foundation ADVERSITY

four Four eyes see more than
two COOPERATION

fox fox may grow grey, but
never AGE

fox should not be on the
jury JUSTICE

quick brown fox jumps over the
lazy dog WORDS

sleeping fox counts
hens CHARACTER

free best things in life are
free MONEY

only free cheese is in a
mousetrap TEMPTATION

There's no such thing as a free
lunch TEMPTATION

Thought is free OPINION

freedom passion for freedom never
dies POLITICS

freits He that follows freits FUTURE

French Excuse (or pardon)
my French APOLOGY AND
EXCUSES

No more Latin, no more
French EDUCATION

Friday Friday's child is loving and
giving GENEROSITY

friend Access—your flexible
friend DEBT AND BORROWING

earth is man's only
friend ENVIRONMENT

enemy of my enemy is my
friend ENEMIES

friend in need is a friend
indeed FRIENDSHIP

Hold a true friend with both your
hands FRIENDSHIP

Lend your money, and lose
your friend DEBT AND
BORROWING

Life without a friend, is
death FRIENDSHIP

Phone a friend COOPERATION

friends Be kind to your
friends FRIENDSHIP

best of friends must part MEETING
AND PARTING

Even your closest friends
won't HEALTH

Save us from our
friends FRIENDSHIP

Short reckonings make long
friends DEBT AND BORROWING

1We have no friends but the
mountains DANGER

friendship hedge between keeps
friendship green NEIGHBOURS

pot boils, friendship
lives HOSPITALITY

frog child of a frog is a frog FAMILY
frog in a well knows nothing
of SELF-ESTEEM AND SELF-ASSERTION
frond As one fern frond dies,
another LEADERSHIP
frosts So many mists in March, so
many frosts SPRING
fruit fire is winter's fruit WINTER
He that would eat fruit EFFORT
September blow soft till the
fruit's AUTUMN
Stolen fruit are
sweet TEMPTATION
tree is known by its
fruit CHARACTER
When all fruit fails, welcome
haws NECESSITY
frying Keep one eye on the
frying-pan COOKING
Fuji wise man will climb Mount Fuji
once TRAVEL
full Full cup, steady hand CAUTION
It's ill speaking between a full
man FOOD
fullness Out of the fullness of the
heart FEELINGS
funeral Dream of a funeral DREAMS
One funeral makes many DEATH
furrow old horse does not spoil the
furrow AGE
further Go further and fare
worse SATISFACTION AND
DISCONTENT
fury Hell hath no fury like a woman
scorned WOMEN
furze When the furze is in
bloom LOVE
future future's bright, the future's
Orange FUTURE
man's best reputation for his
future REPUTATION

There's no future like the
present FUTURE
gain No pain, no gain EFFORT
Nothing venture, nothing
gain THOROUGHNESS
One man's loss is another
man's gain CIRCUMSTANCE AND
SITUATION
There's no great loss without
CIRCUMSTANCE AND SITUATION
galaxy long time ago in a galaxy far,
far away TIME
game After the game, the king and
the pawn DEATH
Lookers-on see most of the
game ACTION AND INACTION
gamekeeper old poacher makes the
best gamekeeper WAYS AND MEANS
garbage Garbage in, garbage
out COMPUTING
garden book is like a garden BOOKS
More things grow in the
garden GARDENS
Select a proper site for your
garden GARDENS
gardener It is not enough for a
gardener FLOWERS
garment Silence is a woman's best
garment WOMEN
gather Drops that gather one
by one QUANTITIES AND
QUALITIES
gaze Only the eagle can gaze
at the sun STRENGTH AND
WEAKNESS
generation One generation plants
the trees TREES
generations It takes three
generations to make RANK
generous Be just before you're
generous JUSTICE

It is easy to be generous with GENEROSITY

genius Genius is an infinite capacity ABILITY

gentleman You may know a gentleman by RANK

germs Kills all known germs ENVIRONMENT

get I didn't get where I am today EFFORT

more you get the more you want GREED

Mounties always get their man COUNTRIES AND PEOPLES

ghosties From ghoulies and ghosties FEAR

ghoulies From ghoulies and ghosties FEAR

gift Life is the best gift LIFE

Never look a gift horse in the mouth GRATITUDE

gifts Fear the Greeks bearing gifts TRUST AND TREACHERY

gill Every herring must hang by its own gill RESPONSIBILITY

ginger Every good quality is contained in ginger HEALTH

Local ginger is not hot FAMILIARITY

older the ginger, the more pungent AGE

girdle good name is better than a golden girdle REPUTATION

girls All dancing girls are nineteen YOUTH

give Give a man a fish, and you feed CHARITY

Give and take is fair play JUSTICE

Give a thing, and take a thing GENEROSITY

He gives twice who gives quickly GENEROSITY

giving Friday's child is loving and giving GENEROSITY

Glasgow Glasgow's miles better BRITISH TOWNS AND REGIONS

glass hammer shatters glass, but forges steel WAYS AND MEANS

Those who live in glass houses GOSSIP

glitters All that glitters is not gold QUANTITIES AND QUALITIES

globally Think globally, act locally ENVIRONMENT

gloria Sic transit gloria mundi TRANSIENCE

glove Touch not the cat but a glove CATS

gloves cat in gloves catches no mice CAUTION

gnat Chess is a sea where a gnat may drink SPORTS AND GAMES

Don't strain at a gnat, and swallow BELIEF

go Go further and fare worse SATISFACTION AND DISCONTENT

Go in, stay in CAUTION

Light come, light go POSSESSIONS

Quickly come, quickly go LOYALTY

goal paths are many, but the goal is the same WAYS AND MEANS

God All things are possible with God GOD

Call on God, but row away CAUTION

church is God between four walls CHRISTIAN CHURCH

Every man for himself and God for us all SELF-INTEREST

God helps them that help themselves GOD

God is high above, and the
tsar GOVERNMENT
God made the country COUNTRY
AND THE TOWN
God makes the back to the
burden SYMPATHY
God never sends mouths FOOD
God sends meat, but the
Devil COOKING
God's in his heaven; all's right
OPTIMISM AND PESSIMISM
God sleeps in the stone,
dreams HUMAN RACE
God tempers the wind to the
shorn lamb SYMPATHY
God writes straight with crooked
lines GOD
Man proposes, God
disposes FATE
Man's extremity is God's
opportunity RELIGION
May God in his mercy look
down BRITISH TOWNS AND
REGIONS
mills of God grind slowly FATE
nature of of God is a circle GOD
nearer the church, the farther
from God CHRISTIAN CHURCH
Poverty comes from
God POVERTY
Prayer to God, and service to
the tsar PREPARATION AND
READINESS
Put your trust in God, and
keep PRACTICALITY
robin and the wren are
God's BIRDS
There's probably no God GOD
voice of the people is the voice of
God POLITICS
Where God builds a church
GOOD AND EVIL

You cannot serve God and
Mammon MONEY
Your soul may belong to God
ARMED FORCES
godliness Cleanliness is next to
godliness BEHAVIOUR
gods gods do not subtract LEISURE
gods send nuts to those AGE
Take the goods the gods
provide OPPORTUNITY
Whom the gods love die
young YOUTH
Whom the gods would
destroy MIND
goes As Maine goes, so goes the
nation POLITICS
Steady as she goes CAUTION
What goes around comes
around JUSTICE
going If you don't know
where you are
going TRAVEL
When the going gets
tough CHARACTER
gold All that glitters is not
gold QUANTITIES AND
QUALITIES
Gold may be bought too
dear VALUE
If gold rusts, what will iron
do CORRUPTION
inch of gold cannot buy
time TIME
It is good to make a bridge of
gold WAYS AND MEANS
golden golden key can open any
door CORRUPTION
golden rule of life is BEGINNING
good name is better than a golden
girdle REPUTATION
Speech is silver, but silence is
golden SILENCE

good All good things must come to an end ENDING

Any publicity is good ADVERTISING

Bad money drives out good MONEY

Better a good cow CHARACTER

change is as good as a rest CHANGE

Confession is good for the soul HONESTY

End good, all good ENDING

Every good boy deserves favour MUSIC

Every good quality is contained in ginger HEALTH

good beginning makes a good BEGINNING

Good behaviour is the last BEHAVIOUR

good die young VIRTUE

Good fences make good neighbours NEIGHBOURS

good horse cannot be of a bad colour APPEARANCE

good leader is also a good follower LEADERSHIP

Good medicine always has a bitter taste MEDICINE

Good men are scarce VIRTUE

good name is better than a golden girdle REPUTATION

good reputation stands still REPUTATION

good seaman is known in bad weather SEA

Good seed makes a bad crop CAUSES AND CONSEQUENCES

Good soup is made in an old pot EXPERIENCE

good time was had by all HAPPINESS

Good to forgive, best to forget FORGIVENESS

Good wine needs no bush ADVERTISING

Guinness is good for you DRINK

Have you read any good books READING

He is a good dog who goes to church BEHAVIOUR

Hope is a good breakfast HOPE

If something sounds too good to be true EXCELLENCE

If you can't be good, be careful CAUTION

It is good fishing in troubled waters OPPORTUNITY

It's good to talk SPEECH

liar ought to have a good memory LIES

Never bid the Devil good morrow PROBLEMS AND SOLUTIONS

Never do evil that good may come BEHAVIOUR

No good deed goes unpunished VIRTUE

No news is good news NEWS AND JOURNALISM

One good turn deserves another COOPERATION

One who sees something good NEWS AND JOURNALISM

secret is either too good to keep SECRECY

test of good manners is MANNERS

There are as good fish in the sea LOVE

There is no good flock without DOGS

There is nothing so good for the inside HORSES

You can have too much of a good thing EXCESS

goods Ill gotten goods never thrive CRIME AND PUNISHMENT
Take the goods the gods provide OPPORTUNITY

goose Christmas is coming, and the goose CHRISTMAS
What's sauce for the goose JUSTICE

gorse When the gorse is out of bloom LOVE

gossip Gossip is the lifeblood of society GOSSIP
Gossip is vice GOSSIP

gossips Whoever gossips to you GOSSIP

grain There is no proverb without a grain SAYINGS

granaries All autumns do not fill granaries AUTUMN

grand Seriously, though, he's doing a grand ACHIEVEMENT

grandmother Don't teach your grandmother ADVICE

grass grass is always greener ENVY
When elephants fight, it is the grass POWER
While the grass grows, the steed ACHIEVEMENT

gratitude Don't overload gratitude GRATITUDE

graves If you want revenge, dig two graves REVENGE

Gray Gray's Inn for walks LAW

great Death is the great leveller DEATH
great book is a great evil BOOKS
Great minds think alike THINKING
Great oaks from little acorns CAUSES AND CONSEQUENCES
soldier of the Great War, known unto ARMED FORCES

Wink at sma' fauts, ye hae great anes MISTAKES

greater greater the sinner, the greater the saint GOOD AND EVIL
greater the truth, the greater the libel GOSSIP

greatness If any man seek for greatness FAME

greed Need makes greed GREED

Greek When Greek meets Greek SIMILARITY AND DIFFERENCE

Greeks Fear the Greeks bearing gifts TRUST AND TREACHERY

green Blue and green should never be DRESS
Give a man a fish, and you feed CHARITY
Green Christmas, white Easter WEATHER
green Yule makes a fat churchyard CHRISTMAS
hedge between keeps friendship green NEIGHBOURS
If I keep a green bough in my heart HAPPINESS

greener grass is always greener ENVY

grey All cats are grey in the dark SIMILARITY AND DIFFERENCE
fox may grow grey AGE
grey mare is the better horse MARRIAGE

grief Grief is the price we pay for love MOURNING
He that conceals his grief SORROW

grieve Do not grieve that rose trees have thorns SATISFACTION AND DISCONTENT

grind mill cannot grind with the water that OPPORTUNITY

---

mills of God grind slowly FATE

grist All is grist that comes to the mill OPPORTUNITY

Groucho I am a Marxist—of the Groucho POLITICS

grow Ill weeds grow apace GOOD AND EVIL

More things grow in the garden GARDENS

guessing Punctuality is the art of guessing PUNCTUALITY

guest first day a guest, the second day HOSPITALITY

guest is like the morning dew HOSPITALITY

Treat your guest as a guest for two days HOSPITALITY

guests Fish and guests stink after three days HOSPITALITY

guide Let your conscience be your guide CONSCIENCE

guilty guilty conscience needs no accuser CONSCIENCE

guilty flee when no man pursueth GUILT

guilty one always runs GUILT

Not guilty, but don't do it again GUILT

We are all guilty GUILT

We name the guilty men GUILT

guinea Worth a guinea a box VALUE

Guinness Guinness is good for you DRINK

gum So much chewing gum for the eyes BROADCASTING

gun Have gun, will travel TRAVEL

gunner cobbler to his last and the gunner KNOWLEDGE

guns Guns don't kill people MURDER

guy No more Mr Nice Guy CHANGE

penny for the guy MONEY

guys Nice guys finish last SPORTS AND GAMES

habit Custom is mummified by habit CUSTOM AND HABIT

habits Old habits die hard CUSTOM AND HABIT

had What you've never had SATISFACTION AND DISCONTENT

You cannot lose what you never had POSSESSIONS

Haig Don't be vague, ask for Haig CERTAINTY AND DOUBT

hair Beauty draws with a single hair BEAUTY

half Do not meet troubles half way WORRY

Half a loaf is better than no bread SATISFACTION AND DISCONTENT

half is better than the whole MODERATION

Half the truth is often a whole lie LIES

One half of the world does not know KNOWLEDGE

Two boys are half a boy WORK

Well begun is half done BEGINNING

Halifax From Hell, Hull, and Halifax BRITISH TOWNS AND REGIONS

hall It is merry in hall when beards wag all HOSPITALITY

halloo Don't halloo till you are out of the wood OPTIMISM AND PESSIMISM

halved trouble shared is a trouble halved COOPERATION

Hope deferred makes the heart
sick HOPE

If it were not for hope, the
heart HOPE

It is a poor heart that never
rejoices HAPPINESS

larger the body, the bigger the
heart BODY

Out of the fullness of the
heart FEELINGS

Put a stout heart to a stey
brae DETERMINATION

way to a man's heart is
through MEN

What the eye doesn't see, the
heart IGNORANCE

Writing is a picture of the writer's
heart WRITING

heat If you don't like the heat, get
out STRENGTH AND WEAKNESS

heated only thing a heated argument ever ARGUMENT

heaven Crosses are ladders that lead
to heaven SUFFERING

From Madrid to heaven TOWNS
AND CITIES

God's in his heaven; all's right
OPTIMISM AND PESSIMISM

Heaven protects children,
sailors DANGER

Hell is where heaven is
not HAPPINESS

If you want to see heaven CAUSES
AND CONSEQUENCES

Marriages are made in
heaven MARRIAGE

mind enlightened is like
heaven MIND

heaviest heaviest baggage for the
traveller TRAVEL

hedge hedge between keeps
friendship green NEIGHBOURS

Heineken Heineken refreshes the
parts DRINK

heir Winter is summer's
heir WINTER

hell From Hell, Hull, and
Halifax BRITISH TOWNS AND
REGIONS

Hell hath no fury like a woman
scorned WOMEN

Hell is where heaven is
not HAPPINESS

road to hell is paved with ACTION
AND INACTION

help Do not call a wolf to help
you ENEMIES

God helps them that help
themselves GOD

Help you to salt, help you to
sorrow MISFORTUNES

large family, quick help FAMILY

mouse may help a lion POWER

helps Every little
helps COOPERATION

God helps them that help
themselves GOD

hen Better an egg today than a hen
tomorrow PRESENT

whistling woman and a crowing
hen WOMEN

hens sleeping fox counts
hens CHARACTER

herbs Better a dinner of
herbs FEELINGS

here Here be dragons TRAVEL

Here's tae us; wha's like us
SELF-ESTEEM AND SELF-ASSERTION

We're here Because We're
here FATE

heresy Turkeys, heresy, hops, and
beer CHANGE

hero No man is a hero to his
valet FAMILIARITY

heron white heron is a bird of BIRDS

herring Every herring must hang by its own gill RESPONSIBILITY

hesitates He who hesitates is lost INDECISION

hey Hey, hey, LBJ, how many kids WARFARE

hide No fist is big enough to hide the sky GOVERNMENT
Those who hide can find SECRECY
You can't hide an awl in a sack SECRECY

high God is high above, and the tsar GOVERNMENT
mountains are high, and the emperor GOVERNMENT

higher higher the monkey climbs AMBITION

hills Blue are the hills that are far FAMILIARITY

himself Every man for himself and God for us all SELF-INTEREST
Every man for himself, and the Devil SELF-INTEREST

hire labourer is worthy of his hire WORK

history History is a fable HISTORY
History is fiction HISTORY
History is written by the victors HISTORY
History repeats itself HISTORY
Make poverty history POVERTY
What's hit is history KNOWLEDGE

hit What's hit is history KNOWLEDGE

hog Every hog has his Martinmas FATE

hogs Pigs get fat, but hogs get GREED

hold Hold a true friend with both your hands FRIENDSHIP
What you have, hold POSSESSIONS

Holdfast Brag is a good dog, but Holdfast WORDS AND DEEDS

hole When you are in a hole, stop digging APOLOGY AND EXCUSES

home Charity begins at home CHARITY
East, west, home's best HOME
Englishman's home is his castle HOME
Go abroad and you'll hear news of home TRAVEL
Home is home HOME
Home is home, as the Devil said LAW
Home is where the heart is HOME
Home is where the mortgage is HOME
There's no place like home HOME
Who goes home? POLITICS
woman's place is in the home WOMEN

Homer Homer sometimes nods MISTAKES

honestly Get the money honestly if you can MONEY
Sell honestly, but not honesty HONESTY

honesty Honesty is more praised than practised HONESTY
Honesty is the best policy HONESTY
Sell honestly, but not honesty HONESTY

honey bee sucks honey where the spider CHARACTER
Honey catches more flies than vinegar WAYS AND MEANS

One day honey, one day
onions CIRCUMSTANCE AND
SITUATION
Where bees are, there is
honey WORK
honi *Honi soit qui mal y pense* GOOD
AND EVIL
honour post of honour is the post of
danger DANGER
prophet is not without
honour FAMILIARITY
There is honour among
thieves COOPERATION
hope Fear less, hope more; Eat
less LIFESTYLES
He that lives in hope dances to an
ill tune HOPE
Hope deferred makes the heart
sick HOPE
Hope for the best and prepare
for PREPARATION AND READINESS
Hope is a good breakfast HOPE
Hope is the pillar of the
world HOPE
Hope springs eternal HOPE
If it were not for hope, the
heart HOPE
In the kingdom of hope HOPE
To plant a tree is to plant
hope TREES
While there's life there's
hope HOPE
hopefully It is better to travel
hopefully HOPE
hopes smaller the lizard, the greater
its hopes AMBITION
hops Turkeys, heresy, hops, and
beer CHANGE
horn Blow your own horn, even
if ADVERTISING
horns Fate can be taken by the
horns FATE

horse Don't put the cart before the
horse PATIENCE
good horse cannot be of a bad
colour APPEARANCE
grey mare is the better
horse MARRIAGE
If two ride on a horse RANK
If you have a horse of your
own DEBT AND
BORROWING
Never look a gift horse in the
mouth GRATITUDE
No foot, no horse HORSES
old horse does not spoil the
furrow AGE
One may steal a
horse REPUTATION
short horse is soon
curried WORK
swiftest horse cannot overtake
the word WORDS
You can take a horse to the
water DEFIANCE
horseback Set a beggar on
horseback POWER
Sickness arrives on
horseback SICKNESS
horses Horses for courses ABILITY
If wishes were horses,
beggars OPTIMISM AND PESSIMISM
hospitality Food without
hospitality is
medicine HOSPITALITY
Hospitality and medicine must
be HOSPITALITY
hot Hot water does not burn
down FUTILITY
little pot is soon hot ANGER
Local ginger is not
hot FAMILIARITY
Strike while the iron is
hot OPPORTUNITY

hour darkest hour is just before dawn OPTIMISM AND PESSIMISM

One hour's sleep before midnight SLEEP

hours Six hours' sleep for a man SLEEP

Some sleep five hours; nature requires SLEEP

house Better one house spoiled than two MARRIAGE

dog is a lion in his own house DOGS

Learning is better than house and land KNOWLEDGE

When house and land are gone KNOWLEDGE

houses Fools build houses and wise men FOOLS

how How now, brown cow SPEECH

howling howlin' coyote ain't stealin' no chickens HONESTY

Hubert Praise from Sir Hubert PRAISE AND FLATTERY

Hull From Hell, Hull, and Halifax BRITISH TOWNS AND REGIONS

human To err is human but to really COMPUTING

To err is human (to forgive divine) MISTAKES

hundred buyer has need of a hundred eyes BUYING AND SELLING

When angry count a hundred ANGER

hundredth Only the camel knows the hundredth NAMES

hunger Hunger drives the wolf out of the wood NECESSITY

Hunger is the best sauce EATING

Winter thunder, summer hunger WEATHER

hungry hungry man is an angry man FOOD

satisfied person does not know the hungry SELF-INTEREST

hurry Always in a hurry, always behind HASTE AND DELAY

Don't hurry—start early HASTE AND DELAY

Hurry no man's cattle PATIENCE

hurt Don't cry before you're hurt COURAGE

What you don't know can't hurt you IGNORANCE

husband husband is always the last to know IGNORANCE

I married my husband for life MEN

hyphens If you take hyphens seriously WORDS

I I before e, except after c WORDS

ice rich man gets his ice in summer WEALTH

ideas All words are pegs to hang ideas on WORDS

idle Better be idle than ill doing IDLENESS

Devil finds work for idle hands IDLENESS

idle brain is the devil's workshop IDLENESS

Idle people have the least leisure IDLENESS

idleness Idleness is the root of all evil IDLENESS

ifs If ifs and ans were pots and pans OPTIMISM AND PESSIMISM

ignorance Ignorance is bliss IGNORANCE

Ignorance is voluntary
misfortune IGNORANCE
Ignorance of the law is no
excuse LAW
ignorant Science has no enemy but
the ignorant SCIENCE
ill Better be idle than ill
doing IDLENESS
Doing nothing is ill IDLENESS
He that has an ill
name REPUTATION
He that lives in hope dances to an
ill tune HOPE
Ill gotten goods never thrive
CRIME AND PUNISHMENT
Ill weeds grow apace GOOD
AND EVIL
It's an ill bird that fouls its own
nest LOYALTY
It's an ill wind that blows
nobody OPTIMISM AND
PESSIMISM
It's ill speaking between a full
man FOOD
It's ill waiting for dead men's
shoes AMBITION
Never speak ill of the
dead REPUTATION
imitation Imitation is the sincerest
form of flattery PRAISE AND
FLATTERY
important What is the most
important
thing HUMAN RACE
impressions First impressions
are BEGINNING
impune Nemo me impune
lacessit DEFIANCE
in Go in, stay in CAUTION
inch inch ahead is darkness FUTURE
inch of gold cannot buy
time TIME

indecision Indecision is
fatal INDECISION
indeed friend in need is a friend
indeed FRIENDSHIP
industry Necessity sharpens
industry NECESSITY
Science finds, industry
applies TECHNOLOGY
infinite Genius is an infinite
capacity ABILITY
infirmities Dreams retain the
infirmities of DREAMS
inherit We do not inherit the
earth ENVIRONMENT
injury Don't add insult to
injury WORDS AND
DEEDS
ink ink of a scholar is holier
than EDUCATION
inn Gray's Inn for walks LAW
inquisition Nobody expects the
Spanish Inquisition SURPRISE
inside There is nothing so
good for the inside HORSES
insult Don't add insult to injury
WORDS AND DEEDS
interest Worry is interest paid on
trouble WORRY
interesting May you live in
interesting times CIRCUMSTANCE
AND SITUATION
invention Necessity is the
mother of invention NECESSITY
invited Business goes where it is
invited BUSINESS
Ireland England's difficulty is
Ireland's COUNTRIES AND PEOPLES
iron If gold rusts, what will iron
do CORRUPTION
Iron sharpens iron CHARACTER
Strike while the iron is
hot OPPORTUNITY

Isfahan Isfahan is half the world TOWNS AND CITIES

ivy Ee, it was agony, Ivy SUFFERING

Jack All work and no play makes Jack LEISURE

Every Jack has his Jill MEN AND WOMEN

good Jack makes a good Jill MEN AND WOMEN

Jack is as good as his master EMPLOYMENT

Jack of all trades and master of none EMPLOYMENT

jade Everything has a price, but jade is VALUE

jam Jam tomorrow and jam yesterday PRESENT

January warm January, a cold May WEATHER

Jeannie Jeannie, Jeannie, full of hopes CHILDREN

Jerusalem Next year in Jerusalem TOWNS AND CITIES

jest Many a true word is spoken in jest TRUTH

jewel Fair play's a jewel JUSTICE

Jill Every Jack has his Jill MEN AND WOMEN

good Jack makes a good Jill MEN AND WOMEN

Jim It's life, Jim, but not as we know it LIFE

Jim'll fix it PROBLEMS AND SOLUTIONS

jingle single bracelet does not jingle COOPERATION

job Never send a boy to do a man's job YOUTH

join If you can't beat them, join them WAYS AND MEANS

journey Is your journey really necessary TRAVEL

longest journey begins with a single BEGINNING

Jove Jove but laughs at lovers' perjury LOVE

joy Shared joy is double joy SYMPATHY

Strength through joy STRENGTH AND WEAKNESS

judge Do not judge a tree by its bark APPEARANCE

Don't judge a man until CRITICISM

Judge not, that ye be not judged PREJUDICE AND TOLERANCE

No one should be judge in his own LAW

judged Judge not, that ye be not judged PREJUDICE AND TOLERANCE

June dripping June sets all in tune SUMMER

jury fox should not be on the jury JUSTICE

just Be just before you're generous JUSTICE

Just say no DETERMINATION

Just when you thought it was safe DANGER

justice Justice delayed is justice denied JUSTICE

We all love justice JUSTICE

justifies end justifies the means WAYS AND MEANS

keep It is one thing to keep your morals BEHAVIOUR

Keep a thing seven years POSSESSIONS

Keep one eye on the frying-pan COOKING

Keep your own shop BUSINESS

secret is either too good to keep SECRECY

Three may keep a secret SECRECY

It's life, Jim, but not as we know it LIFE
It's not what you know CORRUPTION
It's not what you know OPPORTUNITY
last one to know about the sea IGNORANCE
less you know, the better you sleep IGNORANCE
One half of the world does not know KNOWLEDGE
satisfied person does not know the hungry SELF-INTEREST
Sch ... you know who SECRECY
To know all is to forgive all FORGIVENESS
What you don't know can't hurt you IGNORANCE
You never know what you can do COURAGE
You should know a man seven years NEIGHBOURS
knowledge Knowledge and timber KNOWLEDGE
Knowledge is power KNOWLEDGE
larger the shoreline of knowledge KNOWLEDGE
little knowledge is a dangerous thing KNOWLEDGE
known Kills all known germs ENVIRONMENT
man is known by the company he FAMILIARITY
soldier of the Great War, known unto ARMED FORCES
knows frog in a well knows nothing of SELF-ESTEEM AND SELF-ASSERTION
Necessity knows no law NECESSITY
Only the camel knows the hundredth NAMES

Who knows most, speaks least SPEECH
kumara kumara does not speak of its own SELF-ESTEEM AND SELF-ASSERTION
laborare Laborare est orare RELIGION
labour Labour isn't working POLITICS
labourer labourer is worthy of his hire WORK
ladders Crosses are ladders that lead to heaven SUFFERING
ladies Lady Margaret Hall for ladies EDUCATION
lady And all because the lady loves Milk Tray EFFORT
Faint heart never won fair lady COURAGE
opera isn't over till the fat lady sings ENDING
lamb bleating of the lamb excites the tiger TEMPTATION
God tempers the wind to the shorn lamb SYMPATHY
land Every land has its own law COUNTRIES AND PEOPLES
Learning is better than house and land KNOWLEDGE
When house and land are gone KNOWLEDGE
You buy land, you buy stones BUYING AND SELLING
lands cat always lands on its feet CATS
lane It is a long lane that has no turning PATIENCE
lang Lang may yer lum reek HOME
language nation without a language is COUNTRIES AND PEOPLES
large large family, quick help FAMILY

Little pitchers have large
ears SECRECY
larger larger the body, the bigger
the heart BODY
larger the shoreline of
knowledge KNOWLEDGE
larks If the sky falls we shall catch
larks EFFORT
last cobbler to his last and the
gunner KNOWLEDGE
He laughs last, laughs
longest REVENGE
husband is always the last to
know IGNORANCE
It is the last straw EXCESS
last drop makes the cup run
over EXCESS
last one to know about the
sea IGNORANCE
Let the cobbler stick to his
last KNOWLEDGE
Nice guys finish last SPORTS
AND GAMES
When the last tree is
cut ENVIRONMENT
late Better late than
never PUNCTUALITY
early man never borrows
from the late PREPARATION AND
READINESS
It is never too late to
learn EDUCATION
It is never too late to
mend CHANGE
It's too late to shut the
stable-door FORESIGHT
later Cathedral time is five minutes
later PUNCTUALITY
Latin No more Latin, no more
French EDUCATION
laugh Do not laugh at the fallen
SUCCESS AND FAILURE

Laugh and the world laughs with
you SYMPATHY
Let them laugh that win SUCCESS
AND FAILURE
laughs earth laughs at him
who ENVIRONMENT
He who laughs last, laughs
longest REVENGE
Jove but laughs at lovers'
perjury LOVE
Laugh and the world laughs with
you SYMPATHY
Love laughs at locksmiths LOVE
laughter Laughter is the best
medicine MEDICINE
law Every land has its own
law COUNTRIES AND
PEOPLES
Hard cases make bad law LAW
Ignorance of the law is no
excuse LAW
Necessity knows no
law NECESSITY
One law for the rich JUSTICE
Possession is nine points of the
law LAW
Self-preservation is the first
law of nature
SELF-INTEREST
laws Laws of
Thermodynamics SCIENCE
more laws, the more thieves and
bandits LAW
New lords, new laws CHANGE
lawyer man who is his own lawyer
has a fool LAW
lazy Long and lazy, little and
loud WOMEN
quick brown fox jumps over the
lazy dog WORDS
lead If the people will
lead LEADERSHIP

If you are not the lead
dog LEADERSHIP
leader good leader is also a good
follower LEADERSHIP
Take me to your
leader LEADERSHIP
leads man who reads is the man
who leads READING
leap Look before you
leap CAUTION
learn It is never too late to
learn EDUCATION
Live and learn EXPERIENCE
Never too old to
learn EDUCATION
We must learn to walk
before PATIENCE
learned Nobody is born
learned CLERGY
learning Learning is a treasure that
follows KNOWLEDGE
Learning is better than house and
land KNOWLEDGE
sea of learning has no
end KNOWLEDGE
There is no royal road to
learning EDUCATION
Travelling is learning TRAVEL
leather There is nothing like
leather WAYS AND MEANS
leave Always leave the party
when HOSPITALITY
leaves Falling leaves have to
return HOME
He who leaves succeeds SUCCESS
AND FAILURE
led army of stags led by a lio-
n ARMED FORCES
leeks Eat leeks in March and
ramsons in May HEALTH
legs Do not add legs to the
snake EXCESS

leisure busiest men have the most
leisure LEISURE
Idle people have the least
leisure IDLENESS
Marry in haste and repent at
leisure MARRIAGE
There is luck in leisure PATIENCE
lemon answer is a lemon
SATISFACTION AND DISCONTENT
lemons If life hands you
lemons ADVERSITY
lend Lend your money, and
lose your friend DEBT AND
BORROWING
lender Neither a borrower, nor a
lender be DEBT AND BORROWING
length Length begets
loathing SPEECH
lengthening Travelling is one way
of lengthening life TRAVEL
lengthens As the day lengthens, so
the cold WEATHER
leopard leopard does not change his
spots CHANGE
less Fear less, hope more; Eat
less LIFESTYLES
Less is more MODERATION
less you know, the better you
sleep IGNORANCE
Of two evils choose the
less CHOICE
let Let's be careful CAUTION
Let sleeping dogs lie CAUTION
Let well alone CAUTION
Let your conscience be your
guide CONSCIENCE
Live and let live PREJUDICE AND
TOLERANCE
letter Beauty is a good
letter BEAUTY
Change the name and not the
letter MARRIAGE

Do not close a letter without reading it LETTERS

love letter sometimes costs more LETTERS

Someone, somewhere, wants a letter LETTERS

leveller Death is the great leveller DEATH

liar liar ought to have a good memory LIES

liar's candle lasts till evening LIES

libel greater the truth, the greater the libel GOSSIP

liberal conservative is a liberal who's CRIME AND PUNISHMENT

liberté Liberté! Égalité! Fraternité! POLITICS

library library is a repository of medicine BOOKS

lick It is a poor cook that cannot lick COOKING

lie As a tree falls, so shall it lie DEATH

Deceit is a lie DECEPTION

Half the truth is often a whole lie LIES

If you lie down with dogs FAMILIARITY

lie can go around the world LIES

One seldom meets a lonely lie LIES

lies camera never lies TECHNOLOGY

life Art is long and life is short LIFE

best things in life are free MONEY

dog is for life, not just for Christmas DOGS

golden rule of life is BEGINNING

If life hands you lemons ADVERSITY

I married my husband for life MEN

It's life, Jim, but not as we know it LIFE

Life begins at forty AGE

Life begins on the day you start GARDENS

Life is a sexually transmitted disease LIFE

Life is harder than crossing a field LIFE

Life isn't all beer and skittles LIFE

Life is the best gift LIFE

Life's a bitch, and then you die LIFE

Life without a friend, is death FRIENDSHIP

Medicine can prolong life, but MEDICINE

Travelling is one way of lengthening life TRAVEL

Variety is the spice of life CHANGE

While there's life there's hope HOPE

lifeblood Gossip is the lifeblood of society GOSSIP

light Light come, light go POSSESSIONS

Light for all NEWS AND JOURNALISM

Light the blue touch paper DANGER

Many hands make light work COOPERATION

lighthouse It is dark at the foot of the lighthouse IGNORANCE

lightly Touch the earth lightly ENVIRONMENT

lightning Lightning never strikes twice CHANCE AND LUCK

like Here's tae us; wha's like us SELF-ESTEEM AND SELF-ASSERTION

If you don't like the heat, get out STRENGTH AND WEAKNESS

Like breeds like SIMILARITY AND
DIFFERENCE

Like father, like son FAMILY

Like master, like man WORK

Like mother, like
daughter FAMILY

Like people, like priest CLERGY

Like will to like SIMILARITY AND
DIFFERENCE

You're going to like this LIKES
AND DISLIKES

liked I liked it so much, I bought the
company BUSINESS

Lincoln Lincoln was, London
is BRITISH TOWNS AND REGIONS

line Not a day without a line ART

linen Never choose your women or
linen APPEARANCE

One does not wash one's dirty
linen SECRECY

lining Every cloud has a silver
lining OPTIMISM AND PESSIMISM

link You are the weakest link
STRENGTH AND WEAKNESS

lion army of stags led by a
lion ARMED FORCES

dog is a lion in his own
house DOGS

live dog is better than a dead
lion LIFE

March comes in like a lion SPRING

mouse may help a lion POWER

When the lion shows its
teeth DANGER

lions Christians to the lions
CHRISTIAN CHURCH

Until the lions produce their
own HISTORY

lip There's many a slip 'twixt cup
and lip MISTAKES

lips Loose lips sink ships GOSSIP

My lips are sealed SECRECY

lipstick You can put lipstick on a
pig FUTILITY

listen If I listen, I have the
advantage SPEECH

Listen a thousand times,
and speak once SPEECH

Stop-look-and-listen CAUTION

listeners Listeners never hear
good SECRECY

little Big fish eat little fish POWER

Every little helps COOPERATION

Few have too much, and fewer
too little WEALTH

little absence does much
good ABSENCE

Little children, little
sorrows CHILDREN

Little fish are sweet QUANTITIES
AND QUALITIES

little knowledge is a dangerous
thing KNOWLEDGE

Little pitchers have large
ears SECRECY

little pot is soon hot ANGER

Little strokes fell great
oaks DETERMINATION

Little things please little
minds VALUE

Love me little, love me
long LOYALTY

Many a little makes a mickle
QUANTITIES AND QUALITIES

There is no little enemy ENEMIES

live Come live with me and you'll
know FAMILIARITY

Eat to live, not live to
eat EATING

If you want to live and thrive
CHANCE AND LUCK

Live and learn EXPERIENCE

Live and let live PREJUDICE AND
TOLERANCE

live dog is better than a dead
lion LIFE

Man cannot live by bread
alone LIFE

They that live longest, see
most EXPERIENCE

Threatened men live long WORDS
AND DEEDS

lived And they all lived happily ever
after ENDING

lives Careless talk costs
lives GOSSIP

cat has nine lives CATS

He lives long who lives
well VIRTUE

He that lives in hope dances to an
ill tune HOPE

living Be happy while y'er
leevin LIFE

Envy feeds on the
living ENVY

Saturday's child works hard for a
living WORK

lizard smaller the lizard, the greater
its hopes AMBITION

Lizzie Lizzie Borden took an
axe MURDER

loaf Half a loaf is better than no
bread SATISFACTION AND
DISCONTENT

slice off a cut loaf isn't
missed IGNORANCE

loathing Length begets
loathing SPEECH

local Local ginger is not
hot FAMILIARITY

locally Think globally, act
locally ENVIRONMENT

locksmiths Love laughs at
locksmiths LOVE

loft September blow soft till the
fruit's AUTUMN

log No matter how long a log
floats CHANGE

London Lincoln was,
London is BRITISH TOWNS
AND REGIONS

London Bridge is broken down
BRITISH TOWNS AND REGIONS

lone lone sheep is in danger from
the wolf SOLITUDE

lonely One seldom meets a lonely
lie LIES

long Art is long and life is
short LIFE

Be the day weary or be the day
long TIME

He lives long who lives
well VIRTUE

How long is a piece of string
QUANTITIES AND QUALITIES

It is a long lane that has no
turning PATIENCE

Kings have long arms POWER

Lang may yer lum reek HOME

Long and lazy, little and
loud WOMEN

Long foretold, long
last WEATHER

long time ago in a galaxy far, far
away TIME

Love me little, love me
long LOYALTY

Never is a long time TIME

stern chase is a long
chase DETERMINATION

Threatened men live long WORDS
AND DEEDS

longest He who laughs last, laughs
longest REVENGE

longest journey begins with a
single BEGINNING

longest way home is the
shortest PATIENCE

They that live longest, see
most   EXPERIENCE
look Look before you
leap   CAUTION
Stop-look-and-listen   CAUTION
lookers Lookers-on see most
of the game   ACTION AND
INACTION
loose Loose lips sink ships   GOSSIP
lord abomination unto the Lord,
but   LIES
Everybody loves a lord   RANK
lords New lords, new laws   CHANGE
lose Heads I win, tails you lose
WINNING AND LOSING
Lend your money, and lose
your friend   DEBT AND
BORROWING
What you lose on the swings
WINNING AND LOSING
You cannot lose what you never
had   POSSESSIONS
You win a few, you lose a
few   SUCCESS AND
FAILURE
losers Finders keepers (losers
weepers)   POSSESSIONS
loses tale never loses in the
telling   GOSSIP
loss One man's loss is another
man's gain   CIRCUMSTANCE AND
SITUATION
There's no great loss without
CIRCUMSTANCE AND SITUATION
lost For want of a nail the shoe was
lost   PREPARATION AND READINESS
He who hesitates is
lost   INDECISION
No one was ever lost on a straight
road   PREPARATION AND READINESS
There is nothing lost by
civility   MANNERS

'Tis better to have loved and
lost   LOVE
What a neighbour gets is not
lost   NEIGHBOURS
lottery Marriage is a
lottery   MARRIAGE
louder Actions speak louder than
words   WORDS AND DEEDS
louse Sue a beggar and catch a
louse   FUTILITY
lousy Lousy but loyal   LOYALTY
love All's fair in love and
war   JUSTICE
course of true love never did run
smooth   LOVE
fence between makes love more
CAUSES AND CONSEQUENCES
Grief is the price we pay for
love   MOURNING
It is best to be off with the old
love   LOVE
Love and a cough   LOVE
Love begets love   LOVE
Love is blind   LOVE
Love laughs at locksmiths   LOVE
love letter sometimes costs
more   LETTERS
Love makes the world go
round   LOVE
Love makes time pass   LOVE
Love me, love my dog   DOGS
Love will find a way   LOVE
Love your enemy   ENEMIES
Love your neighbour, but
don't   NEIGHBOURS
Lucky at cards, unlucky in love
CHANCE AND LUCK
Make love not war   LIFESTYLES
Of soup and love, the first is
best   FOOD
One cannot love and be
wise   LOVE

Pity is akin to love   SYMPATHY

To understand your parents'
love   PARENTS

We all love justice   JUSTICE

Whom the gods love die
young   YOUTH

You do not marry the person you
love   MARRIAGE

loved better to have loved   LOVE

Lovell cat, the rat, and Lovell the
dog   GOVERNMENT

lovers Jove but laughs at lovers'
perjury   LOVE

quarrel of lovers is the
renewal   LOVE

loves Everybody loves a
lord   RANK

Misery loves company   SORROW

loving Friday's child is loving and
giving   GENEROSITY

loyal Lousy but loyal   LOYALTY

luck Devil's children have the
Devil's luck   CHANCE AND LUCK

Fools for luck   CHANCE AND LUCK

great fortune depends on luck
CHANCE AND LUCK

There is luck in leisure   PATIENCE

There is luck in odd numbers
CHANCE AND LUCK

luckier harder I work, the
luckier   CHANCE AND LUCK

lucky It is better to be born
lucky   CHANCE AND LUCK

Lucky at cards, unlucky in love
CHANCE AND LUCK

Third time lucky   CHANCE
AND LUCK

Throw a lucky man into the
sea   CHANCE AND LUCK

lum Lang may yer lum reek   HOME

lunch Breakfast like a king, lunch
like   EATING

There's no such thing as a free
lunch   TEMPTATION

Macgregor Where Macgregor sits is
the head   RANK

mad Don't get mad, get
even   REVENGE

made Here's one I made
earlier   PREPARATION AND
READINESS

Madrid From Madrid to heaven
TOWNS AND CITIES

Mahomet If the mountain
will not come to
Mahomet   NECESSITY

Maine As Maine goes, so goes the
nation   POLITICS

make Happiness is what you
make   HAPPINESS

If you don't make
mistakes   MISTAKES

Make do and mend   THRIFT

Make love not war   LIFESTYLES

maketh Manners maketh
man   MANNERS

mal Honi soit qui mal y pense   GOOD
AND EVIL

Mammon You cannot serve
God and Mammon
MONEY

man Am I not a man and a
brother   HUMAN RACE

child is the father of the
man   CHARACTER

Clothes make the man   DRESS

earth is man's only
friend   ENVIRONMENT

Every elm has its man   TREES

Like master, like man   WORK

Man cannot live by bread
alone   LIFE

Man fears Time, but Time
fears   TIME

man is as old as he feels   MEN AND WOMEN

Man is a wolf to man   HUMAN RACE

man is known by the company he   FAMILIARITY

Man is the enemy of   IGNORANCE

Man is the measure   HUMAN RACE

Manners maketh man   MANNERS

Man proposes, God disposes   FATE

man who is born in a stable   CHARACTER

Mounties always get their man   COUNTRIES AND PEOPLES

Never send a boy to do a man's job   YOUTH

Nine tailors make a man   DRESS

No moon, no man   CHILDREN

Oxo gives a meal man-appeal   FOOD

Six hours' sleep for a man   SLEEP

way to a man's heart is through   MEN

Whatever man has done   ACHIEVEMENT

manage You can only manage what you can   MANAGEMENT

manager No manager ever got fired   COMPUTING

Manchester What Manchester says today   BRITISH TOWNS AND REGIONS

mangoes Eat the mangoes. Do not count the trees   WAYS AND MEANS

mankind All mankind is divided into three   HUMAN RACE

manners Other times, other manners   CHANGE

Striking manners are bad manners   MANNERS

test of good manners is   MANNERS

manure Money, like manure, does no good   MONEY

many Many a little makes a mickle   QUANTITIES AND QUALITIES

Many a mickle makes a muckle   QUANTITIES AND QUALITIES

Many hands make light work   COOPERATION

So many men, so many opinions   OPINION

march Eat leeks in March and ramsons in May   HEALTH

March borrowed from April three days   SPRING

March comes in like a lion   SPRING

On the first of March, crows begin   SPRING

peck of March dust is worth a king's   SPRING

So many mists in March, so many frosts   SPRING

mare A mare usque ad mare   COUNTRIES AND PEOPLES

mare grey mare is the better horse   MARRIAGE

Money makes the mare to go   MONEY

Nothing so bold as a blind mare   IGNORANCE

marines Tell that to the marines   BELIEF

market He that cannot abide a bad market   BUSINESS

markets Bull markets climb a wall of worry   BUSINESS

marriage Marriage is a lottery   MARRIAGE

There goes more to marriage   MARRIAGE

marriages Marriages are made in heaven   MARRIAGE

married I married my husband for
  life MEN
  young man married is
  a MARRIAGE
marry Marry in haste and repent at
  leisure MARRIAGE
  Marry in May, rue for
  aye WEDDINGS
  Never marry for money,
  but MARRIAGE
marrying Building and marrying of
  children ARCHITECTURE
Martinmas Every hog has his
  Martinmas FATE
martyrs blood of the martyrs
  CHRISTIAN CHURCH
Marxist I am a Marxist—of the
  Groucho POLITICS
mass Meat and mass CHRISTIAN
  CHURCH
master eye of a master does more
  work EMPLOYMENT
  Fire is a good servant, but a
  bad master WAYS AND
  MEANS
  Jack is as good as his
  master EMPLOYMENT
  Jack of all trades and master of
  none EMPLOYMENT
  Like master, like man WORK
  When the pupil is ready, the
  master EDUCATION
masters No man can serve
  two masters CHOICE
matters What matters is what
  works WAYS AND MEANS
may April and May are keys to the
  whole year SPRING
  April showers bring forth May
  flowers SPRING
  Eat leeks in March and ramsons in
  May HEALTH

He that will not when he
  may OPPORTUNITY
Marry in May, rue for
  aye WEDDINGS
May chickens come
  cheeping SPRING
Ne'er cast a clout till May be
  out DRESS
Sell in May and go away BUYING
  AND SELLING
swarm in May is worth a load of
  hay SUMMER
warm January, a cold
  May WEATHER
meal Oxo gives a meal
  man-appeal FOOD
means end justifies the means
  WAYS AND MEANS
measure Man is the measure of all
  things HUMAN RACE
  Measure seven times, cut once
  PREPARATION AND READINESS
  There is measure in all
  things MODERATION
measures Exceptional times
  require NECESSITY
meat After meat, mustard EATING
  God sends meat, but the
  Devil COOKING
  Meat and mass CHRISTIAN
  CHURCH
  nearer the bone, the sweeter the
  meat QUANTITIES AND QUALITIES
  One man's meat is another
  man's poison LIKES AND
  DISLIKES
medicine Food without hospitality
  is medicine HOSPITALITY
  Good medicine always has a bitter
  taste MEDICINE
  Hospitality and medicine must
  be HOSPITALITY

Laughter is the best
medicine MEDICINE
library is a repository of
medicine BOOKS
Medicine can prolong life,
but MEDICINE
Your food is your
medicine HEALTH
meet Do not meet troubles half
way WORRY
Extremes meet SIMILARITY AND
DIFFERENCE
meets When Greek meets
Greek SIMILARITY AND DIFFERENCE
memory liar ought to have a good
memory LIES
Our memory is always at
fault MIND
men best of men are but men at
best HUMAN RACE
mend It is never too late to
mend CHANGE
Make do and mend THRIFT
mending woman and a ship ever
want mending WOMEN
mercy May God in his mercy
look down BRITISH TOWNS AND
REGIONS
merit Merit in appearance
is APPEARANCE
merrier more the merrier
QUANTITIES AND QUALITIES
merry cherry year, a merry
year SUMMER
Eat, drink and be merry, for
tomorrow LIFESTYLES
It is merry in hall when beards
wag all HOSPITALITY
mice cat in gloves catches no
mice CAUTION
Keep no more cats than will catch
mice MODERATION

When the cat's away, the mice
will OPPORTUNITY
mickle Many a little makes a
mickle QUANTITIES AND
QUALITIES
Many a mickle makes a muckle
QUANTITIES AND QUALITIES
midnight One hour's sleep before
midnight SLEEP
might Might is right POWER
mightier pen is mightier than the
sword WAYS AND MEANS
mile miss is as good as a
mile MISTAKES
miles Essex stiles, Kentish
miles BRITISH TOWNS AND REGIONS
Every two miles the water
changes TRAVEL
Glasgow's miles better BRITISH
TOWNS AND REGIONS
Walking ten thousand
miles EXPERIENCE
Walking ten thousand
miles KNOWLEDGE
milk Feeding a snake with
milk CHARACTER
It is no use crying over spilt
milk MISFORTUNES
Why buy a cow when milk is so
cheap SEX
milka Drinka Pinta Milka HEALTH
mill All is grist that comes to the
mill OPPORTUNITY
mill cannot grind with the water
that OPPORTUNITY
million If you really want to make a
million WEALTH
mills mills of God grind
slowly FATE
mind mind enlightened is like
heaven MIND
Mind has no sex MIND

mind is a terrible thing to
waste   MIND

Out of sight, out of
mind   ABSENCE

Travel broadens the
mind   TRAVEL

wise man changes his
mind   FOOLS

minds Great minds think
alike   THINKING

Little things please little
minds   VALUE

miracles age of miracles is
past   SURPRISE

mirror Mirror, mirror on the
wall   BEAUTY

mischief mother of mischief is no
bigger   CAUSES AND CONSEQUENCES

misery Misery loves
company   SORROW

misfortune Ignorance is voluntary
misfortune   IGNORANCE

misfortunes Misfortunes never
come singly   MISFORTUNES

miss miss is as good as a
mile   MISTAKES

You never miss the water till the
well   GRATITUDE

missed slice off a cut loaf isn't
missed   IGNORANCE

misses person who misses his
chance   OPPORTUNITY

missing One of our aircraft is
missing   ARMED FORCES

mistake Shome mistake,
shurely   MISTAKES

mistakes If you don't make
mistakes   MISTAKES

mists So many mists in March,
so many frosts   SPRING

mixen Better wed over the
mixen   FAMILIARITY

mockingbird mockingbird has no
voice   BIRDS

moderation Moderation in all
things   MODERATION

moment Enjoy the present
moment   PRESENT

To question and ask is a
moment's shame   THINKING

Monday Monday's child is fair of
face   BEAUTY

They that wash on
Monday   HOUSEWORK

money bulls make money, the
bears make   BUYING AND
SELLING

fool and his money are soon
parted   FOOLS

Get the money honestly if you
can   MONEY

Lend your money, and lose your
friend   DEBT AND BORROWING

Money can't buy
happiness   MONEY

Money has no smell   MONEY

Money is like sea water   MONEY

Money isn't everything   MONEY

Money is power   MONEY

Money is the root of all
evil   MONEY

Money like manure, does no
good   MONEY

Money makes a man   WEALTH

Money makes money   WEALTH

Money makes the mare to
go   MONEY

Money talks   MONEY

Never marry for money,
but   MARRIAGE

Time is money   MONEY

When money speaks, the
truth   CORRUPTION

You pays your money   CHOICE

---

moneyless moneyless man goes fast through POVERTY

monk cowl does not make the monk APPEARANCE

monkey higher the monkey climbs AMBITION
rusty monkey wrench DETERMINATION
Softlee, softlee, catchee monkey PATIENCE
What can a monkey know of the taste VALUE

monkeys Even monkeys sometimes fall off a tree MISTAKES
If you pay peanuts, you get monkeys VALUE

months Nine months of winter WEATHER

monument You'll die facing the monument CRIME AND PUNISHMENT

monumentum Si monumentum requiris, circumspice ARCHITECTURE

moon No moon, no man CHILDREN

morals It is one thing to keep your morals BEHAVIOUR

more Fear less, hope more; Eat less LIFESTYLES
Less is more MODERATION
more arguments you win, the less ARGUMENT
more butter, the worse cheese FOOD
More haste, less speed HASTE AND DELAY
more laws, the more thieves and bandits LAW
more the merrier QUANTITIES AND QUALITIES
More things grow in the garden GARDENS

more you get the more you want GREED
Much would have more GREED
whole is more than the sum QUANTITIES AND QUALITIES

morning guest is like the morning dew HOSPITALITY
morning daylight appears plainer TIME
Morning dreams come true DREAMS
morning knows no more than the evening SLEEP

morrow Never bid the Devil good morrow PROBLEMS AND SOLUTIONS

mortgage Home is where the mortgage is HOME

mortuis De mortuis nil nisi bonum REPUTATION

Moses For every Pharaoh there is a Moses COURAGE
Moses took a chance CHANCE AND LUCK

moss rolling stone gathers no moss CIRCUMSTANCE AND SITUATION

most Who knows most, speaks least SPEECH

mother Absence is the mother of disillusion ABSENCE
Diligence is the mother of CHANCE AND LUCK
Like mother, like daughter FAMILY
mother of mischief is no bigger CAUSES AND CONSEQUENCES
mother understands what the child PARENTS
Necessity is the mother of invention NECESSITY

Summer is the mother of the poor SUMMER

mount wise man will climb Mount Fuji once TRAVEL

mountain If the mountain will not come to Mahomet NECESSITY

man who removes a mountain PATIENCE

One mountain cannot accommodate two LEADERSHIP

mountains Beyond mountains there are more DETERMINATION

Faith will move mountains BELIEF

mountains are high, and the emperor GOVERNMENT

We have no friends but the mountains DANGER

Mounties Mounties always get their man COUNTRIES AND PEOPLES

mouse It's the second mouse that gets PREPARATION AND READINESS

mouse may help a lion POWER

One for the mouse, one for the crow NATURE

mousetrap only free cheese is in a mousetrap TEMPTATION

mouth Never look a gift horse in the mouth GRATITUDE

shut mouth catches no flies SILENCE

mouths God never sends mouths but FOOD

Out of the mouths of babes— KNOWLEDGE

moutons Revenons á ces moutons DETERMINATION

move Did the earth move for you SEX

When you pray, move your feet RELIGION

moved shall not be moved DETERMINATION

moves If it moves, salute it ARMED FORCES

much Few have too much, and fewer too little WEALTH

Much would have more GREED

Sow much, reap much CAUSES AND CONSEQUENCES

You can have too much of a good thing EXCESS

muck Where there's muck there's brass MONEY

muckle Many a mickle makes a muckle QUANTITIES AND QUALITIES

mulberry With time and patience the mulberry leaf PATIENCE

mule If you lead your mule to the top PROBLEMS AND SOLUTIONS

multitude Charity covers a multitude of sins FORGIVENESS

mummified Custom is mummified by habit CUSTOM AND HABIT

mummy Mummy, what's that man for? POLITICS

murder Killing no murder MURDER

Murder will out MURDER

museum ace caff with quite a nice museum HOSPITALITY

music Music helps not the toothache MUSIC

When the music changes CHANGE

must What must be, must be FATE

mustard After meat, mustard EATING

nail For want of a nail the shoe was lost PREPARATION AND READINESS

nail that sticks up is certain to MANAGEMENT

One nail drives out another SIMILARITY AND DIFFERENCE

name Change the name and not the letter MARRIAGE

Give a dog a bad name and hang GOSSIP

good name is better than a golden girdle REPUTATION

He that has an ill name REPUTATION

We name the guilty men GUILT

names No names, no pack-drill SECRECY

Naples See Naples and die TOWNS AND CITIES

nation As Maine goes, so goes the nation POLITICS

Nation shall speak peace unto BROADCASTING

nation without a language COUNTRIES AND PEOPLES

national national debt, if it is not excessive DEBT AND BORROWING

nature Death is nature's way DEATH

father is a banker provided by nature PARENTS

Nature abhors a vacuum NATURE

Self-preservation is the first law of nature SELF-INTEREST

Some sleep five hours; nature requires SLEEP

You can drive out nature with a pitchfork NATURE

naughty Naughty but nice TEMPTATION

near Near is my kirtle, but nearer my smock SELF-INTEREST

Near is my shirt, but nearer my skin SELF-INTEREST

nearer nearer the bone, the sweeter the meat QUANTITIES AND QUALITIES

nearer the church, the farther from God CHRISTIAN CHURCH

necessary Is your journey really necessary TRAVEL

necessity Make a virtue of necessity NECESSITY

Necessity is the mother of invention NECESSITY

Necessity knows no law NECESSITY

Necessity sharpens industry NECESSITY

nectar Even nectar is a poison EXCESS

need Charity sees the need CHARITY

friend in need is a friend indeed FRIENDSHIP

Need makes greed GREED

Your King and Country need you ARMED FORCES

needle When a pine needle falls in the forest KNOWLEDGE

needles Needles and pins, needles and pins MARRIAGE

needs Needs must when the devil drives NECESSITY

neglected Business neglected BUSINESS

neighbour Love your neighbour, but don't NEIGHBOURS

rotten apple injures its neighbour CORRUPTION

What a neighbour gets is not lost NEIGHBOURS

neighbours Good fences make good neighbours NEIGHBOURS

nemo Nemo me impune lacessit DEFIANCE

nest It's an ill bird that fouls its own nest LOYALTY

nineteen All dancing girls are nineteen YOUTH

no Just say no DETERMINATION
No cross, no crown SUFFERING
No foot, no horse HORSES
No names, no pack-drill SECRECY
No surrender DEFIANCE
There's no such thing as a free lunch TEMPTATION

nobody Everybody's business is nobody's RESPONSIBILITY
Nobody expects the Spanish Inquisition SURPRISE

nod Nod's as good as a wink ADVICE

nods Homer sometimes nods MISTAKES

noise Silence is a still noise SILENCE

north North wind doth blow WEATHER

North-amptonshire Northamptonshire for squires BRITISH TOWNS AND REGIONS

nose Don't cut off your nose to spite REVENGE

nostalgia Nostalgia isn't what it used to be PAST

not Not a day without a line ART
Not guilty, but don't do it again GUILT

nothing Doing nothing is ill IDLENESS
If you have nothing POSSESSIONS
Nothing can bring you peace but PEACE
Nothing comes from nothing VALUE
Nothing for nothing VALUE
Nothing is certain but death CERTAINTY AND DOUBT

Nothing is certain but the unforeseen FORESIGHT
Nothing is for ever CHANGE
Nothing is stolen without hands HONESTY
Nothing so bad but it might have been SYMPATHY
Nothing succeeds like success SUCCESS AND FAILURE
Nothing venture, nothing gain THOROUGHNESS
Nothing venture, nothing have THOROUGHNESS
Something is better than nothing SATISFACTION AND DISCONTENT
There is nothing like leather WAYS AND MEANS

now And now for something CHANGE

nowt Hear all, see all, say nowt SELF-INTEREST
There's nowt so queer as folk HUMAN RACE
When in doubt, do nowt ACTION AND INACTION

nullius Nullius in verba HYPOTHESIS AND FACT

numbers There is luck in odd numbers CHANCE AND LUCK
There is safety in numbers QUANTITIES AND QUALITIES

nuts gods send nuts to those AGE

oak When the oak is before the ash TREES

oaks Great oaks from little acorns CAUSES AND CONSEQUENCES
Little strokes fell great oaks DETERMINATION

obedience first duty of a soldier is obedience ARMED FORCES

obey He that cannot obey cannot command LEADERSHIP

obvious obvious choice is usually CHOICE

odd There is luck in odd numbers CHANCE AND LUCK

odious Comparisons are odious SIMILARITY AND DIFFERENCE

offenders Offenders never pardon FORGIVENESS

offered They offered death CHOICE

old Better be an old man's darling MARRIAGE

Don't throw away the old bucket PREPARATION AND READINESS

For the unlearned, old age is winter AGE

Good soup is made in an old pot EXPERIENCE

man is as old as he feels MEN AND WOMEN

Never too old to learn EDUCATION

old error is always more popular TRUTH

Old habits die hard CUSTOM AND HABIT

old horse does not spoil the furrow AGE

old net is cast aside while the new net YOUTH

old poacher makes the best gamekeeper WAYS AND MEANS

Old sins cast long shadows PAST

Old soldiers never die ARMED FORCES

There's no fool like an old fool AGE

You cannot catch old birds EXPERIENCE

You cannot put an old head EXPERIENCE

You cannot shift an old tree CUSTOM AND HABIT

You can't put new wine in old bottles CHANGE

You can't teach an old dog new tricks CUSTOM AND HABIT

Young folks think old folks to be fools YOUTH

Young men may die, but old men DEATH

Young saint, old devil HUMAN RACE

older older the ginger, the more pungent AGE

omelette You cannot make an omelette PRACTICALITY

once Christmas comes but once a year CHRISTMAS

Once a —, always a — CHARACTER

Once a priest, always CLERGY

one Beware of the man of one book BOOKS

Children: one is one CHILDREN

One for sorrow, two for mirth BIRDS

One good turn deserves another COOPERATION

One mountain cannot accommodate two LEADERSHIP

One step at a time PATIENCE

onions One day honey, one day onions CIRCUMSTANCE AND SITUATION

only Only — shopping days to Christmas CHRISTMAS

open door must be either shut or open CHOICE

Teachers open the
door EDUCATION
opens When one door
shuts, another
opens OPPORTUNITY
opera opera isn't over till the fat
lady sings ENDING
opinions So many men, so many
opinions OPINION
Those who never retract their
opinions OPINION
opportunities Opportunities look
for you OPPORTUNITY
opportunity Every crisis provides
an opportunity OPPORTUNITY
Man's extremity is God's
opportunity RELIGION
Opportunity makes a thief CRIME
AND PUNISHMENT
Opportunity never knocks
for OPPORTUNITY
Opportunity never knocks
twice OPPORTUNITY
orange future's bright, the future's
Orange FUTURE
orare Laborare est orare RELIGION
other Other times, other
manners CHANGE
others Do unto others as you would
they LIFESTYLES
ounce ounce of practice is worth a
pound of WORDS AND DEEDS
out Don't halloo till you are
out of the wood OPTIMISM AND
PESSIMISM
Out of debt, out of danger DEBT
AND BORROWING
Out of sight, out of
mind ABSENCE
truth is out there KNOWLEDGE
overcome We shall
overcome DETERMINATION

overload Don't overload
gratitude GRATITUDE
overpaid Overpaid, overfed,
oversexed EXCESS
oversexed Overpaid, overfed,
oversexed EXCESS
own He who slaps his own
face MISTAKES
Oxo Oxo gives a meal
man-appeal FOOD
oyster world is one's
oyster OPPORTUNITY
oysters Don't eat oysters
unless FOOD
pace It is the pace that
kills STRENGTH AND WEAKNESS
Pace makes the race HORSES
pack-drill No names, no
pack-drill SECRECY
padlock Wedlock is a
padlock MARRIAGE
pain No pain, no gain EFFORT
Pride feels no pain PRIDE
rock in the water does not know
the pain SYMPATHY
paint blind man's wife needs no
paint APPEARANCE
painted black as he is
painted REPUTATION
painter Every painter paints
himself ART
good painter can draw a
devil ART
paints Every painter paints
himself ART
palmam Palmam qui
meruit ACHIEVEMENT
pans If ifs and ands were
pots and pans OPTIMISM AND
PESSIMISM
paper Paper bleeds little WRITING
Paper is patient WRITING

paradise England is the
paradise of women COUNTRIES
AND PEOPLES

pardon Excuse (or pardon) my
French APOLOGY AND EXCUSES
Offenders never
pardon FORGIVENESS

parent art of being a
parent CHILDREN
Caution is the parent of
safety CAUTION

parents Parents want their
children to become PARENTS
To understand your parents'
love PARENTS

parsley Parsley seed goes nine
times GARDENS

parsnips Fine words butter no
parsnips WORDS AND DEEDS

part best of friends must part
MEETING AND PARTING

parted fool and his money are soon
parted FOOLS

parts Heineken refreshes the
parts DRINK

party Always leave the party
when HOSPITALITY

pass And this, too, shall pass
away TRANSIENCE
If the Bermudas let you
pass SEA
Love makes time pass LOVE

passe Tout passe, tout casse LIFE

passeront Ils ne passeront
pas DEFIANCE

passion passion for freedom never
dies POLITICS

past age of miracles is
past SURPRISE
past always looks better PAST
past at least is secure PAST
past is always ahead of us PAST

Things past cannot be
recalled PAST

paternoster No penny, no
paternoster BUSINESS

paths paths are many, but the
goal is the same WAYS AND
MEANS

patience All commend
patience PATIENCE
Patience is a virtue PATIENCE
With time and patience the
mulberry leaf PATIENCE

patient Paper is patient WRITING

Paul If Saint Paul's day be fair and
clear WINTER

pawn After the game, the king and
the pawn DEATH

pay Can't pay, won't
pay DEFIANCE
Crime doesn't pay CRIME AND
PUNISHMENT
He that cannot pay, let him
pray MONEY
If you pay peanuts, you get
monkeys VALUE
No cure, no pay BUSINESS
Pay beforehand was never
well BUSINESS
price we pay for love MOURNING
Service is the rent we
pay CHARITY
Take what you want, and pay for
it RESPONSIBILITY
They that dance must pay the
fiddler POWER

pays Death pays all debts DEATH
He who pays the piper calls the
tune POWER
It pays to advertise ADVERTISING
third time pays for
all DETERMINATION
You pays your money CHOICE

peace If you want peace, you must
  prepare PREPARATION AND
  READINESS
  Nation shall speak peace
  unto BROADCASTING
  Nothing can bring you peace
  but PEACE
  Peace is the dream of the
  wise PEACE

peacock peacock is always
  happy because SELF-ESTEEM AND
  SELF-ASSERTION

peanuts If you pay peanuts, you get
  monkeys VALUE

pears Walnuts and pears
  you plant
  for GARDENS

peck peck of March dust is worth a
  king's SPRING
  We must eat a peck of
  dirt EATING

Peebles Peebles for pleasure
  BRITISH TOWNS AND REGIONS

pegs All words are pegs to hang
  ideas on WORDS

pen pen is mightier than the
  sword WAYS AND MEANS
  What is written with a
  pen WRITING

pence Take care of the
  pence THRIFT

penny bad penny always
  turns up CHARACTER
  In for a penny, in for a
  pound THOROUGHNESS
  No penny, no
  paternoster BUSINESS
  penny for the guy MONEY
  penny saved is a penny
  earned THRIFT
  Penny wise and pound
  foolish THRIFT

pense Honi soit qui mal y pense
  GOOD AND EVIL

people Guns don't kill
  people MURDER
  If the people will lead LEADERSHIP
  Like people, like priest CLERGY
  Power to the people POLITICS
  Proverbs are the coins of the
  people SAYINGS
  To understand the
  people SAYINGS
  voice of the people is the voice of
  God POLITICS

Peoria It'll play in Peoria POLITICS

perfect Practice makes
  perfect WORK

perfection Trifles make
  perfection WORK

perfume Flattery, like perfume
  PRAISE AND FLATTERY

perish Perish the
  thought THINKING

perjury Jove but laughs at lovers'
  perjury LOVE

Persil Persil washes
  whiter HOUSEWORK

personal personal is
  political POLITICS

Pharaoh For every Pharaoh there is
  a Moses COURAGE

phone Phone a friend COOPERATION

pick See a pin and pick it
  up CHANCE AND LUCK

picture Every picture tells a
  story KNOWLEDGE
  One picture is worth ten
  thousand words WORDS
  AND DEEDS
  Writing is a picture of the writer's
  heart WRITING

pie apple-pie without some
  cheese FOOD

Promises, like pie-crust,
are made   TRUST AND
TREACHERY

pies Devil makes his Christmas
pies   LAW

pig What can you expect from a
pig   CHARACTER

You can put lipstick on a
pig   FUTILITY

pigs Pigs get fat, but hogs
get   GREED

Pigs may fly   BELIEF

pile Pile it high, sell it
cheap   BUSINESS

pillar Hope is the pillar of the
world   HOPE

pillow clean conscience is a good
pillow   CONSCIENCE

pills Dr Williams' pink pills for pale
people   MEDICINE

pilot In a calm sea, every man is a
pilot   ACHIEVEMENT

pin He that will not stoop for a
pin   PRIDE

It's a sin to steal a pin   HONESTY

See a pin and pick it up   CHANCE
AND LUCK

pine When a pine needle falls in the
forest   KNOWLEDGE

pink Dr Williams' pink pills for pale
people   MEDICINE

pins Needles and pins, needles and
pins   MARRIAGE

pint You cannot get a quart into a
pint   FUTILITY

pinta Drinka Pinta Milka   HEALTH

piper He who pays the piper
calls the tune   POWER

It takes seven years to make a
piper   MUSIC

pitch He that touches pitch shall be
defiled   GOOD AND EVIL

pitcher pitcher will go to the
well   EXCESS

pitchers Little pitchers have large
ears   SECRECY

pitchfork You can drive out nature
with a pitchfork   NATURE

pitied Better be envied than
pitied   ENVY

pity Pity is akin to love   SYMPATHY

place There's a time and a place
CIRCUMSTANCE AND SITUATION

There's no place like home   HOME

plague Please your eye and
plague   BEAUTY

plan He who fails to plan, plans to
fail   SUCCESS AND FAILURE

I have a cunning plan   THINKING

No plan survives first contact   PREPARATION AND READINESS

plans He who fails to plan, plans to
fail   SUCCESS AND FAILURE

plant best time to plant a tree
was   TREES

Confidence is a plant of slowth
growth   TRUST AND TREACHERY

To plant a tree is to plant
hope   TREES

Walnuts and pears you plant
for   GARDENS

planted Trees planted by the
ancestors   TREES

plants One generation plants the
trees   TREES

play All work and no play makes
Jack   LEISURE

Fair play's a jewel   JUSTICE

Give and take is fair play   JUSTICE

If you play with fire you get
burnt   DANGER

It'll play in Peoria   POLITICS

Play it again, Sam   MUSIC

Turn about is fair play   JUSTICE

Poverty is not a crime   POVERTY
power All power to the
    Soviets   POWER
    Beauty is power   BEAUTY
    Knowledge is power   KNOWLEDGE
    Money is power   MONEY
    Power corrupts   POWER
    Power is like an egg   POWER
    Power to the people   POLITICS
practice ounce of practice is
    worth a pound of   WORDS
    AND DEEDS
    Practice makes perfect   WORK
practise Practise what
    you preach   WORDS AND
    DEEDS
practised Honesty is more
    praised than
    practised   HONESTY
praise Praise the child, and you
    make love to   PARENTS
    Self-praise is no
    recommendation   SELF-ESTEEM
    AND SELF-ASSERTION
praised Honesty is more praised
    than practised   HONESTY
pray He that cannot pay, let him
    pray   MONEY
    When you pray, move your
    feet   RELIGION
prayer Prayer to God, and service to
    the tsar   PREPARATION AND
    READINESS
prays family that prays together
    stays   RELIGION
preach Practise what you preach
    WORDS AND DEEDS
precept Example is better than
    precept   WORDS AND DEEDS
prepare Hope for the best and
    prepare for   PREPARATION AND
    READINESS

If you want peace, you must
    prepare   PREPARATION AND
    READINESS
    To fail to prepare is to prepare
    to fail   PREPARATION AND
    READINESS
prepared Be prepared   PREPARATION
    AND READINESS
present Enjoy the present
    moment   PRESENT
    No time like the
    present   OPPORTUNITY
    There's no future like the
    present   FUTURE
preservation Self-preservation
    is the first law of
    nature   SELF-INTEREST
press You press the button, we do
    the rest   TECHNOLOGY
pressed One volunteer is
    worth two pressed
    men   WORK
pretend We pretend to
    work   EMPLOYMENT
pretty Pretty is as pretty
    does   BEHAVIOUR
prevention Prevention is better
    than cure   FORESIGHT
prey Birds of prey do not
    sing   BIRDS
price Every man has his
    price   CORRUPTION
    Everything has a price, but jade
    is   VALUE
    Grief is the price we pay for
    love   MOURNING
pride Pride feels no pain   PRIDE
    Pride goes before a fall   PRIDE
    Stupidity and pride grow   PRIDE
priest Like people, like
    priest   CLERGY
    Once a priest, always   CLERGY

princes Camels, fleas, and princes ROYALTY

Punctuality is the politeness of princes PUNCTUALITY

print All the news that's fit to print NEWS AND JOURNALISM

probably There's probably no God GOD

procrastination Procrastination is the thief of time HASTE AND DELAY

promises Promises, like pie-crust, are made TRUST AND TREACHERY

proof proof of the pudding is in the eating HYPOTHESIS AND FACT

prophet prophet is not without honour FAMILIARITY

prophets Is Saul also among the prophets ABILITY

proposes Man proposes, God disposes FATE

prosper Cheats never prosper DECEPTION

prosperity Both poverty and prosperity POVERTY

proverb There is no proverb without a grain SAYINGS

proverbs Proverbs are the coins of the people SAYINGS

providence Providence is always on the side of ARMED FORCES

public One does not wash one's dirty linen SECRECY

publicity Any publicity is good publicity ADVERTISING

pudding proof of the pudding is in the eating HYPOTHESIS AND FACT

puddle sun loses nothing by shining into a puddle GOOD AND EVIL

punctuality Punctuality is the art of guessing PUNCTUALITY

Punctuality is the politeness of princes PUNCTUALITY

Punctuality is the soul of business PUNCTUALITY

pungent older the ginger, the more pungent AGE

Sour, sweet, bitter, pungent FATE

pupil When the pupil is ready, the master EDUCATION

purse You can't make a silk purse FUTILITY

pursueth guilty flee when no man pursueth GUILT

push Do not push the river, it will flow FUTILITY

put Never put off till tomorrow HASTE AND DELAY

putt Drive for show, and putt for dough SPORTS AND GAMES

quality Every good quality is contained in ginger HEALTH

Never mind the quality, feel the width QUANTITIES AND QUALITIES

quarrel It takes two to make a quarrel ARGUMENT

quarrel of lovers is the renewal LOVE

quart You cannot get a quart into a pint FUTILITY

queer There's nowt so queer as folk HUMAN RACE

question Ask a silly question and you get FOOLS

civil question deserves a civil answer MANNERS

Fools ask questions that wise men KNOWLEDGE

There are two sides to every question JUSTICE

To question and ask is a moment's shame THINKING

quick quick brown fox jumps over the lazy dog WORDS

quickly He gives twice who gives
quickly GENEROSITY
Quickly come, quickly
go LOYALTY

quiet best doctors are Dr Quiet,
Dr Diet MEDICINE
quiet conscience sleeps in
thunder CONSCIENCE

quote Devil can quote
Scripture SAYINGS

race Pace makes the race HORSES
race is not to the swift, nor the
battle SUCCESS AND FAILURE
Slow and steady wins the
race DETERMINATION

radio Always turn the radio on
before BROADCASTING

rain Blessed are the dead that the
rain DEATH
Now you will feel no
rain WEDDINGS
Rain before seven, fine before
eleven WEATHER
Rain, rain, go away WEATHER
To dream of the dead is a sign of
rain DREAMS

rains Have an umbrella ready
before it rains PREPARATION AND
READINESS
In the woods it rains twice TREES
It never rains but it
pours MISFORTUNES

raise It is easier to raise the
Devil BEGINNING

ramsons Eat leeks in March and
ramsons in May HEALTH

rat cat, the rat, and Lovell the
dog GOVERNMENT
You dirty rat CHARACTER

read Have you read any good
books READING
He that runs may read READING

reading Do not close a letter
without reading it LETTERS

reads man who reads is the man
who leads READING

real Will the real — please stand
up SECRECY

reap As you sow, so you reap
CAUSES AND CONSEQUENCES
Sow an act, and reap CUSTOM
AND HABIT
Sow much, reap much CAUSES
AND CONSEQUENCES

reaps Speech sows, silence
reaps SILENCE

reason There is reason in the
roasting of eggs CAUSES AND
CONSEQUENCES

recalled Things past cannot be
recalled PAST

receive He gives twice who gives
quickly GENEROSITY

receivers If there were no
receivers CRIME AND PUNISHMENT

reckonings Short reckonings make
long friends DEBT AND BORROWING

recommendation Self-praise is no
recommendation SELF-ESTEEM
AND SELF-ASSERTION

red Better red than dead CHOICE
Red sky at night, shepherd's
delight WEATHER

redressed fault confessed is half
redressed FORGIVENESS

reed reed before the wind lives
on STRENGTH AND WEAKNESS

reek Lang may yer lum reek HOME

rejoices It is a poor heart that never
rejoices HAPPINESS

relationship I belong by blood
relationship FAMILY

remedy There is a remedy for
everything DEATH

remember Please to remember the Fifth TRUST AND TREACHERY
Remember the Alamo WARFARE
When you drink water, remember GRATITUDE

removals Three removals are as bad CHANGE

renewal quarrel of lovers is the renewal LOVE

rent Service is the rent we pay CHARITY

repeats History is written by the victors HISTORY

repent Marry in haste and repent at leisure MARRIAGE

republican Not to be a republican at twenty POLITICS

reputation good reputation stands still REPUTATION
man's best reputation for his future REPUTATION

request No flowers by request MOURNING

rest After dinner rest a while EATING
change is as good as a rest CHANGE
You press the button, we do the rest TECHNOLOGY

revenge If you want revenge, dig two graves REVENGE
Revenge is a dish that can be eaten REVENGE
Revenge is sweet REVENGE

revenons Revenons d ces moutons DETERMINATION

revenue Thrift is a great revenue THRIFT

revolution Every revolution was first a thought REVOLUTION AND REBELLION

revolutions Revolutions are not made by REVOLUTION AND REBELLION
Revolutions are not made with REVOLUTION AND REBELLION

reward Virtue is its own reward VIRTUE

rib elephant does not die of one broken rib STRENGTH AND WEAKNESS

rice Talk will not cook rice WORDS AND DEEDS

rich One law for the rich JUSTICE
rich man gets his ice in summer WEALTH

ride If wishes were horses, beggars OPTIMISM AND PESSIMISM

rides He who rides a tiger DANGER

ridiculous From the sublime to the ridiculous SUCCESS AND FAILURE

right customer is always right BUSINESS
Do right and fear no man CONSCIENCE
Even a stopped clock is right twice a day TIME
God's in his heaven; all's right OPTIMISM AND PESSIMISM
He is always right who suspects MISTAKES
Might is right POWER
Two wrongs don't make a right GOOD AND EVIL

ripe Soon ripe, soon rotten YOUTH

rise Early to bed and early to rise HEALTH
In politics, a man must learn to rise POLITICS
stream cannot rise above its source CHARACTER

rising rising tide lifts all boats SUCCESS AND FAILURE

river Do not push the river, it will flow FUTILITY

If you sit by the river long enough PATIENCE

live in the river CIRCUMSTANCE AND SITUATION

river that forgets its source GRATITUDE

sea refuses no river GREED

Where the river is deepest CHARACTER

rivers All rivers run into the sea RIVERS

road No one was ever lost on a straight road PREPARATION AND READINESS

road to hell is paved with ACTION AND INACTION

There is no royal road to learning EDUCATION

Why did the chicken cross the road PROBLEMS AND SOLUTIONS

roads All roads lead to Rome TOWNS AND CITIES

Roads are made by walking TRAVEL

roasting There is reason in the roasting of eggs CAUSES AND CONSEQUENCES

robbery fair exchange is no robbery JUSTICE

robin robin and the wren are God's BIRDS

Robin Robin Hood could brave all weathers WEATHER

rock rock in the water does not know the pain SYMPATHY

rocket Up like a rocket, down like a stick SUCCESS AND FAILURE

rocking Worry is like a rocking chair WORRY

rocks hand that rocks the cradle rules WOMEN

rod Spare the rod and spoil CHILDREN

roll Assistant heads must roll BROADCASTING

rolling rolling stone gathers no moss CIRCUMSTANCE AND SITUATION

Romans When in Rome, do as the Romans do BEHAVIOUR

Rome All roads lead to Rome TOWNS AND CITIES

Rome was not built in a day PATIENCE

When in Rome, do as the Romans do BEHAVIOUR

room There's always room at the top AMBITION

rooster Rooster today, feather duster tomorrow SUCCESS AND FAILURE

root Money is the root of all evil MONEY

No tree takes so deep a root PREJUDICE AND TOLERANCE

roots roots of charity are always green CHARITY

rope Give a man enough rope WAYS AND MEANS

rose Do not grieve that rose trees have thorns SATISFACTION AND DISCONTENT

He who wants a rose PRACTICALITY

No rose without a thorn CIRCUMSTANCE AND SITUATION

roses Take time to smell the roses LEISURE

Time brings roses PATIENCE

rots Winter never rots in the sky WINTER

rotten rotten apple injures its neighbour CORRUPTION
Small choice in rotten apples CHOICE
Soon ripe, soon rotten YOUTH

round Love makes the world go round LOVE

row Call on God, but row away CAUTION

royal There is no royal road to learning EDUCATION

rudder Who won't be ruled by the rudder CAUSES AND CONSEQUENCES

rudderless widow is a rudderless boat MARRIAGE

rue Marry in May, rue for aye WEDDINGS

rule Divide and rule GOVERNMENT
exception proves the rule HYPOTHESIS AND FACT
golden rule of life is BEGINNING
Self-interest is the rule SELF-INTEREST
There is an exception to every rule HYPOTHESIS AND FACT

ruled Who won't be ruled by the rudder CAUSES AND CONSEQUENCES

rules hand that rocks the cradle rules WOMEN
Rules are made to be broken LAW

run All rivers run into the sea RIVERS
You cannot run with the hare TRUST AND TREACHERY

runs guilty one always runs GUILT
He that runs may read READING
He who fights and runs away CAUTION

Russian Scratch a Russian and you find COUNTRIES AND PEOPLES

rust Better to wear out than to rust IDLENESS

rusts If gold rusts, what will iron do CORRUPTION

Sabbath child that is born on the Sabbath CHILDREN

sack You can't hide an awl in a sack SECRECY

sacks Empty sacks will never stand upright POVERTY

safe Better be safe than sorry CAUTION
Just when you thought it was safe DANGER
Safe bind, safe find CAUTION

safety Caution is the parent of safety CAUTION
There is safety in numbers QUANTITIES AND QUALITIES

said They haif said: Quhat say they DEFIANCE
What the soldier said isn't evidence GOSSIP

sailor One cannot become a good sailor EFFORT

sailors Heaven protects children, sailors DANGER

saint Devil was sick, the Devil a saint GRATITUDE
greater the sinner, the greater the saint GOOD AND EVIL
If Saint Paul's day be fair and clear WINTER
On Saint Thomas the Divine WINTER
Young saint, old devil HUMAN RACE

saints There are more saints in Cornwall BRITISH TOWNS AND REGIONS

salt Help you to salt, help you to sorrow MISFORTUNES

salty Those who eat salty fish RESPONSIBILITY

salute If it moves, salute it ARMED FORCES

Sam Play it again, Sam MUSIC

Satan Satan rebuking sin GOOD AND EVIL

satisfied satisfied person does not know the hungry SELF-INTEREST

Saturday Saturday's child works hard for a living WORK

sauce Hunger is the best sauce EATING

What's sauce for the goose JUSTICE

Saul Is Saul also among the prophets ABILITY

save Save the whale ENVIRONMENT

Save us from our friends FRIENDSHIP

saved penny saved is a penny earned THRIFT

say Do as I say, not as I do BEHAVIOUR

Hear all, see all, say nowt SELF-INTEREST

Say it with flowers FLOWERS

They haif said: Quhat say they DEFIANCE

says What everybody says must be true TRUTH

What Manchester says today BRITISH TOWNS AND REGIONS

Who says A must say B NECESSITY

scabbard Two swords do not fit in one scabbard SIMILARITY AND DIFFERENCE

scalded He who has been scalded CAUTION

scarce Good men are scarce VIRTUE

scare Kill the chicken to scare CAUSES AND CONSEQUENCES

scholar ink of a scholar is holier than EDUCATION

school Experience keeps a dear school EXPERIENCE

Never tell tales out of school SECRECY

schoolgirl Keep that schoolgirl complexion APPEARANCE

science Much science, much sorrow SCIENCE

Science finds, industry applies TECHNOLOGY

Science has no enemy but the ignorant SCIENCE

scorned Hell hath no fury like a woman scorned WOMEN

scrambled You can't unscramble scrambled eggs FUTILITY

scratch Scratch a Russian and you find COUNTRIES AND PEOPLES

scream In space no one can hear you scream FEAR

Scripture Devil can quote Scripture SAYINGS

sea All rivers run into the sea RIVERS

Chess is a sea where a gnat may drink SPORTS AND GAMES

He that would go to sea for pleasure SEA

In a calm sea, every man is a pilot ACHIEVEMENT

last one to know about the sea IGNORANCE

Money is like sea water MONEY

sea of learning has no end KNOWLEDGE

sea refuses no river GREED

sea wants to be visited SEA
There are as good fish in the
sea LOVE
Throw a lucky man into the
sea CHANCE AND LUCK
willing foe and sea room ARMED
FORCES
sealed My lips are sealed SECRECY
seaman good seaman is known in
bad weather SEA
second It's the second mouse
that gets PREPARATION AND
READINESS
Second thoughts are
best CAUTION
secret secret is either too good to
keep SECRECY
Three may keep a secret SECRECY
secure past at least is secure PAST
see He who can see three days
ahead FORESIGHT
Lookers-on see most of the
game ACTION AND INACTION
Nice to see you MEETING AND
PARTING
See all your best work go
unnoticed SECRECY
See Naples and die TOWNS AND
CITIES
See no evil, hear no evil, speak no
evil VIRTUE
They that live longest, see
most EXPERIENCE
What the eye doesn't see, the
heart IGNORANCE
What you see is what you
get APPEARANCE
seed   blood of the martyrs
is the seed CHRISTIAN
CHURCH
Every pomegranate has one
seed FOOD

Good seed makes a bad crop
CAUSES AND CONSEQUENCES
seed hidden in the heart of an
apple TREES
seeding One year's seeding makes
seven GARDENS
seeing By seeing one
spot CHARACTER
Seeing is believing BELIEF
seek Seek and ye shall find ACTION
AND INACTION
seekers Seekers are
finders ACHIEVEMENT
seem Be what you would
seem BEHAVIOUR
seen Children should be seen and
not CHILDREN
sees One who sees something
good NEWS AND JOURNALISM
self Deny self for self's sake
SELF-ESTEEM AND SELF-ASSERTION
self-praise Self-praise is no
recommendation SELF-ESTEEM
AND SELF-ASSERTION
sell Don't sell the skin till you have
caught OPTIMISM AND PESSIMISM
Pile it high, sell it cheap BUSINESS
Sell honestly, but not
honesty HONESTY
Sell in May and go away BUYING
AND SELLING
semper Semper eadem CHANGE
send Never send a boy to do a
man's job YOUTH
September September blow soft till
the fruit's AUTUMN
seriously Seriously, though,
he's ACHIEVEMENT
serpent Strike the serpent's
head ENEMIES
servant Fire is a good servant, but a
bad master WAYS AND MEANS

serve You cannot serve God and
  Mammon MONEY
served Youth must be
  served YOUTH
service Prayer to God, and service
  to the tsar PREPARATION AND
  READINESS
  Service is the rent we
  pay CHARITY
set Sow dry and set wet GARDENS
settling In settling an
  island, the first
  building ARCHITECTURE
seven Fall seven times, stand up
  eight DETERMINATION
  Give me a child for the first
  seven EDUCATION
  It takes seven years to make a
  piper MUSIC
  I was a seven-stone
  weakling HEALTH
  Keep a thing seven
  years POSSESSIONS
  Measure seven times, cut once
  PREPARATION AND READINESS
  One year's seeding makes
  seven GARDENS
  Rain before seven, fine before
  eleven WEATHER
  You should know a man seven
  years NEIGHBOURS
sex Mind has no sex MIND
sexually Life is a sexually
  transmitted disease LIFE
shadow Coming events cast their
  shadow FUTURE
shadows Old sins cast long
  shadows PAST
shame Fool me once, shame on
  you DECEPTION
  Tell the truth and shame the
  devil TRUTH

  To question and ask is a moment's
  shame THINKING
shared Shared joy is double
  joy SYMPATHY
  trouble shared is a trouble
  halved COOPERATION
sharpens Iron sharpens
  iron CHARACTER
sharper sharper the storm, the
  sooner it's over OPTIMISM AND
  PESSIMISM
shed You can shed tears that she is
  gone MOURNING
sheep bleating sheep loses a
  bite OPPORTUNITY
  lone sheep is in danger from the
  wolf SOLITUDE
  One might as well be hanged for a
  sheep THOROUGHNESS
  wolves are well fed and the
  sheep DANGER
shepherd Red sky at night,
  shepherd's delight WEATHER
shines Make hay while the sun
  shines OPPORTUNITY
  So much sun as shines
  on WEATHER
shining sun loses nothing by
  shining into a puddle GOOD
  AND EVIL
ship Do not spoil the ship for a
  ha'porth of tar THOROUGHNESS
  One hand for oneself and one for
  the ship SEA
  woman and a ship ever want
  mending WOMEN
ships Loose lips sink ships GOSSIP
shirt Near is my shirt, but nearer
  my skin SELF-INTEREST
shirtsleeves From shirtsleeves
  to shirtsleeves SUCCESS AND
  FAILURE

shoe For want of a nail the shoe was lost PREPARATION AND READINESS

If the shoe fits, wear it NAMES

shoemaker shoemaker's son always goes FAMILY

shoes I cried because I had no shoes MISFORTUNES

It's ill waiting for dead men's shoes AMBITION

You need more than dancing shoes DANCE

shoot When you shoot an arrow of truth TRUTH

shop Keep your own shop BUSINESS

shopping Only — shopping days to Christmas CHRISTMAS

shore I sit on the shore, and wait for the wind PATIENCE

shoreline larger the shoreline of knowledge KNOWLEDGE

shorn God tempers the wind to the shorn lamb SYMPATHY

short Art is long and life is short LIFE

short cut is often a wrong cut WAYS AND MEANS

short horse is soon curried WORK

Short reckonings make long friends DEBT AND BORROWING

shortest longest way home is the shortest PATIENCE

show Drive for show, and putt for dough SPORTS AND GAMES

show must go on DETERMINATION

Tell me and I'll forget. Show me and TEACHING

showers April showers bring forth May flowers SPRING

shrouds Shrouds have no pockets MONEY

shut door must be either shut or open CHOICE

It's too late to shut the stable-door FORESIGHT

shut mouth catches no flies SILENCE

shuts When one door shuts, another opens OPPORTUNITY

shy Once bitten, twice shy EXPERIENCE

sick Devil was sick, the Devil a saint GRATITUDE

Hope deferred makes the heart sick HOPE

sickly bloody war and a sickly season ARMED FORCES

sickness Sickness arrives on horseback SICKNESS

side bread never falls but on its buttered side MISFORTUNES

Providence is always on the side of ARMED FORCES

sides There are two sides to every question JUSTICE

sight Out of sight, out of mind ABSENCE

silence Silence is a still noise SILENCE

Silence is a woman's best garment WOMEN

Silence means consent SILENCE

Speech is silver, but silence is golden SILENCE

Speech sows, silence reaps SILENCE

silent It is the calm and silent water DANGER

silk You can't make a silk purse FUTILITY

silly Ask a silly question and you get FOOLS

silver Every cloud has a silver lining OPTIMISM AND PESSIMISM

Speech is silver, but silence is
golden   SILENCE

similia *Similia similibus*
curantur   MEDICINE

sin It's a sin to steal a pin   HONESTY

Satan rebuking sin   GOOD
AND EVIL

sincerest Imitation is the sincerest
form of flattery   PRAISE AND
FLATTERY

sing Birds of prey do not
sing   BIRDS

Little birds that can
sing   COOPERATION

Sing before breakfast,
cry   FEELINGS

singing singing army and a   ARMED
FORCES

single Beauty draws with a single
hair   BEAUTY

longest journey begins with a
single   BEGINNING

single arrow is easily
broken   COOPERATION

single bracelet does not
jingle   COOPERATION

singly Misfortunes never come
singly   MISFORTUNES

sings opera isn't over till the fat lady
sings   ENDING

sinner greater the sinner, the
greater the saint   GOOD
AND EVIL

sins Charity covers a multitude of
sins   FORGIVENESS

Old sins cast long shadows   PAST

sir Praise from Sir Hubert   PRAISE
AND FLATTERY

site Select a proper site for your
garden   GARDENS

sitting Are you sitting comfortably?   BEGINNING

It is as cheap sitting as
standing   ACTION AND
INACTION

sixpence Bang goes
sixpence   THRIFT

sixty-two Where were you in
'62?   ABSENCE

size One size does not fit all   WAYS
AND MEANS

skin Beauty is only skin
deep   BEAUTY

Don't sell the skin till you
have caught   OPTIMISM AND
PESSIMISM

fair skin hides seven
defects   APPEARANCE

Near is my shirt, but nearer my
skin   SELF-INTEREST

There is more than one way
to skin a cat   WAYS
AND MEANS

When a tiger dies it leaves its
skin   REPUTATION

skittles Life isn't all beer and
skittles   LIFE

sky If the sky falls we shall catch
larks   EFFORT

No fist is big enough to hide the
sky   GOVERNMENT

Red sky at night, shepherd's
delight   WEATHER

Winter never rots in the
sky   WINTER

Women hold up half the
sky   WOMEN

slap Slip, slop, slap   HEALTH

slaps He who slaps his own
face   MISTAKES

sleep beginning of health is
sleep   SLEEP

less you know, the better you
sleep   IGNORANCE

One hour's sleep before
midnight SLEEP
Six hours' sleep for a
man SLEEP
Some sleep five hours; nature
requires SLEEP
We never sleep SLEEP
sleeping Let sleeping dogs
lie CAUTION
sleeping fox counts
hens CHARACTER
sleeps quiet conscience sleeps in
thunder CONSCIENCE
slice slice off a cut loaf isn't
missed IGNORANCE
slip Slip, slop, slap HEALTH
There's many a slip 'twixt cup and
lip MISTAKES
slop Slip, slop, slap HEALTH
slow Confidence is a plant of slow
growth TRUST AND TREACHERY
Slow and steady wins the
race DETERMINATION
Slow but sure PATIENCE
slowly Make haste slowly HASTE
AND DELAY
small Better are small fish than an
empty dish SATISFACTION AND
DISCONTENT
Small choice in rotten
apples CHOICE
Small is beautiful QUANTITIES AND
QUALITIES
Wink at sma' fauts, ye hae great
anes MISTAKES
smaller smaller the lizard, the
greater its hopes AMBITION
smell Money has no smell MONEY
Take time to smell the
roses LEISURE
smock Near is my kirtle, but nearer
my smock SELF-INTEREST

smoke No smoke without
fire REPUTATION
smoking Smoking can seriously
damage SMOKING
smooth course of true love
never did run
smooth LOVE
snake Do not add legs to the
snake EXCESS
Feeding a snake with
milk CHARACTER
Once bitten by a snake CAUTION
Poke a bush, a snake
comes CAUTION
sneezes Coughs and sneezes spread
diseases SICKNESS
soap Flattery is soft soap PRAISE
AND FLATTERY
soar However high a bird may
soar ENVIRONMENT
sober Wanton kittens make sober
cats YOUTH
society Gossip is the lifeblood of
society GOSSIP
soft Flattery is soft soap PRAISE AND
FLATTERY
soft answer turneth away
wrath ANGER
softly Softlee, softlee, catchee
monkey PATIENCE
soil answer lies in the soil GARDENS
soldier Every Turk is born a
soldier COUNTRIES AND PEOPLES
first duty of a soldier ARMED
FORCES
soldier of the Great War,
known unto ARMED
FORCES
What the soldier said isn't
evidence GOSSIP
soldiers Old soldiers never
die ARMED FORCES

someone Someone, somewhere, wants a letter LETTERS

something And now for something CHANGE

Something is better than nothing SATISFACTION AND DISCONTENT

son Like father, like son FAMILY

My son is my son till he gets him PARENTS

shoemaker's son always goes FAMILY

songless believer is a songless bird BELIEF

sons Clergymen's sons always CLERGY

soon Soon ripe, soon rotten YOUTH

sooner sooner begun, the sooner done BEGINNING

sorrow Help you to salt, help you to sorrow MISFORTUNES

Much science, much sorrow SCIENCE

One for sorrow, two for mirth BIRDS

sorrows Little children, little sorrows CHILDREN

sorry Better be safe than sorry CAUTION

sorts It takes all sorts CHARACTER

soul Brevity is the soul of wit SPEECH

Confession is good for the soul HONESTY

eyes are the window of the soul BODY

Punctuality is the soul of business PUNCTUALITY

Your soul may belong to God ARMED FORCES

sound Empty vessels make the most sound FOOLS

soup Good soup is made in an old pot EXPERIENCE

Of soup and love, the first is best FOOD

sour Sour, sweet, bitter, pungent FATE

source river that forgets its source GRATITUDE

stream cannot rise above its source CHARACTER

Soviets All power to the Soviets POWER

sow As you sow, so you reap CAUSES AND CONSEQUENCES

If you do not sow in the spring AUTUMN

Sow an act, and reap CUSTOM AND HABIT

Sow corn in clay GARDENS

Sow dry and set wet GARDENS

sow may whistle, though it has ABILITY

Sow much, reap much CAUSES AND CONSEQUENCES

They that sow the wind CAUSES AND CONSEQUENCES

sows Speech sows, silence reaps SILENCE

space In space no one can hear you scream FEAR

Watch this space NEWS AND JOURNALISM

Spanish Nobody expects the Spanish Inquisition SURPRISE

spare Spare at the spigot THRIFT

Spare the rod and spoil CHILDREN

Spare well and have to spend THRIFT

speak kumara does not speak of its own SELF-ESTEEM AND SELF-ASSERTION

Listen a thousand times,
and speak once SPEECH
Never speak ill of the
dead REPUTATION
See no evil, hear no evil, speak no
evil VIRTUE
Some folks speak from
experience EXPERIENCE
Speak as you find REPUTATION
speaks Everyone speaks well of the
bridge MANNERS
Who knows most, speaks
least SPEECH
species female of the species is more
deadly WOMEN
speculate If you don't
speculate BUSINESS
speech Speech is silver, but silence is
golden SILENCE
Speech sows, silence
reaps SILENCE
speed More haste, less speed
HASTE AND DELAY
spend Spare well and have to
spend THRIFT
What you spend, you
have POSSESSIONS
spice Variety is the spice of
life CHANGE
spider bee sucks honey where the
spider CHARACTER
When spider webs
unite COOPERATION
spigot Spare at the spigot THRIFT
spilt It is no use crying over spilt
milk MISFORTUNES
spindle Do not fold, spindle
or COMPUTING
spite Don't cut off your nose to
spite REVENGE
spoil Do not spoil the ship for a
ha'porth of tar THOROUGHNESS

Spare the rod and spoil CHILDREN
Too many cooks spoil the
broth WORK
spoiled Better one house spoiled
than two MARRIAGE
spoils One spoonful of tar spoils a
barrel QUANTITIES AND QUALITIES
spoonful One spoonful of tar spoils
a barrel QUANTITIES AND QUALITIES
spot By seeing one spot CHARACTER
spots leopard does not change his
spots CHANGE
spring If you do not sow in the
spring AUTUMN
Spring forward, fall back TIME
springs Hope springs eternal HOPE
spy I spy strangers POLITICS
squires Northamptonshire for
squires BRITISH TOWNS AND
REGIONS
stable It's too late to shut the
stable-door FORESIGHT
man who is born in a
stable CHARACTER
stables Care, and not fine
stables HORSES
stabs Stabs heal, but bad words
never WORDS AND DEEDS
stags army of stags led by a
lion ARMED FORCES
stand Empty sacks will never stand
upright POVERTY
Fall seven times, stand up
eight DETERMINATION
Will the real — please stand
up SECRECY
standing It is as cheap sitting as
standing ACTION AND INACTION
stars I pointed out to you the
stars KNOWLEDGE
start Don't hurry—start
early HASTE AND DELAY

Life begins on the day you start GARDENS

started I've started so I'll finish BEGINNING

starve Feed a cold and starve a fever SICKNESS

stays family that prays together stays RELIGION

steady Slow and steady wins the race DETERMINATION

Steady as she goes CAUTION

steal It's a sin to steal a pin HONESTY

One may steal a horse REPUTATION

stealin' howlin' coyote ain't stealin' no chickens HONESTY

steals He who steals an egg will steal a camel HONESTY

steed While the grass grows, the steed ACHIEVEMENT

steel hammer shatters glass, but forges steel WAYS AND MEANS

step It is the first step BEGINNING

One step at a time PATIENCE

stern stern chase is a long chase DETERMINATION

stey Put a stout heart to a stey brae DETERMINATION

stick It is easy to find a stick to beat a dog APOLOGY AND EXCUSES

Let the cobbler stick to his last KNOWLEDGE

Throw dirt enough, and some will stick REPUTATION

Up like a rocket, down like a stick SUCCESS AND FAILURE

sticks nail that sticks up is certain to MANAGEMENT

Sticks and stones may break my bones WORDS

stiles Essex stiles, Kentish miles BRITISH TOWNS AND REGIONS

still Silence is a still noise SILENCE

Still achieving, still pursuing ACHIEVEMENT

still tongue makes a wise head SILENCE

Still waters run deep CHARACTER

stink Fish and guests stink after three days HOSPITALITY

stinks fish always stinks from the head LEADERSHIP

stir more you stir it CAUTION

stitch stitch in time saves nine CAUTION

stolen Nothing is stolen without hands HONESTY

Stolen fruit are sweet TEMPTATION

Stolen waters are sweet TEMPTATION

stone God sleeps in the stone, dreams HUMAN RACE

Stone-dead hath no fellow DEATH

You cannot get blood from a stone FUTILITY

stones Sticks and stones may break my bones WORDS

You buy land, you buy stones BUYING AND SELLING

stools Between two stools one falls INDECISION

stoop He that will not stoop for a pin PRIDE

stop Stop-look-and-listen CAUTION

Stop me and buy one FOOD

stopped Even a stopped clock is right twice a day TIME

storm After a storm comes a calm PEACE
Any port in a storm NECESSITY
sharper the storm, the sooner it's over OPTIMISM AND PESSIMISM
stormy It was a dark and stormy night BEGINNING
story everyday story of country folk COUNTRY AND THE TOWN
Every picture tells a story KNOWLEDGE
One story is good till another is told HYPOTHESIS AND FACT
stout Put a stout heart to a stey brae DETERMINATION
stove cook is no better than her stove COOKING
straight God writes straight with crooked lines GOD
No one was ever lost on a straight road PREPARATION AND READINESS
strain Don't strain at a gnat, and swallow BELIEF
Let the train take the strain TRAVEL
strand You're never alone with a Strand SMOKING
strange Politics makes strange bedfellows POLITICS
stranger Fact is stranger than fiction TRUTH
tears of the stranger are only water SYMPATHY
Truth is stranger than fiction TRUTH
strangers I spy strangers POLITICS
straw drowning man will clutch at a straw HOPE
It is the last straw EXCESS
straw vote only shows which way POLITICS

You cannot make bricks without straw FUTILITY
straws Straws tell which way the wind blows KNOWLEDGE
stream stream cannot rise above its source CHARACTER
strength Strength through joy STRENGTH AND WEAKNESS
Union is strength COOPERATION
stretch Stretch your arm no further than THRIFT
strike Strike while the iron is hot OPPORTUNITY
strikes Lightning never strikes twice CHANCE AND LUCK
Three strikes and you're out CRIME AND PUNISHMENT
striking It is a striking coincidence that COUNTRIES AND PEOPLES
Striking manners are bad manners MANNERS
string How long is a piece of string QUANTITIES AND QUALITIES
strokes Different strokes for different folks CHOICE
Little strokes fell great oaks DETERMINATION
stronger There is one thing stronger than THINKING
stubborn Facts are stubborn things HYPOTHESIS AND FACT
stupidity Stupidity and pride grow PRIDE
style style is the man CHARACTER
sublime From the sublime to the ridiculous SUCCESS AND FAILURE
succeed If at first you don't succeed DETERMINATION
succeeds He who leaves succeeds SUCCESS AND FAILURE
Nothing succeeds like success SUCCESS AND FAILURE

success Nothing succeeds like success SUCCESS AND FAILURE
only place where success comes before SUCCESS AND FAILURE
Success has many fathers, while failure SUCCESS AND FAILURE

sue Sue a beggar and catch a louse FUTILITY

sufficient Sufficient unto the day is the evil WORRY

sum whole is more than the sum QUANTITIES AND QUALITIES

summer One swallow does not make a summer SUMMER
rich man gets his ice in summer WEALTH
Summer is the mother of the poor SUMMER
Winter is summer's heir WINTER
Winter thunder, summer hunger WEATHER

sun Do not argue against the sun ARGUMENT
Happy is the bride the sun shines on WEDDINGS
Make hay while the sun shines OPPORTUNITY
Never let the sun go down on FORGIVENESS
Only the eagle can gaze at the sun STRENGTH AND WEAKNESS
So much sun as shines on WEATHER
sun loses nothing by shining into a puddle GOOD AND EVIL
There is nothing new under the sun FAMILIARITY
Turn your face to the sun OPTIMISM AND PESSIMISM

sunny If Candlemas day be sunny and bright WINTER

superiority Equality is difficult, but superiority LEADERSHIP

sups He who sups with the devil CAUTION

sure Slow but sure PATIENCE

surrender No surrender DEFIANCE

suspects He is always right who suspects MISTAKES

Sussex Sussex won't be druv BRITISH TOWNS AND REGIONS

swallow Don't strain at a gnat, and swallow BELIEF
It is idle to swallow the cow DETERMINATION
One swallow does not make a summer SUMMER

swarm swarm in May is worth a load of hay SUMMER

sweep If every one would sweep his own SELF-INTEREST

sweeps It beats as it sweeps as it cleans HOUSEWORK

sweet By a sweet tongue and kindness BEHAVIOUR
Little fish are sweet QUANTITIES AND QUALITIES
Revenge is sweet REVENGE
Sour, sweet, bitter, pungent FATE
Stolen fruit are sweet TEMPTATION
Stolen waters are sweet TEMPTATION
Words are sweet, but they never take WORDS AND DEEDS

sweeter nearer the bone, the sweeter the meat QUANTITIES AND QUALITIES

sweetest From the sweetest wine, the tartest SIMILARITY AND DIFFERENCE

swift race is not to the swift, nor the battle SUCCESS AND FAILURE

swiftest swiftest horse cannot overtake the word WORDS

swim Fish, to taste good, must swim COOKING

swings What you lose on the swings WINNING AND LOSING

Swithin Saint Swithin's day, if thou be fair SUMMER

sword pen is mightier than the sword WAYS AND MEANS
Whosoever draws his sword against REVOLUTION AND REBELLION

swords Two swords do not fit in one scabbard SIMILARITY AND DIFFERENCE

tablets Keep taking the tablets MEDICINE

tailors Nine tailors make a man DRESS

tails Heads I win, tails you lose WINNING AND LOSING

take Give a thing, and take a thing GENEROSITY
Take away Aberdeen and twelve BRITISH TOWNS AND REGIONS
Take me to your leader LEADERSHIP
Take the goods the gods provide OPPORTUNITY
Take what you want, and pay for it RESPONSIBILITY

takes It takes all sorts CHARACTER
It takes two to make a bargain COOPERATION
It takes two to tango COOPERATION

taking Keep taking the tablets MEDICINE

tale tale never loses in the telling GOSSIP

tales Dead men tell no tales SECRECY
Never tell tales out of school SECRECY

talk Careless talk costs lives GOSSIP
If you can talk, you can sing ABILITY
It's good to talk SPEECH
Talk is cheap WORDS AND DEEDS
Talk of the Devil MEETING AND PARTING
Talk will not cook rice WORDS AND DEEDS
There isn't much to talk about HOSPITALITY
We have ways of making you talk POWER

talks Money talks MONEY

tall tall tree attracts the wind FAME

tango It takes two to tango COOPERATION

tank Put a tiger in your tank TRAVEL

tar Do not spoil the ship for a ha'porth of tar THOROUGHNESS
One spoonful of tar spoils a barrel QUANTITIES AND QUALITIES

tartest From the sweetest wine, the tartest SIMILARITY AND DIFFERENCE

taste Every man to his taste LIKES AND DISLIKES
Fish, to taste good, must swim COOKING
Good medicine always has a bitter taste MEDICINE
What can a monkey know of the taste VALUE

tastes Tastes differ   LIKES AND
DISLIKES
There is no accounting for
tastes   LIKES AND DISLIKES
teach Don't teach your
grandmother   ADVICE
You can't teach an old dog new
tricks   CUSTOM AND HABIT
teacher Experience is the best
teacher   EXPERIENCE
teachers Teachers open the
door   EDUCATION
teaches He teaches ill who teaches
all   TEACHING
He that teaches himself has a fool
for   TEACHING
Who teaches me for a day is my
father   TEACHING
tears tears of the stranger are only
water   SYMPATHY
You can shed tears that she is
gone   MOURNING
teeth When the lion shows its
teeth   DANGER
Winter either bites with its
teeth   WINTER
wolf may lose his teeth, but
never   AGE
tell Dead men tell no tales   SECRECY
Don't ask, don't tell   SECRECY
Never tell tales out of
school   SECRECY
Tell me and I'll forget. Show me
and   TEACHING
Tell that to the marines   BELIEF
Tell the truth and shame the
devil   TRUTH
Time will tell   TIME
telling tale never loses in the
telling   GOSSIP
tempers God tempers the wind to
the shorn lamb   SYMPATHY

tennis Anyone for tennis?   SPORTS
AND GAMES
test Test before you trust   TRUST
AND TREACHERY
test of good manners is   MANNERS
that Been there, done that, got the
T-shirt   TRAVEL
thermodynamics Laws of
Thermodynamics   SCIENCE
thicker Blood is thicker than
water   FAMILY
thief Hang a thief when
he's young   CRIME AND
PUNISHMENT
Opportunity makes a thief   CRIME
AND PUNISHMENT
postern door makes a
thief   OPPORTUNITY
Procrastination is the thief of
time   HASTE AND DELAY
Set a thief to catch a thief   WAYS
AND MEANS
thieves Little thieves are hanged   CRIME AND PUNISHMENT
more laws, the more thieves and
bandits   LAW
There is honour among
thieves   COOPERATION
When thieves fall out   CRIME AND
PUNISHMENT
thing If a thing's worth
doing   EFFORT
You can have too much of a good
thing   EXCESS
think Think globally, act
locally   ENVIRONMENT
third third time is the charm
CHANCE AND LUCK
Third time lucky   CHANCE
AND LUCK
third time pays for
all   DETERMINATION

---

thirsty Dig the well before you are thirsty PREPARATION AND READINESS

Thomas On Saint Thomas the Divine WINTER

thorn No rose without a thorn CIRCUMSTANCE AND SITUATION

thorns Do not grieve that rose trees have thorns SATISFACTION AND DISCONTENT

He who plants thorns CAUSES AND CONSEQUENCES

thought Action without thought ACTION AND INACTION

Every revolution was first a thought REVOLUTION AND REBELLION

Perish the thought THINKING

Thought is free OPINION

wish is father to the thought OPINION

thoughts First thoughts are best INDECISION

Second thoughts are best CAUTION

thread If everyone gives a thread CHARITY

threatened Threatened men live long WORDS AND DEEDS

three All mankind is divided into three HUMAN RACE

Fish and guests stink after three days HOSPITALITY

From clogs to clogs is only three SUCCESS AND FAILURE

He who can see three days ahead FORESIGHT

It takes three generations to make RANK

Three acres and a cow POLITICS

Three may keep a secret SECRECY

Three removals are as bad CHANGE

Three strikes and you're out CRIME AND PUNISHMENT

Three things are not to be trusted DANGER

Two is company, but three is none FRIENDSHIP

threes Bad things come in threes MISFORTUNES

thrift Most people consider thrift a fine virtue THRIFT

Thrift is a great revenue THRIFT

thrive He that will thrive must first ask HOUSEWORK

If you want to live and thrive CHANCE AND LUCK

Ill gotten goods never thrive CRIME AND PUNISHMENT

throw Throw a lucky man into the sea CHANCE AND LUCK

Throw dirt enough, and some will stick REPUTATION

thunder quiet conscience sleeps in thunder CONSCIENCE

Winter thunder, summer hunger WEATHER

Thursday Thursday's child has far to go TRAVEL

tide rising tide lifts all boats SUCCESS AND FAILURE

Time and tide wait for no man OPPORTUNITY

tie It is a tie between men READING

tiger bleating of the lamb excites the tiger TEMPTATION

He who rides a tiger DANGER

Put a tiger in your tank TRAVEL

When a tiger dies it leaves its skin REPUTATION

till Says Tweed to Till RIVERS

timber Knowledge and timber KNOWLEDGE

time Cathedral time is five minutes
later PUNCTUALITY
good time was had by
all HAPPINESS
long time ago in a galaxy far, far
away TIME
Love makes time pass LOVE
Man fears Time, but Time
fears TIME
Never is a long time TIME
No time like the
present OPPORTUNITY
Procrastination is the thief
of time HASTE AND
DELAY
stitch in time saves nine CAUTION
Take time to smell the
roses LEISURE
There is always a first
time BEGINNING
There is a time for
everything TIME
There's a time and a place
CIRCUMSTANCE AND SITUATION
third time is the charm CHANCE
AND LUCK
Those who do not find time for
exercise HEALTH
Time and tide wait for no
man OPPORTUNITY
Time brings roses PATIENCE
Time flies TRANSIENCE
Time is a great healer TIME
Time is money MONEY
Time will tell TIME
Time works wonders TIME
With time and patience the
mulberry leaf PATIENCE
Work expands so as to fill the
time WORK
times Exceptional times
require NECESSITY

May you live in interesting
times CIRCUMSTANCE AND
SITUATION
Other times, other
manners CHANGE
Times change and we with
time CHANGE
Top people take *The Times* NEWS
AND JOURNALISM
tobacco Coffee without
tobacco SMOKING
today Better an egg today than a
hen tomorrow PRESENT
I didn't get where I am
today EFFORT
Today you; tomorrow
me FUTURE
told One story is good till
another is told HYPOTHESIS
AND FACT
tomorrow All the flowers of
tomorrow FLOWERS
Better an egg today than a hen
tomorrow PRESENT
Eat, drink and be merry, for
tomorrow LIFESTYLES
Jam tomorrow and jam
yesterday PRESENT
Never put off till tomorro-
w HASTE AND DELAY
Today you; tomorrow
me FUTURE
Tomorrow is another
day FUTURE
Tomorrow is often the
busiest day FUTURE
Tomorrow never
comes FUTURE
Yesterday has gone,
tomorrow is yet PRESENT
Yesterday is ashes; tomorrow is
wood PRESENT

tongue By a sweet tongue and
kindness BEHAVIOUR
still tongue makes a wise
head SILENCE

too Too many cooks spoil the
broth WORK

tools bad workman blames his
tools APOLOGY AND EXCUSES

toothache Music helps not the
toothache MUSIC

top If you lead your mule to the
top PROBLEMS AND SOLUTIONS
There's always room at the
top AMBITION
Top people take *The Times* NEWS
AND JOURNALISM

touch Light the blue touch
paper DANGER
Touch the earth
lightly ENVIRONMENT

touches He that touches
pitch shall be defiled GOOD
AND EVIL

tout *Tout passe, tout casse* LIFE

trade Every man to his trade WORK
There are tricks in every
trade BUSINESS
Trade follows the flag BUSINESS
Two of a trade never agree
SIMILARITY AND DIFFERENCE

trades Jack of all trades and master
of none EMPLOYMENT

*traduttore Traduttore
traditore* SAYINGS

trail Crime leaves a trail CRIME AND
PUNISHMENT

train Let the train take the
strain TRAVEL

trained We trained
hard MANAGEMENT

*transit Sic transit gloria
mundi* TRANSIENCE

travel better to travel
hopefully HOPE
Have gun, will travel TRAVEL
Travel broadens the
mind TRAVEL

traveller heaviest baggage for the
traveller TRAVEL

travelling Travelling is
learning TRAVEL
Travelling is one way of
lengthening life TRAVEL

travels He travels the fastest who
travels alone SOLITUDE
He who travels fast, travels
alone COOPERATION

tray And all because the lady loves
Milk Tray EFFORT

Tre By Tre, Pol, and Pen NAMES

treasure Learning is a treasure that
follows KNOWLEDGE

treat Treat a man as he is, and
that RELATIONSHIPS

tree As a tree falls, so shall it
lie DEATH
best time to plant a tree
was TREES
Do not judge a tree by its
bark APPEARANCE
Even monkeys sometimes fall off a
tree MISTAKES
falls far from the tree FAMILY
No tree takes so deep a
root PREJUDICE AND TOLERANCE
tall tree attracts the wind FAME
To plant a tree is to plant
hope TREES
tree is known by its
fruit CHARACTER
When the last tree is
cut ENVIRONMENT
woman, a dog, and a walnut
tree WOMEN

You can count the apples
on one tree QUANTITIES AND
QUALITIES
You cannot shift an old tree
CUSTOM AND HABIT
trees Eat the mangoes. Do
not count the trees WAYS
AND MEANS
One generation plants the
trees TREES
Trees planted by the
ancestors TREES
tricks There are tricks in every
trade BUSINESS
You can't teach an old dog new
tricks CUSTOM AND HABIT
trifles Trifles make
perfection WORK
trip Clunk, click, every trip TRAVEL
trouble Never trouble
trouble CAUTION
There will be trouble if the
cobbler KNOWLEDGE
trouble shared is a trouble
halved COOPERATION
When an elephant is in
trouble SUCCESS AND FAILURE
Worry is interest paid on
trouble WORRY
troubled It is good fishing
in troubled
waters OPPORTUNITY
troubles Do not meet troubles half
way WORRY
true course of true love never did
run smooth LOVE
If something sounds too good to
be true EXCELLENCE
Many a true word is spoken in
jest TRUTH
Morning dreams come
true DREAMS

What everybody says must be
true TRUTH
What is new cannot be true
CUSTOM AND HABIT
trust Put your trust in God, and
keep PRACTICALITY
Test before you trust TRUST AND
TREACHERY
Trust in Allah, but tie up your
camel CAUTION
trusted Three things are not to be
trusted DANGER
truth Children and fools tell the
truth HONESTY
greater the truth, the greater the
libel GOSSIP
Half the truth is often a whole
lie LIES
Tell the truth and shame the
Devil TRUTH
There is truth in
wine DRUNKENNESS
truth is out there KNOWLEDGE
Truth is stranger than
fiction TRUTH
Truth lies at the bottom of a
well TRUTH
Truth makes the Devil
blush TRUTH
Truth will out TRUTH
When money speaks, the
truth CORRUPTION
When war is declared, Truth is the
first WARFARE
When you shoot an arrow of
truth TRUTH
try We're number two. We try
harder EFFORT
trying You should make a point of
trying EXPERIENCE
tsar God is high above, and the
tsar GOVERNMENT

Prayer to God, and service to the tsar PREPARATION AND READINESS

tub Every tub must stand on its own bottom STRENGTH AND WEAKNESS

Tuesday If it's Tuesday, this must be Belgium TRAVEL

tune America is a tune COUNTRIES AND PEOPLES

dripping June sets all in tune SUMMER

He that lives in hope dances to an ill tune HOPE

He who pays the piper calls the tune POWER

There's many a good tune AGE

Turk Every Turk is born a soldier COUNTRIES AND PEOPLES

turkeys Turkeys, heresy, hops, and beer CHANGE

turn Even a worm will turn NECESSITY

One good turn deserves another COOPERATION

Turn about is fair play JUSTICE

Turn your face to the sun OPTI-MISM AND PESSIMISM

turning It is a long lane that has no turning PATIENCE

tweed Says Tweed to Till RIVERS

twelve Take away Aberdeen and twelve BRITISH TOWNS AND REGIONS

twice Even a stopped clock is right twice a day TIME

He gives twice who gives quickly GENEROSITY

In the woods it rains twice TREES

Lightning never strikes twice CHANCE AND LUCK

Twice-cooked cabbage is death FOOD

twig As the twig is bent EDUCATION

two Between two stools one falls INDECISION

bird in the hand is worth two CAUTION

If two ride on a horse RANK

If you have two coins LIFESTYLES

If you run after two hares INDECISION

If you want revenge, dig two graves REVENGE

It takes two to make a bargain COOPERATION

It takes two to make a quarrel ARGUMENT

It takes two to tango COOPERATION

No man can serve two masters CHOICE

One for sorrow, two for mirth BIRDS

One mountain cannot accommodate two LEADERSHIP

There are two sides to every question JUSTICE

Treat your guest as a guest for two days HOSPITALITY

Two blacks don't make a white GOOD AND EVIL

Two boys are half a boy WORK

Two heads are better than one THINKING

Two is company, but three is none FRIENDSHIP

Two of a trade never agree SIMILARITY AND DIFFERENCE

Two swords do not fit in one scabbard SIMILARITY AND DIFFERENCE

Two wrongs don't make a right GOOD AND EVIL

We're number two. We try harder EFFORT

While two dogs are fighting ARGUMENT

You cannot carry two watermelons FUTILITY

You have two chances CHANCE AND LUCK

tyranny Democracy is better than tyranny POLITICS

umbrella Don't put up your umbrella before CAUTION

Have an umbrella ready before it rains PREPARATION AND READINESS

unaccustomed Unaccustomed as I am SPEECH

unbelieving Believing has a core of unbelieving BELIEF

undersold Never knowingly undersold BUSINESS

understand To understand the people SAYINGS

understands mother understands what the child PARENTS

undone What's done cannot be undone PAST

unexpected unexpected always happens SURPRISE

unforeseen Nothing is certain but the unforeseen FORESIGHT

union Union is strength COOPERATION

united United we stand, divided we COOPERATION

When spider webs unite COOPERATION

unlearned For the unlearned, old age is winter AGE

unlucky Lucky at cards, unlucky in love CHANCE AND LUCK

unnoticed See all your best work go unnoticed SECRECY

unpunished No good deed goes unpunished VIRTUE

unrepentant Forgiving the unrepentant FORGIVENESS

unscramble You can't unscramble scrambled eggs FUTILITY

unwilling committee is a group of the unwilling MANAGEMENT

up Up like a rocket, down like a stick SUCCESS AND FAILURE

What goes up must come down FATE

us Here's tae us; wha's like us SELF-ESTEEM AND SELF-ASSERTION

used Nostalgia isn't what it used to be PAST

Would you buy a used car from this man TRUST AND TREACHERY

vacuum Nature abhors a vacuum NATURE

vague Don't be vague, ask for Haig CERTAINTY AND DOUBT

vain In vain the net is spread FUTILITY

valet No man is a hero to his valet FAMILIARITY

variety Variety is the spice of life CHANGE

varlet ape's an ape, a varlet's a varlet CHARACTER

venture Nothing venture, nothing gain THOROUGHNESS

Nothing venture, nothing have THOROUGHNESS

verba Nullius in verba HYPOTHESIS AND FACT

vero Se non è vero, è molto ben trovato TRUTH

vessels Empty vessels make the most sound FOOLS

---

vice Gossip is vice GOSSIP

victors History is written by the victors HISTORY

victory army knows how to gain a victory ARMED FORCES
Dig for victory GARDENS

view Distance lends enchantment to the view APPEARANCE

village It takes a village to raise a child CHILDREN

virtue Adversity is the foundation of virtue ADVERSITY
Make a virtue of necessity NECESSITY
Most people consider thrift a fine virtue THRIFT
Patience is a virtue PATIENCE
Virtue is its own reward VIRTUE

vision Vision without action is a daydream WORDS AND DEEDS

visited sea wants to be visited SEA

vodka Vodka is an aunt of wine DRINK

voice mockingbird has no voice BIRDS
voice of the people is the voice of God POLITICS

voluntary Ignorance is voluntary misfortune IGNORANCE

volunteer One volunteer is worth two pressed men WORK

Vorsprung Vorsprung durch Technik TECHNOLOGY

vote straw vote only shows which way POLITICS
Vote early and vote often POLITICS

votes Votes for women WOMEN

wait All things come to those who wait PATIENCE

I sit on the shore, and wait for the wind PATIENCE
Time and tide wait for no man OPPORTUNITY

waiting It's ill waiting for dead men's shoes AMBITION

walk If you can walk, you can dance ABILITY
We must learn to walk before PATIENCE

walking Let your fingers do the walking TECHNOLOGY
Roads are made by walking TRAVEL
Walking ten thousand miles EXPERIENCE
Walking ten thousand miles KNOWLEDGE

walks Gray's Inn for walks LAW

wall Bull markets climb a wall of worry BUSINESS
Mirror, mirror on the wall BEAUTY
wall between both best preserves NEIGHBOURS
weakest go to the wall STRENGTH AND WEAKNESS

walls Walls have ears SECRECY

walnut woman, a dog, and a walnut tree WOMEN

walnuts Walnuts and pears you plant for GARDENS

want For want of a nail the shoe was lost PREPARATION AND READINESS
If you want peace, you must prepare PREPARATION AND READINESS
If you want something done ACTION AND INACTION

more you get the more you
want   GREED

Wilful waste makes woeful
want   THRIFT

wanton Wanton kittens make sober
cats   YOUTH

wants Someone, somewhere, wants
a letter   LETTERS

war All's fair in love and
war   JUSTICE

bloody war and a sickly
season   ARMED FORCES

Business is war   BUSINESS

Councils of war never
fight   INDECISION

Daddy, what did you do in the
Great War   ARMED FORCES

Make love not war   LIFESTYLES

soldier of the Great War, known
unto   ARMED FORCES

War will cease when men refuse
to fight   WARFARE

When war is declared, Truth is the
first   WARFARE

warm warm January, a cold
May   WEATHER

wash One does not wash one's dirty
linen   SECRECY

They that wash on
Monday   HOUSEWORK

washes One hand washes the
other   COOPERATION

Persil washes whiter   HOUSEWORK

waste Haste makes waste   HASTE
AND DELAY

mind is a terrible thing to
waste   MIND

Wilful waste makes woeful
want   THRIFT

watch Watch this space   NEWS AND
JOURNALISM

watched watched pot never
boils   PATIENCE

water Blood is thicker than
water   FAMILY

Dirty water will quench
fire   SEX

Every two miles the water
changes   TRAVEL

Hot water does not burn
down   FUTILITY

It is the calm and silent
water   DANGER

mill cannot grind with the water
that   OPPORTUNITY

rock in the water does not know
the pain   SYMPATHY

tears of the stranger are only
water   SYMPATHY

When drinking water, remember
the   PARENTS

When you drink water,
remember   GRATITUDE

Where water flows, a
channel   PATIENCE

You can take a horse to the
water   DEFIANCE

You never miss the water till the
well   GRATITUDE

watermelons You cannot
carry two
watermelons   FUTILITY

waters It is good fishing in
troubled waters   OPPORTUNITY

Still waters run deep   CHARACTER

Stolen waters are
sweet   TEMPTATION

Watson Elementary, my dear
Watson   THINKING

way Love will find a way   LOVE

Straws tell which way the wind
blows   KNOWLEDGE

straw vote only shows which
way POLITICS
There is more than one way to
skin a cat WAYS AND MEANS
way one eats is the way one
works EATING
wilful man must have his
way DETERMINATION
ways There are more ways of killing
a cat WAYS AND MEANS
There are more ways of killing a
dog WAYS AND MEANS
We have ways of making you
talk POWER
we We're here Because We're
here FATE
weakest chain is no stronger than
its weakest COOPERATION
weakest go to the wall STRENGTH
AND WEAKNESS
You are the weakest link
STRENGTH AND WEAKNESS
weakling I was a seven-stone
weakling HEALTH
weapon bayonet is a weapon with a
worker WARFARE
wear Better to wear out than to
rust IDLENESS
If the cap fits, wear it NAMES
If the shoe fits, wear it NAMES
weary Be the day weary or be the
day long TIME
weather sea wants to be
visited SEA
There is no such thing as bad
weather WEATHER
weathers Robin Hood could brave
all weathers WEATHER
webs When spider webs
unite COOPERATION
wed Better wed over the
mixen FAMILIARITY

wedding One wedding brings
another WEDDINGS
wedlock Wedlock is a
padlock MARRIAGE
Wednesday Wednesday's child is
full of woe SORROW
weeds Ill weeds grow apace GOOD
AND EVIL
weepers Finders keepers (losers
weepers) POSSESSIONS
well Didn't she do well?
ACHIEVEMENT
Dig the well before you are
thirsty PREPARATION AND
READINESS
frog in a well knows nothing
of SELF-ESTEEM AND SELF-ASSERTION
He lives long who lives
well VIRTUE
If you want a thing done well
SELF-INTEREST
Let well alone CAUTION
pitcher will go to the well EXCESS
Truth lies at the bottom of a
well TRUTH
Well begun is half
done BEGINNING
wells You have drunk from wells
you did not PAST
west East, west, home's best HOME
Two swords do not fit in one
scabbard SIMILARITY AND
DIFFERENCE
wet Let's get out of these wet
clothes DRINK
Sow dry and set wet GARDENS
whale Save the
whale ENVIRONMENT
what It's not what you
know OPPORTUNITY
What you see is what you
get APPEARANCE

window eyes are the window of the soul BODY

winds You cannot control the winds MANAGEMENT

wine From the sweetest wine, the tartest SIMILARITY AND DIFFERENCE

Good wine needs no bush ADVERTISING

There is truth in wine DRUNKENNESS

Vodka is an aunt of wine DRINK

When the wine is in, the wit DRUNKENNESS

You can't put new wine in old bottles CHANGE

wing bird never flew on one wing GENEROSITY

wink Wink at sma' fauts, ye hae great anes MISTAKES

wins Who dares wins DANGER

winter fire is winter's fruit WINTER

For the unlearned, old age is winter AGE

Nine months of winter WEATHER

One kind word warms three winter SYMPATHY

winter does not go without WINTER

Winter either bites with its teeth WINTER

Winter is summer's heir WINTER

Winter never rots in the sky WINTER

Winter thunder, summer hunger WEATHER

wisdom beginning of wisdom is to call things NAMES

wise fool may give a wise man ADVICE

Fools ask questions that wise men KNOWLEDGE

Fools build houses and wise men FOOLS

It is a wise child that knows PARENTS

It is easy to be wise after the event FORESIGHT

One cannot love and be wise LOVE

Peace is the dream of the wise PEACE

Penny wise and pound foolish THRIFT

still tongue makes a wise head SILENCE

wise man changes his mind FOOLS

wise man will climb Mount Fuji once TRAVEL

word to the wise is enough ADVICE

wish wish is father to the thought OPINION

wishes If wishes were horses, beggars OPTIMISM AND PESSIMISM

wit Brevity is the soul of wit SPEECH

When the wine is in, the wit DRUNKENNESS

wiving Hanging and wiving go by destiny FATE

woe Wednesday's child is full of woe SORROW

wolf caribou feeds the wolf STRENGTH AND WEAKNESS

Do not call a wolf to help you ENEMIES

Fear makes the wolf bigger FEAR

Hunger drives the wolf out of the wood NECESSITY

lone sheep is in danger from the wolf SOLITUDE

Man is a wolf to man HUMAN RACE

wolf may lose his teeth, but never AGE

wolves wolves are well fed and the sheep DANGER

woman Hell hath no fury like a woman scorned WOMEN

Silence is a woman's best garment WOMEN

whistling woman and a crowing hen WOMEN

woman, a dog, and a walnut tree WOMEN

woman and a ship ever want mending WOMEN

woman's place is in the home WOMEN

woman's work is never done HOUSEWORK

women England is the paradise of women COUNTRIES AND PEOPLES

Never choose your women or linen APPEARANCE

Votes for women WOMEN

Women and children first DANGER

Women hold up half the sky WOMEN

wonders Time works wonders TIME

Wonders will never cease SURPRISE

wood Don't halloo till you are out of the wood OPTIMISM AND PESSIMISM

Hunger drives the wolf out of the wood NECESSITY

woods Fields have eyes and woods have ears SECRECY

In the woods it rains twice TREES

wool Many go out for wool AMBITION

Much cry and little wool EFFORT

word Englishman's word is his bond COUNTRIES AND PEOPLES

Many a true word is spoken in jest TRUTH

One kind word warms three winter SYMPATHY

swiftest horse cannot overtake the word WORDS

word to the wise is enough ADVICE

words Actions speak louder than words WORDS AND DEEDS

All words are pegs to hang ideas on WORDS

Fine words butter no parsnips WORDS AND DEEDS

Hard words break no bones WORDS

One picture is worth ten thousand words WORDS AND DEEDS

Stabs heal, but bad words never WORDS AND DEEDS

Words are sweet, but they never take WORDS AND DEEDS

work All work and no play makes Jack LEISURE

Devil finds work for idle hands IDLENESS

end crowns the work ENDING

eye of a master does more work EMPLOYMENT

Go to work on an egg EATING

harder I work, the luckier CHANCE AND LUCK

If you won't work you shan't eat IDLENESS

It is not work that kills, but worry WORRY